Microsoft Dynamics 365 Business Central Cookbook

Effective recipes for developing and deploying applications with Dynamics 365 Business Central

Michael Glue

BIRMINGHAM - MUMBAI

Microsoft Dynamics 365 Business Central Cookbook

Copyright © 2019 Packt Publishing

All rights reserved. No part of this book may be reproduced, stored in a retrieval system, or transmitted in any form or by any means, without the prior written permission of the publisher, except in the case of brief quotations embedded in critical articles or reviews.

Every effort has been made in the preparation of this book to ensure the accuracy of the information presented. However, the information contained in this book is sold without warranty, either express or implied. Neither the author, nor Packt Publishing or its dealers and distributors, will be held liable for any damages caused or alleged to have been caused directly or indirectly by this book.

Packt Publishing has endeavored to provide trademark information about all of the companies and products mentioned in this book by the appropriate use of capitals. However, Packt Publishing cannot guarantee the accuracy of this information.

Commissioning Editor: Richa Tripathi
Acquisition Editor: Shriram Shekhar
Content Development Editor: Divya Vijayan
Senior Editor: Afshaan Khan
Technical Editor: Ketan Kamble
Copy Editor: Safis Editing
Project Coordinator: Prajakta Naik
Proofreader: Safis Editing
Indexer: Tejal Daruwale Soni
Production Designer: Nilesh Mohite

First published: August 2019

Production reference: 1080819

Published by Packt Publishing Ltd.
Livery Place
35 Livery Street
Birmingham
B3 2PB, UK.

ISBN 978-1-78995-854-6

www.packtpub.com

To my wife, Jennifer, for having so much patience waiting for me to finish coding well into the evening. You are the absolute best!

To my kids, Emily, Dylan, Jenna, and Ethan, for simply being amazing and always giving me that reason to step away from the computer.

Packt.com

Subscribe to our online digital library for full access to over 7,000 books and videos, as well as industry leading tools to help you plan your personal development and advance your career. For more information, please visit our website.

Why subscribe?

- Spend less time learning and more time coding with practical eBooks and videos from over 4,000 industry professionals

- Improve your learning with Skill Plans built especially for you

- Get a free eBook or video every month

- Fully searchable for easy access to vital information

- Copy and paste, print, and bookmark content

Did you know that Packt offers eBook versions of every book published, with PDF and ePub files available? You can upgrade to the eBook version at www.packt.com and, as a print book customer, you are entitled to a discount on the eBook copy. Get in touch with us at customercare@packtpub.com for more details.

At www.packt.com, you can also read a collection of free technical articles, sign up for a range of free newsletters, and receive exclusive discounts and offers on Packt books and eBooks.

Contributors

About the author

Michael Glue began his Dynamics journey in June 2001, when he became a certified Dynamics NAV developer. Starting with building custom solutions, he later became a product architect, where he focused solely on building repeatable vertical products. Today, Michael works with a talented research and development team as they continue to push their products forward on the Business Central platform. In 2018, Michael was given his first MVP award in Business Applications. Along with his wife, Jennifer, they have four amazing kids and four very active dogs. From coaching his daughters' baseball team, to playing video games with his boys, to watching a good movie with his wife, not a day goes by that is devoid of excitement. You can follow Michael on Twitter (@navbitsbytes).

About the reviewer

Quenneth Surban is an enthusiastic solutions developer in the Philippines. Kicking off his career in 2016, he partnered with Microsoft to build innovative solutions to help businesses simplify their day-to-day operations. Since then, he has become a certified Microsoft Technology Associate on Software Development. More recently, he moved to become a Microsoft Certified Professional on Programming in C#, and also had the opportunity to work with several organizations to build solutions in Office 365, Dynamics 365, and Microsoft Azure. Today, he continues to design and develop solutions whilst closely working with customers to help them add value with these solutions.

Packt is searching for authors like you

If you're interested in becoming an author for Packt, please visit `authors.packtpub.com` and apply today. We have worked with thousands of developers and tech professionals, just like you, to help them share their insight with the global tech community. You can make a general application, apply for a specific hot topic that we are recruiting an author for, or submit your own idea.

Table of Contents

Preface   1

Chapter 1: Let's Get the Basics out of the Way   7
  Technical requirements   8
  Setting up your development sandbox   8
    Getting ready   9
    How to do it...   9
      Option 1 – Sandbox hosted in Business Central   9
      Option 2 – Azure-hosted sandbox   10
      Option 3 – Sandbox in a local container 15
      Option 4 – Local sandbox using installation media   18
    How it works...   20
    See also   20
  Creating a new AL project   21
    Getting ready   21
    How to do it...   21
    How it works...   23
    There's more...   23
  Creating basic entities   24
    Getting ready   24
    How to do it...   24
    How it works...   28
    See also   29
  Creating new business logic   29
    Getting ready   29
    How to do it...   29
    How it works...   34
    See also   34
  Classifying data   34
    Getting ready   35
    How to do it...   35
    How it works...   35
    There's more...   36
    See also   36
  User permissions   37
    Getting ready   37
    How to do it...   37
    How it works...   40
    There's more...   40
    See also   41

Creating new reports 41
Getting ready 41
How to do it... 41
How it works... 49
There's more... 50
See also 50
Adding help links 50
Getting ready 50
How to do it... 51
How it works... 51
See also 52

Chapter 2: Customizing What's Already There 53
Technical requirements 54
Adding fields to base application tables 54
Getting ready 54
How to do it... 55
How it works... 55
See also 56
Modifying the base application interface 56
Getting ready 56
How to do it... 56
How it works... 58
See also 58
Modifying the base application business logic 59
Getting ready 59
How to do it... 59
How it works... 61
See also 62
Using In-client Designer 62
Getting ready 62
How to do it... 63
How it works... 65
See also 65
Using Event Recorder 65
Getting ready 66
How to do it... 66
How it works... 67
See also 68
Replacing base application reports 68
Getting ready 68
How to do it... 69
How it works... 70
See also 71
Adding new profiles and role centers 71

Getting ready	72
How to do it...	72
How it works...	75
See also	76
Adding filter tokens	**76**
Getting ready	76
How to do it...	77
How it works...	78
See also	78
Adding application areas	**79**
Getting ready	79
How to do it...	79
How it works...	81
There's more...	82
See also	82
Chapter 3: Let's Go Beyond	**83**
Technical requirements	**84**
Control add-ins	**84**
Getting ready	84
How to do it...	85
How it works...	89
See also	89
Dependencies	**90**
Getting ready	90
How to do it...	90
How it works...	93
There's more...	94
Translations	**95**
Getting ready	95
How to do it...	95
How it works...	98
There's more...	99
See also	100
Adding new manual setups	**100**
Getting ready	100
How to do it...	101
How it works...	102
There's more...	102
Assisted Setup wizards	**102**
Getting ready	103
How to do it...	103
How it works...	113
Isolated storage	**114**
Getting ready	114

How to do it... | 114
How it works... | 117
See also | 118
Notifications | 118
Getting ready | 119
How to do it... | 119
How it works... | 122
See also | 123
Using the task scheduler | 123
Getting ready | 123
How to do it... | 124
How it works... | 126
See also | 126
.NET interoperability | 126
Getting ready | 127
How to do it... | 127
How it works... | 131
See also | 132
Implementing telemetry events | 132
Getting ready | 132
How to do it... | 133
How it works... | 135
There's more... | 136
See also | 137

Chapter 4: Testing and Debugging - You Just Gotta Do It | 139
Technical requirements | 140
Introducing the debugger | 140
Getting ready | 140
How to do it... | 140
How it works... | 141
There's more... | 143
See also | 143
Debugging SQL | 143
Getting ready | 143
How to do it... | 144
How it works... | 146
See also | 146
The Automated Testing Toolkit | 147
Getting ready | 147
How to do it... | 147
How it works... | 149
See also | 150
Creating a test application | 150
Getting ready | 150

How to do it... 150
How it works... 153
There's more... 153
Creating automated tests 153
Getting ready 153
How to do it... 154
How it works... 156
There's more... 156
See also 157
Testing the UI 157
Getting ready 157
How to do it... 158
How it works... 160
See also 160
UI handlers 160
Getting ready 161
How to do it... 161
How it works... 163
See also 164
Creating a test library 164
Getting ready 164
How to do it... 165
How it works... 166
See also 167

Chapter 5: Old School, Meet New School 169
Technical requirements 169
Converting CAL to AL 170
Getting ready 170
How to do it... 170
How it works... 175
See also 176
There's more... 176
Post-conversion cleanup 177
Getting ready 177
How to do it... 178
How it works... 181
Upgrading data from CAL objects 181
Getting ready 182
How to do it... 183
How it works... 186
There's more... 187

Chapter 6: Making Your App Extensible 189
Technical requirements 189
Publishing events in your code 190

Getting ready   190
How to do it...   191
How it works...   192
See also   192
Enums   192
Getting ready   193
How to do it...   193
How it works...   195
See also   196
The Discovery design pattern   196
Getting ready   197
How to do it...   197
How it works...   201
See also   202
The Handled design pattern   202
Getting ready   202
How to do it...   203
How it works...   204
See also   205
The Variant Façade design pattern   205
Getting ready   206
How to do it...   206
How it works...   209
See also   209
The Argument Table design pattern   209
Getting ready   210
How to do it...   210
How it works...   213
See also   214

Chapter 7: Business Central for All   215
Technical requirements   216
Consuming external web services   216
Getting ready   216
How to do it...   217
How it works...   220
See also   221
Publishing your own web service   221
Getting ready   221
How to do it...   221
How it works...   223
See also   224
Enabling basic authentication   224
Getting ready   224
How to do it...   224

How it works... 226
There's more... 226
See also 226
The Business Central API – exploring with Postman 227
Getting ready 227
How to do it... 227
How it works... 228
There's more... 229
See also 229
The Business Central API – retrieving data 229
Getting ready 229
How to do it... 230
How it works... 232
There's more... 233
See also 234
The Business Central API – creating data 234
Getting ready 234
How to do it... 234
How it works... 236
There's more... 237
See also 237
The Business Central API – publishing a custom endpoint 237
Getting ready 238
How to do it... 238
How it works... 240
See also 241
Power Platform – using Microsoft Power BI 241
Getting ready 242
How to do it... 242
How it works... 246
There's more... 247
See also 247
Power Platform – using Microsoft Flow 247
Getting ready 248
How to do it... 248
How it works... 253
There's more... 254
See also 255
Power Platform – using Microsoft PowerApps 255
Getting ready 255
How to do it... 256
How it works... 264
There's more... 265
See also 266
Consuming Azure Functions 266

Getting ready 266
How to do it... 267
How it works... 272
See also 273

Chapter 8: DevOps - Don't Live without It 275
Technical requirements 276
Creating an Azure DevOps project 277
Getting ready 277
How to do it... 277
How it works... 279
See also 281
Creating a code repository 281
Getting ready 281
How to do it... 281
How it works... 282
There's more... 283
See also 284
Connecting an AL project to Azure DevOps 284
Getting ready 284
How to do it... 285
How it works... 289
There's more... 289
See also 290
Installing a pipeline agent 290
Getting ready 290
How to do it... 290
How it works... 294
See also 295
Creating a build pipeline 296
Getting ready 296
How to do it... 296
How it works... 304
See also 305
Creating a release pipeline 305
Getting ready 306
How to do it... 306
How it works... 314
See also 315
Enabling branch policies 316
Getting ready 316
How to do it... 316
How it works... 323
There's more... 325
See also 325

Chapter 9: Time to Share Your Application!   327
  Technical requirements   327
  Developing for multiple platforms   328
    Getting ready   328
    How to do it...   329
    How it works...   330
    See also   331
  Protecting your Intellectual Property   331
    Getting ready   331
    How to do it...   331
    How it works...   332
    There's more...   332
    See also   333
  Signing your application   333
    Getting ready   333
    How to do it...   334
    How it works...   335
    There's more...   336
    See also   336
  Installation logic   336
    Getting ready   337
    How to do it...   337
    How it works...   339
    See also   339
  Upgrade logic   339
    Getting ready   340
    How to do it...   340
    How it works...   342
    See also   343
  Installing applications with PowerShell   343
    Getting ready   344
    How to do it...   344
    How it works...   345
    See also   345
  Upgrading applications with PowerShell   346
    Getting ready   346
    How to do it...   347
    How it works...   348
    See also   349
  Deploying a tenant customization   349
    Getting ready   350
    How to do it...   350
    How it works...   351
    See also   352

Other Books You May Enjoy
353

Index
357

Preface

Microsoft Dynamics 365 Business Central is a complete business management application. It can be used to streamline business processes in your company, connect individual departments across the company, and enhance customer interactions.

OK, that first part was really professional-sounding, right? Now, let's get into what this cookbook is going to do for you, and, quite simply, it's going to help you get things done. This book will help you get familiar with the latest development features and tools for building applications for Business Central. You'll find recipes that will help you build and test applications that can be deployed to the cloud, or on-premises. For the old-schoolers out there, you'll also learn how to take your existing Dynamics NAV customizations and move them to the new AL language platform.

Also, if you haven't figured it out already, we're going to be using very normal language here. We're trying to keep things light. After all, developing applications is fun, so why not have fun while learning to do it as well?!

Who this book is for

This book is for Dynamics developers and administrators who want to become efficient in developing and deploying applications in Business Central.

A basic level of knowledge and understanding of the AL programming language, along with an understanding of Dynamics application development and administration, is assumed.

What this book covers

Chapter 1, *Let's Get the Basics out of the Way*, explains how to set up an AL development sandbox, either locally or online, and then goes through basic topics that will typically be a part of all Business Central applications that you create.

Chapter 2, *Customizing What's Already There*, explains how you can customize the base Business Central application.

Chapter 3, *Let's Go Beyond*, explains topics that are not necessarily going to be implemented in every application, but are extremely powerful tools to be aware of for when the need arises.

Chapter 4, *Testing and Debugging - You Just Gotta Do It*, explains how to create automated tests for your Business Central application, and how you can use the debugger to track down issues.

Chapter 5, *Old School, Meet New School*, explains how to convert Dynamics NAV solutions to Business Central applications.

Chapter 6, *Making Your App Extensible*, explains things you can do in order to give other developers the ability to extend and customize your application.

Chapter 7, *Business Central for All*, explains the things that you can do in your Business Central application to connect a Business Central system to other external services and applications.

Chapter 8, *DevOps - Don't Live without It*, explains how to use Azure DevOps to track source code changes, and to automate the building and deploying of your application.

Chapter 9, *Time to Share Your Application!*, explains how to deliver your application to customers, both on-premises and online.

To get the most out of this book

Although this book starts with some entry-level topics, it is expected that you have a general understanding of how to program using the AL programming language. If you plan on using a local, container-based development sandbox, you will need to have a basic level understanding of Docker and PowerShell.

Download the example code files

You can download the example code files for this book from your account at www.packt.com. If you purchased this book elsewhere, you can visit www.packtpub.com/support and register to have the files emailed directly to you.

You can download the code files by following these steps:

1. Log in or register at www.packt.com.
2. Select the **SUPPORT** tab.
3. Click on **Code Downloads & Errata**.
4. Enter the name of the book in the **Search** box and follow the on screen instructions.

Once the file is downloaded, please make sure that you unzip or extract the folder using the latest version of:

- WinRAR/7-Zip for Windows
- Zipeg/iZip/UnRarX for Mac
- 7-Zip/PeaZip for Linux

The code bundle for the book is also hosted on GitHub at `https://github.com/PacktPublishing/Microsoft-Dynamics-365-Business-Central-Cookbook`. In case there's an update to the code, it will be updated on the existing GitHub repository.

We also have other code bundles from our rich catalog of books and videos available at `https://github.com/PacktPublishing/`. Check them out!

Code in Action

Visit the following link to see the code being executed:

`http://bit.ly/2YUg1tI`

Download the color images

We also provide a PDF file that has color images of the screenshots/diagrams used in this book. You can download it here:
`http://www.packtpub.com/sites/default/files/downloads/9781789958546_ColorImages.pdf`.

Conventions used

There are a number of text conventions used throughout this book.

`CodeInText`: Indicates code words in text, database table names, folder names, filenames, file extensions, pathnames, dummy URLs, user input, and Twitter handles. Here is an example: "We can do that by adding code to the `OnInsert()` trigger of the table so that our logic executes every time a record is inserted."

A block of code is set as follows:

```
"startupObjectId": 50101
"startupObjectType": "Page"
```

Bold: Indicates a new term, an important word, or words that you see onscreen. For example, words in menus or dialog boxes appear in the text like this. Here is an example: "Your web browser will open and, once you log in, you will be presented with your new **Television Show List** page."

 Warnings or important notes appear like this.

 Tips and tricks appear like this.

Sections

In this book, you will find several headings that appear frequently (*Getting ready, How to do it..., How it works..., There's more...,* and See also).

To give clear instructions on how to complete a recipe, use these sections as follows:

Getting ready

This section tells you what to expect in the recipe and describes how to set up any software or any preliminary settings required for the recipe.

How to do it...

This section contains the steps required to follow the recipe.

How it works...

This section usually consists of a detailed explanation of what happened in the previous section.

There's more...

This section consists of additional information about the recipe in order to make you more knowledgeable of it.

See also

This section provides helpful links to other useful information for the recipe.

Get in touch

Feedback from our readers is always welcome.

General feedback: If you have questions about any aspect of this book, mention the book title in the subject of your message and email us at customercare@packtpub.com.

Errata: Although we have taken every care to ensure the accuracy of our content, mistakes do happen. If you have found a mistake in this book, we would be grateful if you would report this to us. Please visit www.packtpub.com/submit-errata, selecting your book, clicking on the Errata Submission Form link, and entering the details.

Piracy: If you come across any illegal copies of our works in any form on the Internet, we would be grateful if you would provide us with the location address or website name. Please contact us at copyright@packt.com with a link to the material.

If you are interested in becoming an author: If there is a topic that you have expertise in, and you are interested in either writing or contributing to a book, please visit authors.packtpub.com.

Reviews

Please leave a review. Once you have read and used this book, why not leave a review on the site that you purchased it from? Potential readers can then see and use your unbiased opinion to make purchase decisions, we at Packt can understand what you think about our products, and our authors can see your feedback on their book. Thank you!

For more information about Packt, please visit packtpub.com.

Let's Get the Basics out of the Way 1

Microsoft Dynamics 365 Business Central is a complete business application management system. With it comes an exciting new development platform and tools. Using AL, the primary development language, and Visual Studio Code, the primary development tool, you can create incredibly rich and feature-packed Business Central applications to fit the needs of virtually any customer.

In this chapter, we're going to go over the basics (yes, exactly like the title says!). Some of the recipes in this chapter are very simple, and you might wonder what the point of them is, but don't discount them. There is a reason behind each one, and I'll explain them along the way.

We will start this chapter with a recipe for setting up your development sandbox. After all, we can't build any applications without a place to test them! Once we have our sandbox in place, we will install and configure Visual Studio Code in order to connect it to the sandbox. We'll then move on through a set of recipes that will show you some of the basic components that almost every application you build will have.

In this chapter, we will cover the following recipes:

- Setting up your development sandbox
- Creating a new AL project
- Creating basic entities
- Creating new business logic
- Classifying data
- User permissions
- Creating new reports
- Adding help links

Technical requirements

In order to complete the recipes in this chapter (and this book, for that matter!), you need to install Visual Studio Code on your machine. You will use this to code your AL applications, but you can also use it for a myriad of other programming languages and scripts. You can read and obtain Visual Studio Code at `https://code.visualstudio.com/`.

If you plan on using a Docker container on your local machine, then you'll also need to install Docker. You're going to want to make sure you install the right edition, based on your OS:

- Windows 10: `https://store.docker.com/editions/community/docker-ce-desktop-windows`
- Windows Server: `https://docs.microsoft.com/en-us/virtualization/windowscontainers/quick-start/quick-start-windows-server`

If you have a Business Central license file, you should upload it somewhere that you can access it using a secure URL. For example, you can upload it to either an Azure Storage or Dropbox account. You must be able to get a secure URL for direct download.

Code samples and scripts are available on GitHub. Each of the recipes in this chapter builds on the previous recipe, so you can always download the previous recipe's code to get a quick jump on things if you don't want to work through them all in order. You can download everything you need from `https://github.com/PacktPublishing/Microsoft-Dynamics-365-Business-Central-Cookbook/tree/master/ch1`.

For the reporting recipe, you'll need to have Microsoft Report Builder installed. You can download that from Microsoft Download Center at `https://go.microsoft.com/fwlink/?LinkID=734968`.

Setting up your development sandbox

Well, we're kicking things off with a bang! Our first recipe is probably the longest recipe in this book, but that's because you have choices when it comes to setting up your development sandbox. Will you use a sandbox hosted in Business Central or will you set up your sandbox on a machine? Will that machine be hosted in Azure or on your local machine? Will you use a container or not? The choice is yours, and we'll go through each process in this recipe. By the end of this recipe, you will have a place to do all of your AL coding!

Getting ready

Depending on how you want to set up your development sandbox, you may need to do a few different things to prepare:

- Sign up for or get access to a Business Central subscription
- Sign up for or get access to an Azure subscription for which you can create virtual machines
- Install Docker
- Obtain the latest Business Central installation media

How to do it...

We have four different choices here. If you're super savvy, then by all means, try them all out, but really, you only need to do the one that fits you best.

Option 1 – Sandbox hosted in Business Central

If you want to set up your development sandbox to be hosted in Business Central—which, by the way, is the simplest of all the options—perform the following steps:

1. Sign up for a Microsoft Dynamics 365 Business Central sandbox at `https://aka.ms/getsandboxforbusinesscentral`.

When you sign up for your sandbox, you cannot use a personal email address. You must use either a work or school account.

2. Install the AL Language extension from the Visual Studio Code Marketplace at `https://marketplace.visualstudio.com/items?itemName=ms-dynamics-smb.al`:

There are just two steps to getting your sandbox! Once you go through the signup process, you'll be logged into your sandbox and will be greeted with a message similar to the following:

Option 2 – Azure-hosted sandbox

If you want to use a container hosted on a virtual machine in Azure, perform the following steps:

1. If you have not already done so, you can sign up for an Azure subscription at `https://azure.microsoft.com` and start with a free account.

2. Now that we have an Azure subscription, we need to create a virtual machine within that subscription. This virtual machine will host a Business Central environment inside a Docker container. To make this easy, there is an **Azure Resource Manager** (**ARM**) template available for you to use.

You can access the template at `https://aka.ms/getbc`. Make sure to use your Azure subscription login credentials.

The template contains a lot of options, but for our purposes, we're going to focus on just a few of them. Once you're familiar with the process, take a look at the other options and do things such as connecting your sandbox to an Office 365 account! See the options in the following table:

Option	Comment
Resource Group	Select **Create new** to create a new resource group for this virtual machine. You can name it whatever you like.
Location	Choose the region closest to where you are connecting from. Selecting a region on the other side of the world from you will impact connection performance.
VM Name	Give your machine a name – any name you want! Azure will make sure that the name you choose is acceptable.
Time zone Id	Select the time zone you wish to work in.
Accept EULA	You must accept the **End User License Agreement** (**EULA**) by selecting **Yes** for this option. The EULA can be found at `https://go.microsoft.com/fwlink/?linkid=861843`.
Remote Desktop Access	Use this option to configure whether you are able to use **Remote Desktop Protocol** (**RDP**) to remotely log in to the virtual machine. Set this to an asterisk (*) if you want to connect to this machine from any machine.
VM Admin username	You can leave this as the default value, **vmadmin**, or change it to one that suits you better. This login will be used to remote connect (via RDP) to the machine. This login is configured as the local administrator for the virtual machine.
BC Admin username	You can leave this as the default value, **admin**, or change it to one that suits you better. You will use this login to launch the Business Central Web Client. This user is configured as a super user in the Business Central system.
Admin Password	Set this to any password you want. This password applies to both the virtual machine and BC admin logins. Azure will ensure that the password you enter is strong enough.
BC Docker Image	Here, you can configure the Docker image you wish to use. Set this option to `microsoft/bcsandbox:xx`, where `:xx` represents the country localization you want (for example, `microsoft/bcsandbox:ca` for Canada). For the list of countries available, see `https://hub.docker.com/_/microsoft-businesscentral-sandbox`.
License File URL	If you uploaded a Business Central license to an online storage account, specify the secure URL to the file in this option. You can leave this option blank if you want to use a demo license.

You can get more information on each option in the template by using the '!' icon onscreen, which is directly to the right of each option name.

3. Once you have filled in the ARM template, accept the terms and conditions at the bottom of the screen and then click the **Purchase** button.

Now, you can just sit back and relax, and if your template was configured properly, your virtual machine will be created. Go grab a coffee and check back later.

Make sure you wait at least one hour before logging into the virtual machine. Even after it is successfully created, the machine will go through a series of configurations to create and set up the container.

4. To test the connection to your Azure virtual machine, you need to remotely connect to the machine to get some information from it. You need to use the Azure web portal (`https://portal.azure.com`) to find the address of your virtual machine:
    1. In the Azure web portal, click on **Virtual Machines** in the navigation pane on the left:
        - If you do not see **Virtual Machines**, press **All Services** and search for `Virtual Machines` to select it.
    2. Select the name of the virtual machine that you just created.
    3. Look for the **DNS Name** and take note of the address listed below it:
        - For example, `myvirtualmachine.canadaeast.cloudapp.azure.com`

5. We can monitor the status of the virtual machine configuration by navigating to the virtual machine landing page:
    1. In your web browser, navigate to the **DNS Name** you noted previously.
    2. Click the **View Installation Status** link. Here, you can see when the virtual machine configuration is complete and is ready to use for development.

Once the virtual machine has been fully configured, the landing page will look similar to this:

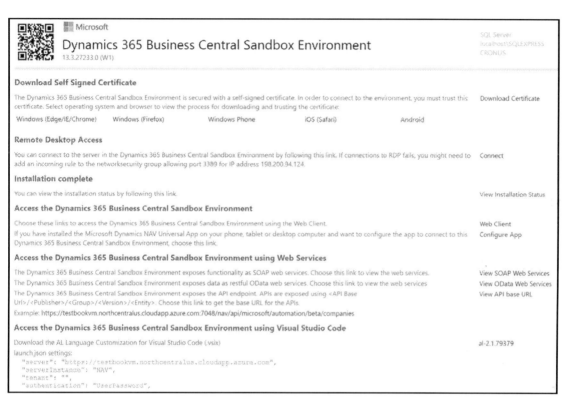

6. Now, we need to take note of a few pieces of information, for later.

    At the bottom of the landing page is a section named **Access the Dynamics 365 Business Central Sandbox Environment using Visual Studio Code**. In this section, take note of the following values:

```
"server": "https://testbookvm.northcentralus.cloudapp.azure.com",
"serverInstance": "NAV",
"tenant": "",
"authentication": "UserPassword",
```

You can also download a remote connection file from the landing page in the event that you want to connect to and work directly within the server.

7. Before we close the landing page, we need to install the security certificate so that we can connect to the sandbox:
    1. On the landing page, click the **Download Certificate** link and save the file to your local machine.
    2. Depending on which web browser you are using, click either the **Windows (Edge/IE/Chrome)** or the **Windows (Firefox)** link and follow the onscreen instructions to install the certificate.

8. Let's check to make sure we can connect to the Business Central Web Client:
    1. Close your web browser and navigate to the landing page for your virtual machine.
    2. Click the Web Client link on the right-hand side of the page.

You should now be looking at the Business Central login page:

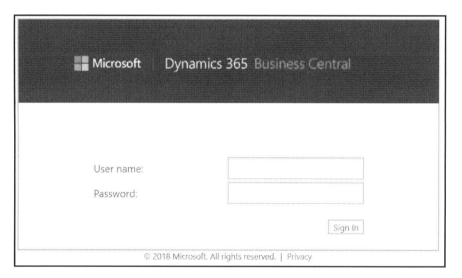

If you get an error about an unsecured connection, try restarting your web browser and/or reinstalling the security certificate.

9. Install the **AL Language** extension from the **Visual Studio Code Marketplace**: https://marketplace.visualstudio.com/items?itemName=ms-dynamics-smb.al.

Option 3 – Sandbox in a local container

If you prefer to have your development sandbox in a container on your local machine, you must have Docker installed and working on your machine. It should be configured to run Windows containers, rather than the default Linux ones. Once you have that, you can perform the following steps:

1. Download `CreateSandboxContainer.ps1` from the GitHub repository.
2. Run **PowerShell ISE** as an administrator and open `CreateSandboxContainer.ps1`.

    Let's look at what the code does. The first line in the script installs **NavContainerHelper**, which is a **PowerShell** module that contains an entire toolbox of commands for interacting with Business Central containers:

    ```
    $install-module navcontainerhelper -force
    ```

    If you would like to read more about NavContainerHelper, there's a wonderful set of blogs about it at https://blogs.msdn.microsoft.com/freddyk/tag/navcontain erhelper/.

3. We have the end-user license agreement. You must manually accept the agreement by setting `$accept_eula = $true`:

    ```
    # set to $true to accept the eula
    (https://go.microsoft.com/fwlink/?linkid=861843)
    $accept_eula = $false
    ```

4. You need to assign your sandbox container a name:

    ```
    # set the name of your container (must be 15 characters or less)
    $containername = ''
    ```

    Docker container names are case-sensitive, so I recommend using lowercase names.

5. You need to define which **Docker** image will be used for the sandbox container. Refer to the link in the script for information on which images are available, as follows:

```
# set image to use to create container (see here for available
images: https://hub.docker.com/_/microsoft-businesscentral-sandbox)
$bcdockerimage = 'mcr.microsoft.com/businesscentral/sandbox:us'
```

6. Set your login credentials. The script will configure the container to be based on a user and password login, so here is where you can define what the username and password will be:

```
# the user you use to login to the Business Central client (is a
SUPER user)
$userName = "admin"
$password = ConvertTo-SecureString -String "Pass@word1" -
AsPlainText -Force
```

If you have a Business Central license, you can upload it to an online storage account and access it with a secure URL. You can put the URL in the script, as follows:

```
# set the secure URL to your Business Central license file (leave
blank to use the demo license)
$licenseFileUri = ''
```

If you upload your license file, you must upload it to a storage account that allows direct download links.

The rest of the script is where the magic happens. First, the username and password that you defined will be converted into PowerShell credential objects, and then the `New-NavContainer` command does all the heavy lifting to create your sandbox:

```
$credential = New-Object -TypeName
"System.Management.Automation.PSCredential" -ArgumentList
$userName, $password

New-NavContainer -accept_eula:$accept_eula `
 -containername $containername `
 -auth UserPassword `
 -Credential $credential `
 -licenseFile $licenseFileUri `
 -includeCSide `
```

```
-alwaysPull `
-doNotExportObjectsToText `
-usessl:$false `
-updateHosts `
-assignPremiumPlan `
-shortcuts Desktop `
-imageName $bcdockerimage `
-useBestContainerOS
```

In order to execute the preceding script, you may need to configure the **Execution Policy** on your machine in order to allow it to run unsigned scripts. You can do that using the `Set-ExecutionPolicy` command-let. For more details, follow `https://docs.microsoft.com/en-us/ powershell/module/microsoft.powershell.security/set- executionpolicy?view=powershell-6`.

7. At this point, if you've filled in all the configuration in the script, you can run it by pressing *F5*. Then, sit back and relax while your container is created. The first thing that will happen is that the Docker image will be downloaded to your machine. This is the longest part of the process because the files are being downloaded, unpacked, and verified. A typical image will be around 10 - 20 GB.

   Once that is finished, the container will be created and should be ready in under 10 minutes.

   Do not close the PowerShell window yet!

8. We need to take note of some important information that we're going to need later. In the **PowerShell** window, look for the following information and save it for later:

```
Web Client          : http://mybccontainer/NAV/
Dev. Server         : http://mybccontainer
Dev. ServerInstance : NAV
```

9. To verify that your machine is working, open your web browser and navigate to the **Web Client** address that was listed in the PowerShell window (see the preceding example).

10. Install the **AL Language** extension from the **Visual Studio Code Marketplace**: `https://marketplace.visualstudio.com/items?itemName=ms- dynamics-smb.al`.

Option 4 – Local sandbox using installation media

If you want to install Business Central onto your local machine using the installation media, you can do that by following these steps:

1. From the installation media, run `setup.exe`.

2. You must accept the licensing terms. Once you do that, click **Advanced Installation Options**.

3. Here, you can choose between two setup options:

   - **Install Demo**: This installs a pre-configuration selection of components without manual intervention.
   - **Choose an installation option**: This allows you to choose which components to install and allows you to select some additional configuration options.

4. Click the **Choose an installation** option so that we can select the components that we need to complete the recipes in this book.

5. Click **Customize...** under the **Developer** option.

6. Make sure that the following components are set to **Run from My Computer**:

   - **AL Development Environment**
   - **Server Administration Tool**
   - **Server**
   - **SQL Server Database Components**
   - **SQL Server Database Components | Demo Database**
   - **Web Server Components**
   - **Dynamics NAV Client | Development Environment (C/SIDE)**

Here is a screenshot for your reference:

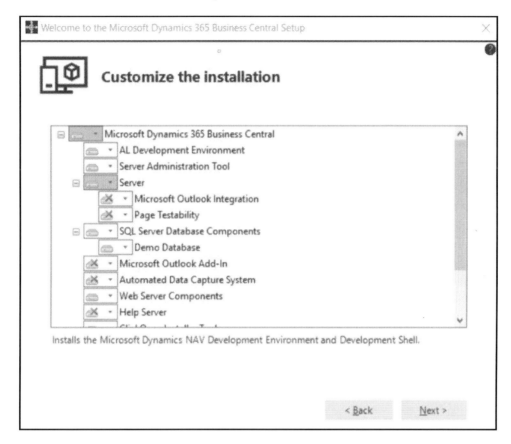

7. Click **Next** and you will see some additional installation parameters. For the purposes of the recipes in this book, you do not need to change anything here.

If you already have a compatible version of **Microsoft SQL Server** installed on your local machine, you can change the **SQL Server** and **SQL Server Instance** parameters to the corresponding ones so that the Business Central installation will use that instead of installing a new instance.

8. Click **Apply** to perform the installation.

If the installation cannot find a compatible version of Microsoft SQL Server, then you will be notified that it will install a new instance. At the time of writing, **Microsoft SQL Server 2016 Express** is the version that will be installed.

9. Once the installation has completed, click **Close** to close the installation wizard.

10. You can verify the installation by opening the Business Central Web Client from t he following URL: `http://localhost:8080/BC130`.

11. Install the **AL Language** extension from the **Visual Studio Code Marketplace** at `https://marketplace.visualstudio.com/items?itemName=ms-dynamics-smb.al`.

How it works...

As you can see, you have a variety of ways you can configure your development sandbox. Personal preference may lead you to choose one way or another, but there are a few things to keep in mind when selecting which configuration to use:

- **Do you need offline access to your development sandbox?** If so, then an Azure-hosted system might not be the right choice for you.
- **Do you need to build for the current Business Central SaaS version?** If so, then you might want to consider setting up your development sandbox to be hosted in Business Central so that it is always on the current release.
- **Do you need to make sure your application will work on a future Business Central release?** If so, you will want to take part in Microsoft's *Ready to Go* (`http://aka.ms/readytogo`) program so that you can gain access to future releases made available via Docker images.
- **Do you need to have multiple versions of Business Central on your local machine?** If so, there's no easier way than using Docker containers to do that!

Each of the processes resulted in the same thing: a development system that will be used to build and test new Business Central applications. Whether it is hosted or not, or a container or local installation, the end result is the same: a development sandbox that you will build and publish your Business Central applications to.

See also

For more information on setting up development sandboxes, you can refer to the *Getting Started With AL* article on the Microsoft Docs website at `https://docs.microsoft.com/en-us/dynamics365/business-central/dev-itpro/developer/devenv-get-started`.

Creating a new AL project

In this recipe, we are going to create a quick and easy sample application. Of course, you can start from a blank slate, but we'll start with the built-in **Hello World** application. It's the easiest way to get your AL development up and running.

Getting ready

You need to have your development sandbox set up and know the address so that you can connect and log in to it. You should have also already installed the AL Language extension in Visual Studio Code. You're definitely going to need that!

How to do it...

1. Open Visual Studio Code.
2. Press *Ctrl + Shift + P* to open the **Command Palette** and type or select **AL:Go!** to create a sample **Hello World** application.
3. When prompted, enter the path to where the new project will be stored. You can leave it as the default path or type in a new one. Press *Enter* to confirm the path.
4. When prompted, you need to select the sandbox type based on what you are working with. You have two options:
    - **Microsoft Cloud Sandbox**: Select this option if you are hosting your development sandbox in Business Central (Option 1 in the *Setting up your development sandbox* section). When you select this option, you will be prompted to log in with your Microsoft account. Use the account under which you created the Business Central sandbox.
    - **Your own server**: Select this option if you chose to put your sandbox in an Azure virtual machine, or on your local machine using a container or the installation media (Options 2 - 4 in the *Setting up your development sandbox* section). When you select this option, you will be prompted to log in. Press **Escape** to cancel the login.
5. This step is only required if you selected **Your own server** in the preceding step. Skip to the next step if you selected **Microsoft Cloud Server**.

    Before we log in to our development sandbox, we need to make sure that we have the correct connection configuration.

This information is stored in the `launch.json` file in the `.vscode` folder. You can view the file's contents by selecting it in the Visual Studio Code **Explorer**.

There are three properties that we need to look at here and set based on how we set up our development sandbox:

server	Here, you need to enter the connection URL into your sandbox. You can leave it at the default (`"http://localhost"`) if you installed your sandbox using the installation media. If you hosted your sandbox on an Azure virtual machine, this will be the `"server":` value that you obtained from the virtual machine landing page. If you have your sandbox in a container on your local machine, this value will be the `Dev. Server` value you obtained from the PowerShell window.
serverInstance	Here, you need to specify the name of your server instance (or service tier name). You can leave it at the default (`"BC130"`) if you installed your sandbox using the installation media. If your sandbox is hosted on an Azure virtual machine, this will be the `"serverInstance":` value that you obtained from the virtual machine landing page. If you have your sandbox in a container on your local machine, this value will be the `Dev. ServerInstance` value you obtained from the PowerShell window.
authentication	This defines the authentication method that will be used to connect to your sandbox. If you installed your sandbox using the installation media, you will set this value to `"Windows"`. If you hosted your sandbox on an Azure virtual machine or it is in a container on your local machine, this value should be set to `"UserPassword"`.

As you're poking around the `launch.json` file, if you press *Enter* to create a new line within the file, you can then press *Ctrl + Space* to see a list of other properties that are available for you to use.

6. Now that we have our configuration set up, we need to download symbols. At this point, Visual Studio Code may have already been prompting you to do that.

   Press *Ctrl + Shift + P* to open the **Command Palette** and type or select **AL: Download Symbols** to download the symbols.

   This will prompt a connection to be made to your development sandbox, and the symbols will be downloaded to your local machine. They will be placed in a folder named `.alpackages`, which you will see in the **Explorer**.

The symbol files are required for you to do any sort of AL development. They contain metadata that describes all the entities that exist in your development sandbox, such as tables, functions, and pages.

Once the symbols have been downloaded, you will see two files in the .alpackages folder, similar to what you can see in the following screenshot:

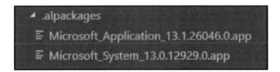

7. Now, it's time to build and publish our application.

    To do that, you can simply press *F5*, which will build the application and then publish it to your development sandbox in debug mode. If you do not want to publish it in debug mode, you can press *Ctrl + F5*.

If you simply want to build your application but are not ready to publish it, you can do that by pressing *Ctrl + Shift + B*, and your application will be built in, but not published to, your development sandbox.

How it works...

Creating the sample application is the quickest way to begin a new AL project. Once you connect your project to your development sandbox and download the symbols, you will be ready to code your AL application.

There's more...

Before you begin creating your new AL application using the sample application, you will need to delete the HelloWorld.al file that is in the sample application.

Creating basic entities

Adding basic entities to your AL application is easy. We're going to take a look at two of them in this recipe: tables and pages. We'll create a new table to track television shows (come on, we need to have some fun with this, right!?) and an associated card and list page.

Getting ready

You're going to need an AL project to work in that's connected to a development sandbox. We will continue to build on the project that we started in this chapter. You can download it from the GitHub link at the start of this chapter.

How to do it...

1. Open your AL project folder in Visual Studio Code. If you have not done so already, delete `HelloWorld.al`.
2. In the Visual Studio Code **Explorer**, right-click and select **New File**. Name this file `Television Show.al`.

   Repeat this process and create two more files:

   - `Television Show List.al`
   - `Television Show Card.al`

 All files that contain AL code need to have an `.al` extension.

3. Let's define the new table.

 You can quickly add the basic structure for a table and field by using the `ttable` and `tfield` snippets. Do this by typing in your chosen snippet name and pressing **Tab**.

In **Explorer**, select `Television Show.al`. In the **Editor** tab, enter the following:

```
table 50100 "Television Show"
{
    fields
    {
        field(1; Code; Code[20])
        {
            NotBlank = true;
        }
        field(2; Name; Text[80])
        {
        }
        field(3; Synopsis; Text[250])
        {
        }
        field(4; Status; Option)
        {
            OptionCaption = 'Active,Finished';
            OptionMembers = Active,Finished;
        }
        field(5; "First Aired"; Date)
        {
        }
    }

    keys
    {
        key(PK; Code)
        { .
            Clustered = true;
        }
    }
}
```

Make sure you save your changes.

4. Now, let's create a card to display the detailed information for our **Television Show** records.

You can quickly add the basic structure for a card page by using the `tpage` snippet. There are multiple types of page snippets, so be sure to select the correct one.

In **Explorer,** select `Television Show Card.al`. In the **Editor** tab, enter the following:

```
page 50100 "Television Show Card"
{
    PageType = Card;
    SourceTable = "Television Show";
    DelayedInsert = true;

    layout
    {
        area(Content)
        {
            group(General)
            {
                field(Code; Code)
                {
                    ApplicationArea = All;
                }
                field(Name; Name)
                {
                    ApplicationArea = All;
                }
                field(Synopsis; Synopsis)
                {
                    ApplicationArea = All;
                }
                field(Status; Status)
                {
                    ApplicationArea = All;
                }
                field("First Aired"; "First Aired")
                {
                    ApplicationArea = All;
                }
            }
        }
    }
}
```

5. Now, we'll build a list page to display the records from our new table.

Only show the most relevant and frequently used information on your list pages.

In **Explorer**, select `Television Show List.al`. In the **Editor** tab, enter the following:

```
page 50101 "Television Show List"
{
    PageType = List;
    ApplicationArea = All;
    UsageCategory = Lists;
    Editable = false;
    CardPageId = "Television Show Card";
    SourceTable = "Television Show";

    layout
    {
        area(Content)
        {
            repeater(Group)
            {
                field(Code; Code)
                {
                    ApplicationArea = All;
                }
                field(Name; Name)
                {
                    ApplicationArea = All;
                }
                field(Status; Status)
                {
                    ApplicationArea = All;
                }
            }
        }
    }
}
```

In order to make your pages (and reports) searchable in the Business Central Web Client, you need to populate `ApplicationArea` and `UsageCategory` in the AL object file.

6. Our basic application is ready to be published for testing. In the `launch.json` file, set the following properties:

```
"startupObjectId": 50101
"startupObjectType": "Page"
```

7. Press *F5* to publish the application to your development sandbox. Your web browser will open and, once you log in, you will be presented with your new **Television Show List** page:

8. Of course, there is not much to see until you enter some records. Try that out by clicking the **+New** button in the ribbon; the **Television Show Card** should open:

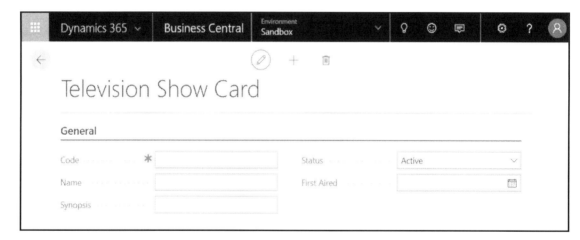

How it works...

We created a basic Business Central application and published it to our development sandbox.

Creating a table allows us to define what data we will capture in our application. We can define a number of properties for each table and field.

In order to display the data in the table, we need to create pages. These allow the user to interact with the data in our application. A list page is the first page that the user will get to when they want to access the data. From this list, they can search, filter existing data, create new data, modify data, and even delete data. When more detailed information is required, the user can navigate from the list page to the card page, which is meant to show more detailed information and actions regarding the data.

See also

We only touched on a very small portion of the full capabilities of tables and pages. You can find more information on tables and pages at the Microsoft Docs website:

- **Tables**: https://docs.microsoft.com/en-us/dynamics365/business-central/dev-itpro/developer/devenv-tables-overview
- **Pages**: https://docs.microsoft.com/en-us/dynamics365/business-central/dev-itpro/developer/devenv-pages-overview

Creating new business logic

Adding a place to store data and interact with it is essential, but in all likelihood, you're going to need to manipulate the data or provide some logic for the user to interact with. In this recipe, we will create some business logic for our application.

Getting ready

We're going to need an AL project that's connected to a development sandbox to work in. We will continue to build on the project that we started in this chapter. You can download it from the GitHub link at the start of this chapter.

How to do it...

1. Open your AL project folder in Visual Studio Code.
2. In the Visual Studio Code **Explorer**, select the Television Show.al file. In the **Editor** tab, add two new fields named Last Aired and Created By, as follows:

```
field(6; "Last Aired"; Date)
{
```

```
    }
    field(7; "Created By"; Code[50])
    {
        Editable = false;
    }
}
```

3. When a new record is added to the Television Show table, we want to know who created it. We can do that by adding code to the `OnInsert()` trigger of the table so that our logic executes every time a record is inserted.

    In the `Television Show.al` file, add the trigger and logic after the `keys` section. All we need to do is set the `Created By` field to the ID of the current user, as follows:

    ```
    trigger OnInsert()
    begin
        "Created By" := UserId();
    end;
    ```

    You can use the `trigger` snippet to create a new trigger.

4. Our next requirement is to make sure that if the user enters the `Last Aired` date, they choose a date that is not earlier than the `First Aired` date. This is simple logic, but it controls our data integrity.

    This is done by adding code to the `InValidate()` trigger of both date fields, since either can be changed independently of the other.

    Since we don't want to write the same code twice, we'll create a new procedure and call it from both fields. The new procedure will validate the dates.

    Start by creating a new procedure. Add this new procedure after the `OnInsert()` trigger you added in the preceding step. The procedure will look like this:

    ```
    local procedure VerifyDates()
    var
        FirstAiredDateCannotBeLaterErr: Label '%1 cannot be earlier
        than %2';
    begin
        if "Last Aired" = 0D then
    ```

```
            exit;

    if "First Aired" > "Last Aired" then
        Error(FirstAiredDateCannotBeLaterErr,
            FieldCaption("Last Aired"),
            FieldCaption("First Aired"));
end;
```

Like I said, it's simple logic, right?

Notice the `Label` variable. These are new to AL and take the place of text constants. You can read more about them at https://docs.microsoft. com/en-us/dynamics365/business-central/dev-itpro/developer/ methods-auto/label/label-data-type.

5. Now that we have our new procedure, we need to call it from each of the date fields. We do that by adding a call to the procedure in the `OnValidate()` trigger of the `First Aired` and `Last Aired` fields. The trigger will look like this:

```
trigger onValidate()
begin
    VerifyDates();
end;
```

Now that we have all of our logic in place, the `Television Show.al` file should look like this:

```
table 50100 "Television Show"
{
    fields
    {
        field(1; Code; Code[20])
        {
            NotBlank = true;
        }
        field(2; Name; Text[80])
        {
        }
        field(3; Synopsis; Text[250])
        {
        }
        field(4; Status; Option)
        {
            OptionCaption = 'Active,Finished';
            OptionMembers = Active,Finished;
        }
        field(5; "First Aired"; Date)
```

```
        {
            trigger onValidate()
            begin
                VerifyDates();
            end;
        }
        field(6; "Last Aired"; Date)
        {
            trigger onValidate()
            begin
                VerifyDates();
            end;
        }
        field(7; "Created By"; Code[50])
        {
            Editable = false;
        }
    }

    keys
    {
        key(PK; Code)
        {
            Clustered = true;
        }
    }

    trigger OnInsert()
    begin
        "Created By" := UserId();
    end;

    local procedure VerifyDates()
    var
        FirstAiredDateCannotBeLaterErr: Label '%1 cannot be
        earlier than %2';
    begin
        if "Last Aired" = 0D then
            exit;

        if "First Aired" > "Last Aired" then
            Error(FirstAiredDateCannotBeLaterErr,
                    FieldCaption("Last Aired"),
                    FieldCaption("First Aired"));
    end;
}
```

6. Before we can test our new logic, we need to add the `Last Aired` field to the **Television Show Card**.
In **Explorer**, select `Television Show Card.al` and add the following code at the end of the `group(General)` section:

```
field("Last Aired"; "Last Aired")
{
    ApplicationArea = All;
}
```

7. We also need to add the `Created By` field to the **Television Show List**.

In **Explorer**, select `Television Show List.al` and add the following code at the end of the `repeater(Group)` section:

```
field("Created By"; "Created By")
{
    ApplicationArea = All;
}
```

8. Press *F5* to build and deploy your application. Once your web browser opens and you log in to your sandbox, you will be on the **Television Show List** page.

Perform the following steps:

1. Click **+New** to open the **Television Show Card**.
2. Populate the **Code** field and press **Tab**.
3. Select any date you want in the **First Aired** field.
4. In the **Last Aired** field, select a date that is earlier than the date you selected in **First Aired**.
5. Click on any other field on the page.

You should see the following error message:

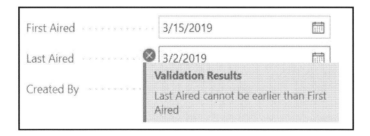

9. Close the **Television Show Card**. You will see that the **Created By** field has been populated for the new record that you just entered:

CODE	NAME	STATUS	CREATED BY
SHOW1	Sample television show	Active	MIKE

How it works...

Triggers are functions that happen based on when predetermined actions occur. When code is placed in these triggers, it is executed whenever the trigger is executed. It is important to note, however, that a trigger can be bypassed using business logic, so you cannot 100% guarantee that a trigger will fire.

The examples we looked at were table triggers that executed when a record was inserted into the table and any time a field was validated. There are many other triggers that are available for you to use in your AL coding. Each different AL object type has its own set of triggers.

See also

You can read more about the different triggers on the Microsoft Docs website at `https://docs.microsoft.com/en-us/dynamics365/business-central/dev-itpro/developer/triggers/devenv-triggers`.

Classifying data

Data privacy is a huge concern for people today. With countless online systems collecting and tracking data from everyone in the world, people want to know that their data is safe and private, and that if they choose to remove their data from a system, it can be done.

Business Central contains features that help you build applications that are compliant with the regulatory requirements for the collecting and handling of personal information.

As an AL developer, you have the ability to identify the type of data that is stored in any new table or field that you create. We will look at how to do this in this recipe.

Getting ready

You're going to need an AL project to work in that's connected to a development sandbox. We will continue to build on the project that we started in this chapter. You can download it from the GitHub link at the start of this chapter.

How to do it...

1. Open your AL project in Visual Studio Code and select the `Television Show.al` file in **Explorer**.
2. For each field that we added to the `Television Show` table, we need to add the `DataClassification` property and assign it a value of `CustomerContent`, as follows:

   ```
   DataClassification = CustomerContent;
   ```

> In the event that a field has multiple properties, the order in which the properties are listed does not matter; however, the properties must be listed before any triggers that are defined.

3. Define the same property to the overall table by adding the following to your AL file, before the `fields` section:

   ```
   DataClassification = CustomerContent;
   ```

How it works...

By specifying the `DataClassification` property for the table and the fields within the table, we have now made our application compliant with data privacy regulations. There are multiple classifications that can be applied to data:

- `CustomerContent`: Content created by users of the system
- `EndUserIdentifiableInformation`: Data that can be used to identify an end user (for example, username and IP address)

- `AccountData`: Data that is part of a customer's billing and payment information (for example, name, address, and email)
- `EndUsePseudonymousIdentifiers`: An identifier that can be used in conjunction with other information to identify an end user (for example, user GUID and user SID)
- `OrganizationIdentifiableInformation`: Data that can be used to find a tenant (for example, Tenant ID).
- `SystemMetadata`: Data generated by the system that cannot be linked to a user or tenant

There's more...

Having the developer define the type of data that your tables and fields contain within the application is just the first step in maintaining data privacy. Business Central contains another feature that lets customers further define the sensitivity of the data in their system. The data sensitivity of a field can be set to one of the following levels:

- Sensitive
- Personal
- Confidential
- Normal

See also

For more information on the two methods for classifying data in Business Central, see the following pages of the Microsoft Docs website:

- Developer: https://docs.microsoft.com/en-us/dynamics365/business-central/dev-itpro/developer/devenv-classifying-data
- Customer: https://docs.microsoft.com/en-us/dynamics365/business-central/dev-itpro/developer/devenv-classifying-data-sensitivity

User permissions

Remember that, when we deliver an application to a customer, we're trying to provide them with the best experience that we can. Nothing's worse than building the best application you can build and everything tests out great, but then you deploy it to the customer and nobody can run it because they don't have any permissions set up. This adds a layer of complexity for the customer that doesn't really need to be there, so the administrator needs to figure out what new entities were added so that they can update their permission sets.

In this recipe, you will see that, with your AL application, you can create a set of user permissions that will be installed when your application is deployed. Then, all an administrator has to do is assign those permissions to the appropriate users!

Getting ready

You're going to need an AL project to work in that's connected to a development sandbox. We will continue to build on the project that we started in this chapter. You can download it from the GitHub link at the start of this chapter.

How to do it...

1. Open up your AL project in Visual Studio Code. Press *Ctrl* + *Shift* + *P* to open the **Command Palette** and type or select **AL: Generate permission set containing current extension objects**.

   Wait... what? That's it? Yeah, it is that easy! When this command runs, it will create a file named `extensionPermissionSet.xml`.

   This file will contain default permissions for every AL object file that you have created in your project:

   - **Tables**: Allow the user to run each table and have full read/write/modify access to the data in the table
   - **Everything else**: Allows the user to execute all other AL object types (such as pages, codeunits, and reports)

Your file should look similar to this:

```xml
<?xml version="1.0" encoding="utf-8"?>
<PermissionSets>
  <PermissionSet RoleID="ALPROJECT1" RoleName="ALProject1">
    <Permission>
      <ObjectType>0</ObjectType>
      <ObjectID>50100</ObjectID>
      <ReadPermission>1</ReadPermission>
      <InsertPermission>1</InsertPermission>
      <ModifyPermission>1</ModifyPermission>
      <DeletePermission>1</DeletePermission>
      <ExecutePermission>0</ExecutePermission>
      <SecurityFilter />
    </Permission>
    <Permission>
      <ObjectType>1</ObjectType>
      <ObjectID>50100</ObjectID>
      <ReadPermission>0</ReadPermission>
      <InsertPermission>0</InsertPermission>
      <ModifyPermission>0</ModifyPermission>
      <DeletePermission>0</DeletePermission>
      <ExecutePermission>1</ExecutePermission>
      <SecurityFilter />
    </Permission>
    <Permission>
      <ObjectType>8</ObjectType>
      <ObjectID>50101</ObjectID>
      <ReadPermission>0</ReadPermission>
      <InsertPermission>0</InsertPermission>
      <ModifyPermission>0</ModifyPermission>
      <DeletePermission>0</DeletePermission>
      <ExecutePermission>1</ExecutePermission>
      <SecurityFilter />
    </Permission>
    <Permission>
      <ObjectType>8</ObjectType>
      <ObjectID>50100</ObjectID>
      <ReadPermission>0</ReadPermission>
      <InsertPermission>0</InsertPermission>
      <ModifyPermission>0</ModifyPermission>
      <DeletePermission>0</DeletePermission>
      <ExecutePermission>1</ExecutePermission>
      <SecurityFilter />
    </Permission>
  </PermissionSet>
</PermissionSets>
```

If you make manual updates to the file that was generated by Visual
Studio Code, and you run the command again to generate the XML file,
your changes will be lost. You can avoid this by renaming the file that was
generated so it doesn't get overwritten. Any manual changes need to be
merged with the generated file.

2. At this point, it's a really good idea to change the `RoleID` and `RoleName` values
in the file. This makes it easier for the administrator who is assigning the
permissions and trying to figure out what each permission set is for.

    Set these properties to the following values:

    ```
    RoleID="TVSHOW"
    RoleName="Television Show"
    ```

If you prefer, you can also manually create a permission set file by
creating an empty XML file, and then using the `tpermsets` and
`tpermset` snippets to quickly build the structure of the file.

3. Now, we can publish our application to make sure that our permission set gets
installed properly.

    In Visual Studio Code, press *F5* to build and publish the application.

4. When your browser opens up, log in to your sandbox and click the 💡 icon at the
top-right of the window in order to open the **Tell Me What You Want to Do**
search page. In the search box, type in `permission sets` and click the link to
open the **PERMISSION SETS** page. In the list of available permission sets, you
should see the **TVSHOW** set that you just created:

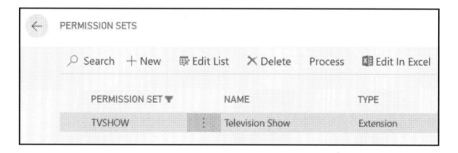

5. Click on the **TVSHOW** permission set row, and on the ribbon at the top, click on **More options | Navigate | Permissions | Permission Set** to open up the permission set details. Here, you can see which permissions are included in the permission set. It should look like this:

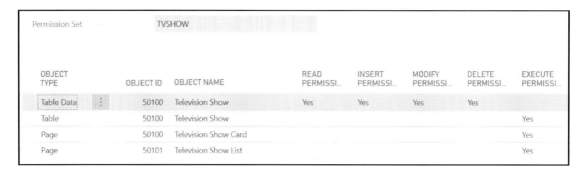

As you can see, our permission set includes full access to the **Television Show** data, and access to run everything that is included in our application.

How it works...

When you create the XML file using the specific structure outlined previously, the AL compiler is able to automatically determine that the file contains permission sets and permissions, and it will automatically load the permission sets into Business Central when your application is installed. This way, the customer does not need to try and figure out what objects have been added, nor do they need to update any existing permission sets that they have already defined.

You can create multiple permission sets within your application, and you can define the permissions in as much detail as you like. For example, you could define two permission sets, where one has only *read-only* access to the data, and the other set has full access, thereby giving the customer the option of assigning different levels of user access.

There's more...

Once your permission sets have been installed, the last step is for the administrator to assign the permission sets to the applicable users. This can be done by either assigning the permission set directly to the user or by assigning the permission set to a user group. By doing this, all users within that group will inherit the new permission set.

See also

You can find more information on managing permissions in Business Central on the Microsoft Docs page

at `https://docs.microsoft.com/en-us/dynamics365/business-central/ui-how-users-p ermissions`.

Creating new reports

In this recipe, we'll look at how you can add a report to your Business Central application. Just a basic report, though – this isn't a lesson on how to create report layouts, which is a whole other topic in itself.

Getting ready

You're going to need an AL project to work on that's connected to a development sandbox. We will continue to build on the project that we started in this chapter. You can download it from the GitHub link at the start of this chapter.

Make sure you have Microsoft Report Builder installed as well!

How to do it...

1. Open up your AL project in Visual Studio Code. In the **Explorer**, right-click and select **New File.** Name the file `Television Shows Report.al`. This report will be a simple list to show the records from the `Television Show` table you added earlier.
2. Now, we need to define the structure of our report dataset.

 You can use the `report` snippet to quickly create the basic structure of a report.

Select the new file and, in the **Editor** tab, enter the following code:

```
report 50100 "Television Shows Report"
{
    UsageCategory = ReportsAndAnalysis;
```

```
        ApplicationArea = All;
        DefaultLayout = RDLC;
        RDLCLayout = 'Television Shows Report.rdl';

        dataset
        {
            dataitem("Television Show"; "Television Show")
            {
                RequestFilterFields = Code, "First Aired", "Last
                Aired", Status;

                column(Code; Code)
                {

                }
                column(Name; Name)
                {

                }
                column(First_Aired; "First Aired")
                {

                }
                column(Last_Aired; "Last Aired")
                {

                }
            }
        }
    }
```

As you can see, in the preceding code, we have defined this report to have an RDLC layout:

```
DefaultLayout = RDLC;
```

We have also defined the name of the layout file:

```
RDLCLayout = 'Television Shows Report.rdl';
```

 A report can be defined with both a Word and an RDLC layout; however, only one can be defined as the default layout. Adding a Word layout to the report would look like `WordLayout = 'Television Shows Report.docx';`.

3. So, how do we create the layout file that we defined in the report AL object file? Of course, you could do it manually, but where's the magic in that? The AL Language extension is going to help you out here. When you build an AL project, if the report layout files that you've defined do not exist, it will create the files for you (with no content, of course – it's not going to do all the work for you!).

Press *Ctrl + Shift + B* to build your AL project.

Notice how in the **Explorer**, a new file named `Television Shows Report.rdlc` was created:

4. The layout that was created for us has an `.rdlc` extension. This is not exactly what we want. By default, this file type will not open using SQL Report Builder, which—for this recipe, at least—is our reporting tool of choice.

Rename the `Television Shows Report.rdlc` layout file and change it to `Television Shows Report.rdl`. This now matches the layout name we defined in the `RDLCLayout` property, and it can now be opened using SQL Report Builder.

5. Now that we have our empty report layout, what do we do next? Well, we need to actually create the layout in that file as it's empty right now. We're going to use Microsoft Report Builder to build a very simple list report layout.

Open **Report Builder** and click **Open** to open the RDL file that you created in your AL project:

Although the layout contents are completely empty, the RDL file does contain the dataset that you defined in the AL object file. You can see this by expanding **Datasets | DataSet_Result** in the **Report Data** pane:

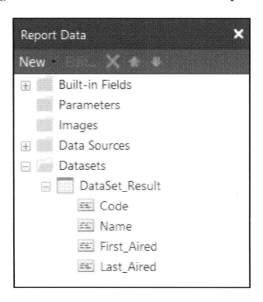

6. Now, we can add a simple table to display the data from the **Television Show** table. We're going to use the built-in wizard for this.

At the top of the Report Builder window, click on the **Insert** tab and then click on **Table | Table Wizard...** to open up the wizard:

7. In the **New Table or Matrix** window, select **Choose an existing dataset in this report or a shared dataset**, and then select the **DataSet_Result** dataset:

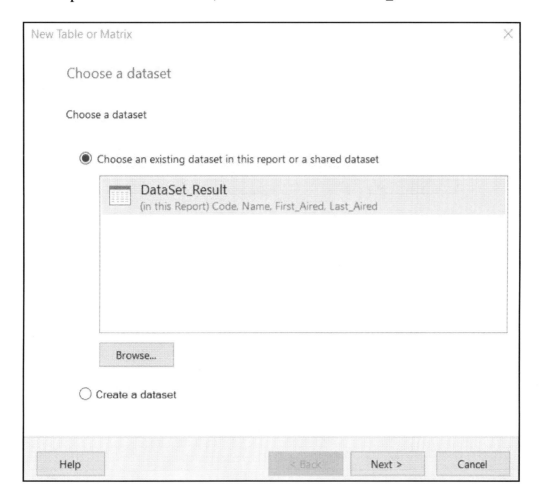

8. Click on **Next**; and you will see the list of available fields:
    1. Click and drag the **Code** field to the **Row groups** section.
    2. Click and drag the remaining fields **(Name, First_Aired** and **Last_Aired**) to the **Values** section.

The wizard should look similar to this:

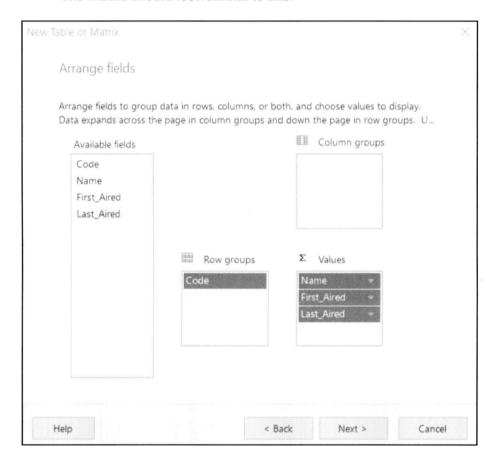

9. Click **Next** to choose the layout options. Uncheck both of the following options:
    - **Show subtotals and grand totals**
    - **Expand/collapse groups**

This is shown in the following screenshot:

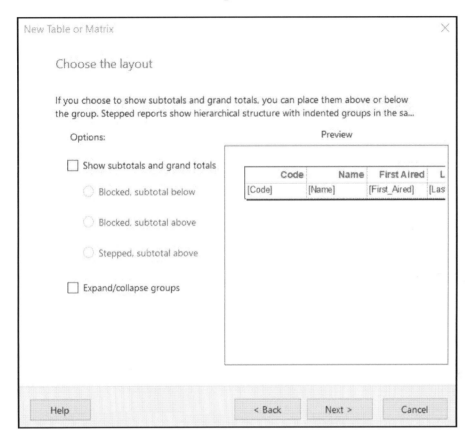

10. Click on **Finish** to close the wizard and add the table to the report layout. The report layout window should now look similar to this:

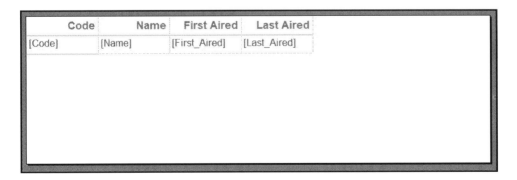

I know – this is not exactly the prettiest layout that's ever been created, but like I said, the point of this recipe is not to learn how to create beautiful reports. We just want to get a report built in our Business Central application.

11. In **Report Builder**, click  at the top left to save the report layout. You can now close the **Report Builder**.

12. We've now created our dataset in an AL file and linked it to a new RDLC layout file. Now, it's time to check out our report.
Press *F5* to build and publish our application.

13. Once your browser is open and you're logged in to the sandbox, use the 🔍 icon at the top-right to search for `Television Shows Report`, and click the link to open the report.

Click **Preview** to run the report onscreen:

At this point, you'll see something such as the following (yes; at this point, you might be realizing that you need to add some **Television Show** entries):

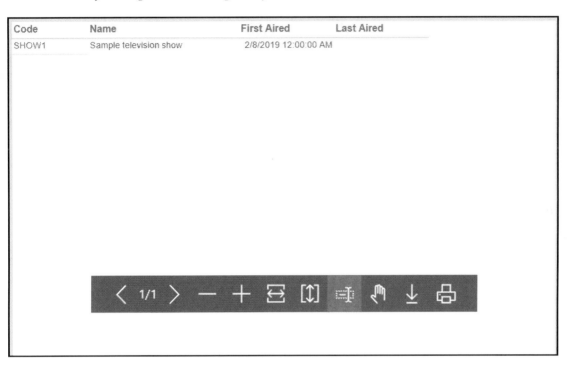

How it works...

A report is made up of two parts:

- **Dataset**: This is an AL file where you will define the tables, fields, filtering, and logic that applies to the report.
- **Layout**: This will be either a Microsoft Word or an RDLC-formatted file and is where you define what the output of the report will look like.

The two parts are linked using properties in the AL file so that when the report is loaded into Business Central, the system knows which layout to use for which report.

There's more...

You can store up to two layouts (one RDLC layout and one for Microsoft Word) with an AL report object, which gives you the ability to deliver different, effectively built-in layout options to the customer. Once the report is installed in Business Central, however, the customer has the ability to further customize those layouts or create an entirely new layout by using the **Custom Report Layouts** feature of Business Central.

See also

You can read more about creating reports on the Microsoft Docs website at `https://docs.microsoft.com/en-us/dynamics365/business-central/dev-itpro/developer/devenv-reports`.

If you would like to learn about how to use **Custom Report Layouts**, check the appropriate page on the Microsoft Docs website at `https://docs.microsoft.com/en-us/dynamics365/business-central/ui-manage-report-layouts`.

Adding help links

You've built an amazing application, you've deployed it to the customer, and now they need help... what do you do? Wouldn't it be nice if you had a dedicated help website for your application? Wouldn't it be nice if, when the user clicked the help icon within your application, they would be taken to that dedicated help website? In this recipe, you'll see how you can make that happen.

Getting ready

You're going to need an AL project to work in that's connected to a development sandbox. We will continue to build on the project that we started in this chapter. You can download it from the GitHub link at the start of this chapter.

How to do it...

1. Open your AL project in Visual Studio Code. In **Explorer**, select the `Television Show List.al` file and add the `HelpLink` page property, as highlighted in the following code:

```
PageType = List;
ApplicationArea = All;
UsageCategory = Lists;
Editable = false;
CardPageId = "Television Show Card";
SourceTable = "Television Show";
HelpLink = 'http://customhelpsite.com/televisionshows';
```

2. Press *F5* to build and publish your application.

3. Once your browser opens and you log in to your sandbox, you will be on the **Television Show List**. Select the ❓ icon at the top right and select **Help**:

   You will be directed to your new custom help link. The link does not point to a real page, as it is just to illustrate the point.

4. Close the **Television Show List** and use the 🔍 icon at the top right to search for `items`. Click the link to open the **Items** list. Select the ❓ icon at the top right and select **Help**. You will see that you're directed to the Microsoft online help website, and not your custom website.

How it works...

When you define a page's `HelpLink` and the user selects the **Help** link in Business Central while on that page, they will be directed to the custom link that's defined for the page. The rest of the pages in the system that are not part of your application will continue to go to the Microsoft online help website.

You can either define page-specific help links or direct all of your pages to a generic landing page. The choice is yours.

As an added bonus, you can also specify help links not only on pages, but also on report request pages and XMLports!

See also

You can read more about adding help links to your AL files on the Microsoft Docs website at https://docs.microsoft.com/en-us/dynamics365/business-central/dev-itpro/ developer/devenv-adding-help-links-from-pages-tables-xmlports.

Customizing What's Already There

2

If you've worked your way through Chapter 1, *Let's Get the Basics out of the Way*, then you know that we've been building a Business Central application that lets us track a list of television shows. Although it's a brand new feature that we have added to Business Central, it's not terribly exciting. Now, let's take that new feature and integrate it into the base Business Central application so that we can track a customer's favorite television shows.

That's right. Not only can you create brand new features, but you can also integrate them into the existing features and logic in Business Central in order to customize the way the system works, which is what this chapter is all about.

In this chapter, we will cover the following recipes:

- Adding fields to base application tables
- Modifying the base application interface
- Modifying the base application business logic
- Using In-client Designer
- Using Event Recorder
- Replacing base application reports
- Adding new profiles and role centers
- Adding filter tokens
- Adding application areas

Technical requirements

We're going to build upon what we started in `Chapter 1`, *Let's Get the Basics out of the Way*, so if you've not worked through that chapter, you should do that now so that you can get your development sandbox set up and Visual Studio Code configured.

Code samples and scripts are available on GitHub. Each of the recipes in this chapter builds on the previous recipe, so you can always download the previous recipe's code to get a quick jump on things if you don't want to work through them all in order. You can download everything from `https://github.com/PacktPublishing/Microsoft-Dynamics-365-Business-Central-Cookbook`.

Adding fields to base application tables

It's one thing to create brand new tables in order to track new information that doesn't exist in Business Central, but what if you just need to track a few additional pieces of data for an entity that is already part of the base application?

This recipe is going to show you how you can add a new field to the `Customer` table.

Some might refer to this process as customizing Business Central, but I'll be referring to it as extending the Business Central application.

Getting ready

You're going to need a Business Central AL development project to work in that's connected to a development sandbox. We will continue to build on the project that we created in `Chapter 1`, *Let's Get the Basics out of the Way*. If you have not completed that chapter, you can download the project from the GitHub link at the beginning of this chapter.

How to do it...

1. Open your AL project folder in Visual Studio Code.
2. In Visual Studio Code's Explorer pane, right-click and create a new file named `Customer Extension.al`. In the **Editor** tab, add the code as follows:

```
tableextension 50100 CustomerExtension extends Customer
{
    fields
    {
        field(50100; "Television Viewing Country"; Option)
        {
            DataClassification = CustomerContent;
            OptionMembers = Canada,"United States","United
            Kingdom";
        }
    }
}
```

Use the `ttableext` snippet to create a **table extension** object and the `tfield` snippet to add new fields.

3. Close and save the `Customer Extension.al` file.

Each Business Central application can contain only one table extension object per table. However, a table can be extended by multiple applications.

How it works...

To add fields to existing base tables, you need to create a **table extension object**. When you do this, you define the table you are going to extend. Once this is done, you simply add your fields as you would any new table. You can add your own logic, properties, and more to your new fields.

When the application gets published, a new companion table will be created in the database to hold the new fields. The Business Central application maintains the link between the companion table and its parent automatically.

See also

You can read more about the table extension object on the Microsoft Docs website at `https://docs.microsoft.com/en-us/dynamics365/business-central/dev-itpro/developer/devenv-table-ext-object`.

Modifying the base application interface

Being able to add new fields to pages, or new actions to the page ribbons, is very common practice, and, luckily for us, it is incredibly easy!

This recipe will show you how to make two changes to the customer card. First, we're going to add a new field, and then we'll add a new action button to the page ribbon.

Getting ready

You're going to need an AL project to work in that's connected to a development sandbox. We will continue to build on the project that we started in Chapter 1, *Let's Get the Basics out of the Way*. You can download that from the GitHub link at the start of this chapter.

Even if you have been working along, you're still going to need to grab a few files from GitHub. Grab the following files from the `ch2/2-modifying-the-base-application-interface` folder and put them in your project folder:

- `Customer Television Show.al`
- `Customer Television Shows.al`

How to do it...

1. Open your AL project folder in Visual Studio Code.
2. In Visual Studio Code's Explorer pane, right-click and create a new file named `Customer Card Extension.al`. In the **Editor** tab, add the following code, which does two things:
   - It adds the `Television Viewing Country` field as the final field in the `General` section.

- It adds a new action button at the end of the `Navigation` group to show the television shows for the given customer:

```
pageextension 50100 CustomerCardExtension extends "Customer
Card"
{
    layout
    {
        addlast(General)
        {
            field("Television Viewing Country";
            "Television Viewing Country")
            {
                ApplicationArea = All;
            }
        }
    }

    actions
    {
        addlast(Navigation)
        {
            action("Customer Television Shows")
            {
                ApplicationArea = All;
                Image = ListPage;
                RunObject = Page "Customer Television
                Shows";
                RunPageLink = "Customer No." = field
                ("No.");
            }
        }
    }
}
```

Use the `tpageext` snippet to create a **page extension** object. You can also use the `tpagefield` and `taction` snippets to create new fields and actions.

3. Now, it's time to test our new additions. Press *F5* to build and publish your application. When your browser opens and you log in to your sandbox, perform the following steps:
    1. Use the ⚲ icon and search for customers to go on the **Customer List**.
    2. Select any customer to drill into the customer card.

First, let's look for the new field that we added. Do you remember where we added it? You should be able to see it on the **General** tab:

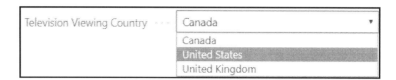

Next, let's check the new action we added. On the customer card, select **Navigate** | **Customer Television Shows**. You may need to first select **More** options to see the **Navigate** link. This will open the **Customer Television Shows** page:

I told you it was easy!

Each Business Central application can contain only one page extension object per page. However, a page can be extended by multiple applications.

How it works...

Similar to extending a table, when you need to make changes to an existing Business Central interface, you do so by creating a **page extension object**, where you can define all the changes that you need to make, including adding, moving, and removing fields, actions, and parts.

See also

You can read more about page extension objects on the Microsoft Docs website at `https://docs.microsoft.com/en-us/dynamics365/business-central/dev-itpro/developer/devenv-page-ext-object`.

Modifying the base application business logic

Being able to enhance and modify the logic within Business Central is incredibly powerful, and it's possible without changing any of the base application source code!

This recipe will show you how to modify the sales document posting routine to add a check to make sure the customer has a favorite television show. I know; it's a completely logical and useful thing for an ERP system to have, right?

Getting ready

You're going to need an AL project to work in that's connected to a development sandbox. We will continue to build on the project that we started in this chapter. You can download this from the GitHub link at the start of this chapter.

How to do it...

1. Open your AL project folder in Visual Studio Code.
2. First, we need to create the new logic that we will implement.

   In Visual Studio Code's Explorer pane, right-click and create a new file named `Check Customer Television Shows.al`. In the **Editor** tab, add the following code, which checks to make sure that there is at least one television show defined as the favorite for the given customer:

```
codeunit 50100 "Check Cust. Television Shows"
{
    procedure CheckCustomerTelevisionShows(CustomerNo:
    Code[20])
    begin
        ValidateFavoriteShowExists(CustomerNo);
    end;

    local procedure ValidateFavoriteShowExists(CustomerNo:
    Code[20])
    var
        CustomerTelevisionShow: Record "Customer Television
        Show";
        NoFavoriteShowErr: Label 'You need to define a favorite
        television show for Customer %1.';
```

```
        begin
            CustomerTelevisionShow.SetRange("Customer No.",
            CustomerNo);
            CustomerTelevisionShow.SetRange(Favorite, true);
            if CustomerTelevisionShow.IsEmpty() then
                Error(NoFavoriteShowErr, CustomerNo);
        end;
    }
```

Use the `tcodeunit` snippet to create a new **codeunit** object, and the `tprocedure` snippet to create new functions.

3. Now that we have our new logic, let's hook it into the sales posting routine. In Visual Studio Code's Explorer pane, right-click and create a new file named `Sales Post Subscribers.al`. In the **Editor** tab, add the following code:

```
codeunit 50101 SalesPostSubscribers
{
    [EventSubscriber(ObjectType::Codeunit, Codeunit::"Sales-Post
    (Yes/No)", 'OnAfterConfirmPost', '', false, false)]
    local procedure OnAfterConfirmPost(SalesHeader: Record "Sales
    Header")
    var
        CheckCustomerTelevisionShows: Codeunit "Check Cust.
        Television Shows";
    begin
        CheckCustomerTelevisionShows.CheckCustomerTelevisionShows
        (SalesHeader."Sell-to Customer No.");
    end;
}
```

Use the `teventsub` snippet to create new event subscribers.

4. Time to test! Press *F5* to build and publish your application. When your browser opens and you log in to your sandbox, perform the following steps:

    1. Use the icon and search for *sales invoices* to go to the **Sales Invoices** page.

    2. Select an existing sales invoice from the list or create a new one:
- Make sure you use an invoice for a customer that has no television shows defined!

    3. Post the sales invoice.

After confirming that you want to post the document, you should see an error similar to the following one:

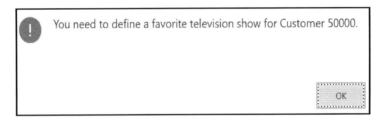

If you want to test further, repeat the preceding process but before you post the invoice, add at least one television show to the customer and mark it as a favorite. Your sales invoice should then post without any error.

For superior performance, try to keep your subscriber codeunits as small as possible. This minimizes the time it takes for the system to load those codeunits into memory when the events are fired. You may also want to consider making your subscribers single instance so they only need to be loaded once per session.

How it works...

In order to change, enhance, or modify the base application logic, we must hook into events using a subscriber. These events are placed throughout the application source code in order to make them extensible to Business Central partners and customers.

The concept of events does mean that you cannot necessarily change every little thing about the system, but it provides a much more controlled way of changing how the system works.

Any time that the event is fired in the application source code, a check is done to see whether there are any active subscribers, and, if so, that the logic in those subscribers is executed.

 When multiple applications subscribe to the same event, you cannot control which application is executed first, so be careful with the code you put into a subscriber. If you are completely reliant on the data looking a certain way, you might run the risk of another application changing it and therefore breaking your logic.

See also

You can read more about subscribers to events on the Microsoft Docs website at `https://docs.microsoft.com/en-us/dynamics365/business-central/dev-itpro/developer/devenv-subscribing-to-events`.

Using In-client Designer

While it's certainly easy enough to code a new page layout in AL, or modify an existing page layout with a page extension, there is another way that you can do this: using **Designer**, which resides directly in the Business Central web client!

This recipe will show you how to launch Designer from Visual Studio Code, make some changes to an existing page layout, and then bring those changes back into your AL project.

Getting ready

You're going to need an AL project to work in that's connected to a development sandbox. We will continue to build on the project that we started in this chapter. You can download that from the GitHub link at the start of this chapter.

How to do it...

1. Open your AL project folder in Visual Studio Code.

2. In order for Designer to work with our AL project, we need to make a small change to the project. Add the following property to the `app.json` file:

   ```
   "showMyCode": true
   ```

3. Press *F6*. This will publish your extension to your sandbox and launch Designer. When your browser opens, you will see that the design mode is active through the box in the top-center of your window:

 While in design mode, you are still looking at the actual data in the system and can interact with the system, just as you would when Designer is not running.

4. While still in design mode, navigate to the **Items** page, and then select any item in order to open the *Item Card*.

   Move your cursor around the page, over the top of various controls on the page. As you move over the fields, you will notice that a triangle appears within the control. For page elements, such as fact boxes, you will notice that the element is highlighted and that the triangle appears within the control. Some examples are as follows:

   We can have a single triangle, as in the following screenshot:

   We can also have double triangles, as shown here:

5. Move your cursor over any field on the page and click the triangle. Select **Remove**. The page will reload with the field now gone:

6. Move your cursor over another field on the page, and then click and drag the triangle to move the field to another location on the page. Release the mouse button to place the field in the new location.

7. Now, let's add a new field to the page:
    1. In the top-center of your screen, in the **Designer** box, click **More**.
    2. Select **+ Field**. A list will open to the right listing all the fields that are available to add to the page.
    3. Drag any field from the list to anywhere on the page.

 Each field in the list will have a status of either **Ready** or **Placed** to indicate whether the field already exists on the page. Note that you can add a field more than once to a page.

8. Now that we're done making our updates to the page, let's save the changes:
    1. In the top-right corner of your browser window, press **Stop designing.**
    2. Uncheck the **Download Code** option.
    3. Press **Save** in the bottom-right corner of your browser window.

9. Now, we pull the changes into our AL project. In Visual Studio Code, press *F7*. This will pull back the changes you just made to the **Item Card**.

10. In Visual Studio Code's Explorer pane, open the `PageExtension50101.al` file and take note of the code in it. The AL code represents the exact changes you made in Designer.

You have just generated AL code by writing no code at all! How cool is that!?

How it works...

By launching Designer from Visual Studio Code, and then saving the changes you make, what you are actually doing is updating the extension that is published in the sandbox with those new changes. Designer is generating the AL code necessary to apply those changes, and, with Visual Studio Code, we can then download that generated code so that we can keep it in our project and further update it manually if required.

 Since Designer changes are stored in the extension, this means that the changes will apply to all users in the system.

See also

You can read more about Designer on the Microsoft Docs website at `https://docs.microsoft.com/en-us/dynamics365/business-central/dev-itpro/developer/devenv-inclient-designer`.

Using Event Recorder

Earlier in this chapter, the *Modifying the base application business logic* recipe showed you how you can modify the existing business logic in Business Central. That recipe showed you what event you needed to subscribe to, but what if you didn't know what events were available to you? What if you know you want to modify a specific processing routine but don't know what events, if any, are in that routine?

Here, **Event Recorder** enters the picture.

With Event Recorder, you can discover what events have been raised in the system, whether they are part of the base application, or whether they are part of another application that's installed.

This recipe will show you how to launch Event Recorder and use it to determine what events are in the sales order release routine.

Getting ready

You're going to need an AL project to work in that's connected to a development sandbox. We will continue to build on the project that we started in this chapter. You can download that from the GitHub link at the start of this chapter.

How to do it...

1. Let's create a simple scenario of releasing a sales order:
    1. Open your browser and log in to your development sandbox.
    2. Go to the **Sales Orders** page and click on any order to open it.
    3. In the ribbon, click on **Release | Reopen** to open the order:
        - Alternatively, you can create a new order, but do not release it.

    Do not close the **Sales Order** page or the web browser tab!

2. Open your AL project folder in Visual Studio Code.
3. Press *Ctrl + Shift + P* to open the **Command Palette** and type or select **AL: Open Events Recorder**. Your web browser will open a new tab. Once you log in to your sandbox, you will see the **Event Recorder** page, as follows:

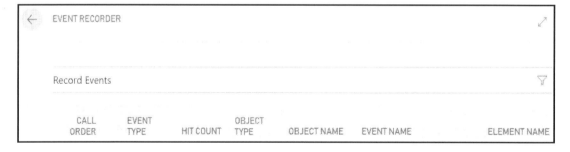

4. On the **Event Recorder** page, click on **Record Events | Start**, and select **Yes** to begin recording events.

    Do not close the **Event Recorder** page or the browser tab!

5. Now, let's perform the process for the events we want to record:
    1. Switch back to the original browser tab with the open sales order.
    2. On the ribbon, click on **Release | Release** to release the order.

6. Now, let's see what events were fired during that process:
    1. Switch back to the browser tab with the **Event Recorder** page.
    2. Click on **Record Events | Stop**, and select **Yes** to view the events that
       were fired.

Results may vary, but you should see something similar to this screenshot:

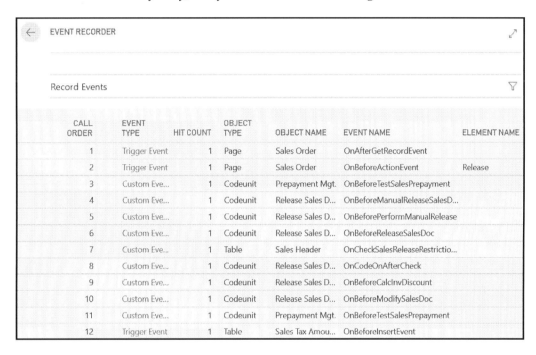

This is a listing of the order in which events were fired during the release of a
sales order.

How it works...

Not knowing what events fire during a routine is a very common scenario when you are
building Business Central applications. Sure, you can dig through the base application
source code to find the answers, but Event Recorder gives you a nice view of what exact
events are fired, the exact order in which they are fired, and how many times they are fired.

This makes it much easier to determine where you hook in any business logic changes that
you want to make, and, as an added bonus, all events will show, even if they are part of
other Business Central applications that are installed.

If you scroll to the far-right of Event Recorder, you will see a link on each row named **Get AL Snippet**. If you select that link, a dialog will appear on screen with the necessary AL code for subscribing to the event listed on that row. Copy that code into your AL project and you're good to go!

See also

You can read more about Event Recorder on the Microsoft Docs website at `https://docs.microsoft.com/en-us/dynamics365/business-central/dev-itpro/developer/devenv-events-discoverability`.

Replacing base application reports

Business Central is jammed full of great reports. Sometimes, however, those reports are not entirely what the user needs to see, and sometimes, adding a custom layout to the report is just not enough as we need to access new logic or new tables and fields. In these scenarios, what we need to do is replace the base report with our own modified version. Luckily for us, this has been made easy using a Business Central application!

This recipe will show you how to replace the **Customer Listing** report with a modified version that shows the television shows defined for the customer.

Getting ready

You're going to need an AL project to work in that's connected to a development sandbox. We will continue to build on the project that we started in this chapter. You can download this from the GitHub link at the start of this chapter.

Even if you have been working along, you'll still need to grab two files from GitHub. Grab the following files from the `ch2/6-replacing-base-application-reports` folder and place them in your project folder:

- `Customer Listing With Television Shows.al`
- `Customer Listing With Television Shows.rdl`

How to do it...

1. First, let's view the existing **Customer Listing** report to see what it looks like:
    1. Open your web browser and go to your Business Central development sandbox.
    2. Using the 💡 icon, search for `Customer Listing` and click the link to run the report.
    3. Click **Preview** to view the report on screen.

    The report should look something like this:

No.	Name and Address / Contact and Phone Number	Customer Posting Group	Blocked Comm ent	Discounts Inv. / Item	Customer Tax Area Code	Terms Fin Chrg	Salesperson Currency Code	Credit Limit ($) / Balance ($)
	Customer Listing							Sunday, March 31, 2019 2:56 PM
	CRONUS Canada, Inc.							Page 1
								MIKE
	All amounts are in CAD.							
10000	Adatum Corporation	DOMESTIC		10000		1M	PS	
	360 Main Street, Suite 1150		No		MB			18,216.96
	Winnipeg, MB R3C 3Z3							
	Robert Townes							
20000	Trey Research	DOMESTIC		20000		14D	PS	
	1950 Meadowvale Blvd.		No		ON			4,908.72
	Missisauga, ON L5N 8L9							
	Helen Ray							

2. In Visual Studio Code, open your AL project.
3. In **Explorer**, create a new file named `Replace Base Reports.al`. In the **Editor** tab, create a new codeunit object and then add the following code:

```al
codeunit 50102 "Replace Base Reports"
{
    [EventSubscriber(ObjectType::Codeunit,
    Codeunit::ReportManagement, 'OnAfterSubstituteReport', '',
    false, false)]
    procedure OnAfterSubstituteReport(ReportId: Integer; var
    NewReportId: Integer)
    begin
        if ReportId = Report::"Customer Listing" then
            NewReportId := Report::"Customer Listing With TV
            Shows";
    end;
}
```

If you do not have the **Customer Listing** report in your development sandbox, you can also perform the preceding example using the **Customer - List** report.

Can it get any easier than this? As you can see from the code, all we need to do is replace the original report that the system was executing with our own modified version.

4. Press *F5* to build and publish your application so that we can test this out. Once it's published, go back and repeat *step 1*, and this time, your report should look something like this (results, of course, will vary based on your data):

As you can see, compared to the original report, we made some pretty drastic changes. We not only changed the report layout, but we also completely changed the dataset too!

Ensure that you substitute a report with one that has a compatible dataset. Some reports that are executed in the source code require specific dataset items because of the way that the logic is written. If you replace the report with an incompatible one, then you will receive errors at runtime.

How it works...

The `OnAfterSubstituteReport` event is fired between when a report is requested to execute and the actual execution. This gives us the chance to intercept that call and replace the report that will be executed.

Don't worry, this event is fired when a user clicks on a report action on a page, or when any of the following commands are executed in the system, which means it will work great for replacing processing reports as well as printed ones:

- Run
- RunModal
- SaveAsHtml
- SaveAsXml
- SaveAsPdf
- SaveAsExcel
- SaveAsWord
- RunRequestPage
- Execute
- Print
- SaveAs

 When the subscriber is executed, if the incoming ReportId and NewReportId parameters do not match, and NewReportId is not –1, then this means that the report has already been substituted by another subscriber (for example, another Business Central application) and you'll need to determine how to handle that.

See also

Check out all the other wonderful things that you can do with reports in your Business Central application on the Microsoft Docs website at https://docs.microsoft.com/en-us/dynamics365/business-central/dev-itpro/developer/devenv-reports.

Adding new profiles and role centers

One of the strengths of Business Central is that it's a role-based experience for every user. If you're a sales-order entry clerk, then when you log in, you will see sales tasks that relate to your job. If you're a warehouse worker, then logging in will take you to tasks that are specific to a warehouse employee. The main point is that every user can have a tailored experience so they only need to navigate through tasks and information that they need to see.

This is done by assigning each user to a profile, which in turn assigns them to a specific role center. That role center is the very first screen that the user sees when they log in, so it's important that the contents of that screen make sense to them.

This recipe will show you how to create a new profile that can be assigned to a user, as well as a new role center for that profile.

Getting ready

You're going to need an AL project to work in that's connected to a development sandbox. We will continue to build on the project that we started in this chapter. You can download that from the GitHub link at the start of this chapter.

Even if you have been working along, you'll still need to grab two files from GitHub. Grab the following files from the `ch2/7-adding-new-profiles-and-role-centers` folder and put them in your project folder:

- `Television Cue.al`
- `Television Role Center Activities.al`

How to do it...

1. In Visual Studio Code, open your AL project.
2. In **Explorer**, create a new file named `Television Role Center.al`, and in the **Editor** tab, start by creating a new **Role Center** page:

   ```
   page 50103 "Television Role Center"
   {
       PageType = RoleCenter;
   }
   ```

3. Add the `layout` section to define what parts will appear in the role center. You can use any existing page part in the system or build new ones.

   In this example, we'll use a new activities part that was created specifically for this role center, as well as a couple of system parts that are common in most role centers:

   ```
   layout
       {
           area(RoleCenter)
   ```

```
    {
        part(Activities; "Television RC Activities")
        {
            ApplicationArea = All;
        }
        part("Report Inbox Part"; "Report Inbox Part")
        {
            ApplicationArea = All;
        }
        part("Power BI Report Spinner Part"; "Power BI
        Report Spinner Part")
        {
            ApplicationArea = All;
        }
    }
}
```

4. After the `layout` section, we'll add a new section named `actions`, so we can define what actions are in the role center:

```
actions
{
}
```

5. The first set of actions we'll define are some lists that we want in the navigation bar. We do that by adding the following code within the `actions` section:

```
area(Embedding)
{
    action("Television Show List")
    {
        RunObject = page "Television Show List";
        Caption = 'Television Shows';
        ApplicationArea = All;
    }
    action("Customer List")
    {
        RunObject = page "Customer List";
        Caption = 'Customers';
        ApplicationArea = All;
    }
}
```

6. Next, we will define a couple of navigation menus with a link under each. This is done by adding the following code after the `area(Embedding)` section:

```
area(Processing)
{
    group(New)
    {
        action(NewCustomer)
        {
            RunPageMode = Create;
            Caption = 'Customer';
            RunObject = page "Customer Card";
            Image = Customer;
            ApplicationArea = All;
        }
    }
    group(Reports)
    {
        action("Television Show Report")
        {
            Caption = 'Television Shows';
            Image = Report;
            RunObject = report "Television Shows Report";
            ApplicationArea = All;
        }
    }
}
```

7. Now that we've created our role center, we need a profile that is associated with it. In Visual Studio Code's Explorer pane, create a new file named `Television Profile.al` and in the **Editor** tab, add the following code:

```
profile "Television Profile"
{
    Description = 'Television Profile';
    RoleCenter = "Television Role Center";
}
```

You can use the `tprofile` snippet to create a new profile object.

8. Now, it's time to try out our new role center! Follow these steps:
    1. Press *F5* to build and publish our application.
    2. In Business Central, click the ⚙ icon at the top-right of the window and select **My Settings.**
    3. Click the assist edit (**...**) icon next to the **Role Center** field to open the list of role centers.
    4. Find and select the **Television Role** entry and click **Ok.**
    5. Click **Ok** to close the **Settings** page.

At this point, your browser will reload and you will now be looking at the new role center you created! Yeah I know, it's not exactly an impressive role center, and it makes absolutely no sense for an ERP system, but who cares? You're learning, right?

How it works...

When creating new role centers for users to be assigned to, you need to create two things:

- A profile
- A role center that is associated to the profile

By first creating a new `Profile` object, when your Business Central application is installed, the new profile will be loaded into the system and will be available to be assigned to users. A profile can be associated to either an existing or a new role center that you include in your application. A profile can only be associated to one role center.

The second step is to create the role center itself. A role center can contain multiple parts, including activity cues, actions to launch processing tasks and reports, parts to show job-specific data, parts that contain external resources such as Power BI reports, or even headlines that contain key information that is important to the user. The basis of creating a new role center is to create a new page object, and then set `PageType = RoleCenter.`

Once the main role center page is created, you can create additional parts by creating new page objects and associating them to the main page. System parts such as Power BI and Report Inbox can also be added to any role center that you create.

Creating new profiles and role centers allows customers to tailor the system for each user based on their job function. This will provide a much friendlier experience for the user as they can concentrate on the tasks and data that are relevant to them. When a user is associated with a profile, they're also associated with the role center for that profile, which means that as soon as they log in to Business Central, they should be greeted with an interface that is relevant to the job they perform.

See also

You can read more about designing and creating role centers, including additional parts not covered in this recipe (for example, headlines), on the Microsoft Docs website at `https://docs.microsoft.com/en-us/dynamics365/business-central/dev-itpro/developer/devenv-designing-role-centers`.

Adding filter tokens

Being able to filter lists of data in Business Central is an incredibly powerful feature. At the basic level, you can filter a list by any field that is in the table, not just what is showing in the list. We can go beyond that though and create our own filter tokens, which will allow us to filter the list in ways that cannot necessarily be done using simple field filters.

This recipe will show you how to add a new filter token that will allow you to quickly filter the **Customer List** page to show only the customers that have television shows defined.

Getting ready

You're going to need an AL project to work in that's connected to a development sandbox. We will continue to build on the project that we started in this chapter. You can download that from the GitHub link at the start of this chapter.

How to do it...

1. Open your AL project folder in Visual Studio Code.
2. In Visual Studio Code's Explorer pane, right-click and create a new file named
   Customers With Television Shows Filter Token.al. In the **Editor** tab,
   create a new codeunit object, and then add the following code:

```
codeunit 50103 "Customers With Shows Filter"
{
    [EventSubscriber(ObjectType::Codeunit,
    Codeunit::TextManagement, 'OnAfterMakeTextFilter',
    '', true, true)]
    local procedure OnAfterMakeTextFilter(var Position: Integer;
    var TextFilterText: Text)
    var
        Customer: Record Customer;
        CustomerTelevisionShows: Record "Customer Television Show";
        CustWithShowsTokenTxt: Label 'CUSTWITHSHOWS';
        MaxCount: Integer;
    begin
        if StrPos(UpperCase(CustWithShowsTokenTxt),
        UpperCase(TextFilterText)) = 0 then
            exit;

        MaxCount := 2000;
        TextFilterText := '';

        if Customer.FindSet() then begin
            repeat
                CustomerTelevisionShows.SetRange("Customer No.",
                Customer."No.");
                if not CustomerTelevisionShows.IsEmpty() then begin
                    MaxCount -= 1;

                    if TextFilterText <> '' then
                        TextFilterText += '|';

                    TextFilterText += Customer."No.";
                end;
            until (Customer.Next() = 0) or (MaxCount <= 0);
        end;
    end;
}
```

3. Now, let's test it! Press *F5* to build and publish your application. Navigate to the **Customers** list page and click the ▽ icon to show the filter pane. Enter a filter value of **%CustWithShows** into the **No.** field and press **Tab**. Note the value that you enter is not case-sensitive:

The list should get filtered down to only show the customers that have television shows defined. If your list is empty, then release the filter, enter some television shows for a customer or two, and try the filter again.

How it works...

In order to add our own filter token, we subscribed to the `OnAfterMakeTextFilter` event that's in the *Text Management* codeunit of the base application. This event is fired at any time that the user types a filter value into a list. By defining our own filter token string, we can then implement custom logic in order to determine which set of records applies to the filter.

Be careful with the filtering logic that you implement. Although you can filter based on whatever logic you like, introducing bad performing logic will not lead to a very nice customer experience if the user has to wait too long for the list to get filtered.

See also

You can check out more on adding new filtering tokens on the Microsoft Docs website at `https://docs.microsoft.com/en-us/dynamics365/business-central/dev-itpro/developer/devenv-adding-filter-tokens`.

Adding application areas

Application areas let you break down your application into multiple user experiences. One example is that you can identify basic as opposed to advanced features so that a new user can turn off the advanced ones until they are more comfortable with the system.

By implementing application areas in your application, when an application area is disabled, all the on screen controls (fields, actions, parts, and so on) are not visible or searchable to the user.

This recipe will show you how to add a new application area to Business Central.

Getting ready

You're going to need an AL project to work in that's connected to a development sandbox. We will continue to build on the project that we started in this chapter. You can download this from the GitHub link at the start of this chapter.

How to do it...

1. Open your AL project folder in Visual Studio Code.
2. First, we need to extend the `Application Area Setup` table in the base application.

   In Visual Studio Code's Explorer pane, right-click and create a new file named `Application Area Setup Extension.al`. In the **Editor** tab, add the following code:

   ```
   tableextension 50101 "Application Area Setup Ext" extends
   "Application Area Setup"
   {
       fields
       {
           field(50100; "Television Shows"; Boolean)
           {
           }
       }
   }
   ```

3. Now, we need to add the logic to allow the new application area to be enabled.

    In Visual Studio Code's Explorer pane, right-click and create a new file named `Enable TV Application Area.al`. In the **Editor** tab, create an empty codeunit like so:

    ```
    codeunit 50104 "Enable TV Application Area"
    {

    }
    ```

4. We need to add a couple of subscribers to our codeunit so that the base application knows about our new application area and when it should be enabled:

    ```
    [EventSubscriber(ObjectType::Codeunit, Codeunit::"Application Area
    Mgmt.", 'OnGetEssentialExperienceAppAreas', '', false, false)]
    local procedure OnGetEssentialExperienceAppAreas(var
    TempApplicationAreaSetup: Record "Application Area Setup"
    temporary)
    begin
        TempApplicationAreaSetup."Television Shows" := true;
    end;

    [EventSubscriber(ObjectType::Codeunit, Codeunit::"Application Area
    Mgmt.", 'OnValidateApplicationAreas', '', false, false)]
    local procedure OnValidateApplicationAreas(ExperienceTierSetup:
    Record "Experience Tier Setup"; TempApplicationAreaSetup: Record
    "Application Area Setup" temporary)
    var
        InvalidErr: Label 'Television Shows should be part of Essential
        in order for the application to work.';
    begin
        if ExperienceTierSetup.Essential then
            if not TempApplicationAreaSetup."Television Shows" then
                Error(InvalidErr);
    end;
    ```

5. Now, let's add two functions to the codeunit. One will allow us to enable the new application area, while the other will establish whether the new application area is already enabled:

    ```
    procedure IsTelevisionShowsEnabled(): Boolean
    var
        AppAreaSetup: Record "Application Area Setup";
        AppAreaMgmtFacade: Codeunit "Application Area Mgmt. Facade";
    begin
    ```

```
    if AppAreaMgmtFacade.GetApplicationAreaSetupRecFromCompany
    (AppAreaSetup, CompanyName()) then
        exit(AppAreaSetup."Television Shows");
end;

procedure EnableTelevisionShows()
var
    AppAreaSetup: Record "Application Area Setup";
    ExperienceTierSetup: Record "Experience Tier Setup";
    AppAreaMgmtFacade: Codeunit "Application Area Mgmt. Facade";
begin
    if ExperienceTierSetup.Get(CompanyName()) then;
    if not ExperienceTierSetup.Essential then
        exit;
    if AppAreaMgmtFacade.GetApplicationAreaSetupRecFromCompany
    (AppAreaSetup, CompanyName()) then begin
        AppAreaSetup."Television Shows" := true;
        AppAreaSetup.Modify();
        AppAreaMgmtFacade.SetupApplicationArea();
    end;
end;
```

6. Now, let's publish our application to verify whether our new application area is available:

   1. Press *F5* to build and publish your application.

   2. Once you log in to your sandbox, use the 💡 icon to go to the **Application Area** page and you will see the new **Television Shows** entry. It will be disabled, as shown here:

Television Shows	☐

How it works...

Using application areas allows you to control the visibility of entire features in Business Central. When you use application areas, every control that you want to be shown when the application area is enabled must be tagged with the application area using the ApplicationArea property. A control can be tagged with multiple application areas.

As soon as you enable any application area, any control that is not tagged with an application area will always be hidden, so be sure that all your controls are tagged before enabling any application areas.

There's more...

Enabling an application area can be done in a couple of different ways, and you can read about both of them at the following links:

- *Manually*: https://docs.microsoft.com/en-us/dynamics365/business-central/ui-experiences.
- *Automatically when the application is installed*: https://docs.microsoft.com/en-us/dynamics365/business-central/dev-itpro/developer/devenv-extending-application-areas#adding-an-application-area.

The next step, after adding your new application area, is to tag all the appropriate controls in your application. If you've been following along in this book, you've seen that we are tagging all of the controls we added with the application area *All*. This is a special application area that is used to tell the system that the control should be shown on screen irrespective of which application areas have been selected. Instead of using all, you'd want to use the new application area(s) that you added with your application.

See also

You can read more about application areas on the Microsoft Docs website at https://docs.microsoft.com/en-us/dynamics365/business-central/dev-itpro/developer/devenv-extending-application-areas.

Let's Go Beyond 3

By this point, we've covered the basics of a Business Central application, and we've learned how to customize the base Business Central platform.

It's time to get a bit more advanced. Are you ready?

We're going to cover some topics that may not apply to every application that you build, but knowing the functionalities that can be built is often crucial, especially when you are designing a solution for a customer. The more tools in your toolbox, the better prepared you'll be!

In this chapter, we will cover the following recipes:

- Control add-ins
- Dependencies
- Translations
- Adding new manual setups
- Assisted Setup wizards
- Isolated storage
- Notifications
- Using the task scheduler
- .NET interoperability
- Implementing telemetry events

Technical requirements

In some of the recipes in this chapter, we're going to build upon the Television Shows application that we started at the beginning of this book. If you've not worked through the book, you might want to do that now so you can get a feel for the project that we're building.

Remember, you need to set up a development sandbox, so if you've not done that yet, then you can check out `Chapter 1`, *Let's Get the Basics Out of the Way*.

Code samples and scripts are available on GitHub. Some of the recipes in this chapter build on previous recipes. You can download the completed recipe code here: `https://github.com/PacktPublishing/Microsoft-Dynamics-365-Business-Central-Cookbook/tree/master/ch3`.

Control add-ins

Control add-ins let you create onscreen elements that are not necessarily part of the standard set of Business Central controls, and also give you the power to create specific controls and interfaces tailored to specific customer needs. This includes big buttons, charts, graphs, and whatever other funky controls you can think of.

This recipe shows you how to add a custom JavaScript control add-in to `Customer Card`.

Getting ready

You're going to need an AL project to work on that's connected to a development sandbox. We will continue to build on the project that we worked on in `Chapter 2`, *Customizing What's Already There*. If you have not completed that chapter, you can download the project from the GitHub link at the start of this chapter.

Even if you have been working along with the book, you're still going to need to grab a few files from GitHub, which you can do by following these steps:

1. In your AL project's, create a new folder (at the same level as `app.json`) named `ControlAddIn`.

2. Get the following files from the `ch3/1-control-addins/code/ControlAddIn` folder on GitHub and put them in the `ControlAddIn` folder you just created:

- `controlAddIn.js`
- `startup.js`
- `style.css`

How to do it...

1. Open your AL project folder in Visual Studio Code.
2. The first thing we need to do is create the control add-in AL object. In the **Explorer**, create a new file named `Television Control AddIn.al` and enter in the following code in the **Editor** tab:

```
controladdin TelevisionControlAddIn
{
    RequestedHeight = 75;
    MinimumHeight = 75;
    MaximumHeight = 75;
    RequestedWidth = 300;
    MinimumWidth = 300;
    MaximumWidth = 300;
    VerticalStretch = true;
    VerticalShrink = true;
    HorizontalStretch = true;
    HorizontalShrink = true;
    StartupScript = 'ControlAddIn/startup.js';
    Scripts = 'ControlAddIn/controlAddIn.js';
    StyleSheets = 'ControlAddIn/style.css';

    procedure SetTelevisionShow(TelevisionShow: JsonObject);
    event ControlReady();
}
```

You can use the `tcontroladdin` snippet to create the default control add-in structure.

If the compiler highlights any issues with the script or style sheet paths, double-check to make sure you created the folder at the right location and that you have the necessary files in that folder.

Note that we define the events and procedures that the control add-in contains, but only the signatures, not the actual source code.

3. Now that we've defined the control add-in in AL, we need to add it to a page. To do this, let's create a new FactBox, which we will then add to `Customer Card`.

   In **Explorer**, create a new file named `Television Control AddIn Factbox.al` and enter the following code in **Editor**:

```
page 50105 "Television Control AddIn Fctbx"
{
    PageType = CardPart;
    SourceTable = Customer;

    layout
    {
        area(Content)
        {

        }
    }
}
```

4. Let's first add the functions that will get the data needed for the control add-in. In our scenario, we want to show what the customer's favorite show is, and provide a way to search for information on the show in an online television database. Enter the following code into **Editor** after the `layout` section:

```
local procedure GetFavoriteTelevisionShow()
var
    CustomerTelevisionShow: Record "Customer Television Show";
    FavoriteShow: JsonObject;
    NoneFoundLbl: Label 'None found';
begin
    CustomerTelevisionShow.SetRange("Customer No.", "No.");
    CustomerTelevisionShow.SetRange(Favorite, true);
    if CustomerTelevisionShow.FindFirst() then begin
        FavoriteShow.Add('name', GetShowName(
        CustomerTelevisionShow."Television Show Code"));
        FavoriteShow.Add('url', MakeTvdbUrl(GetShowName
        (CustomerTelevisionShow."Television Show Code")));
    end else begin
        FavoriteShow.Add('name', NoneFoundLbl);
        FavoriteShow.Add('url', '');
    end,
```

```
        CurrPage.TelevisionControlAddin.SetTelevisionShow(
        FavoriteShow);
end;

local procedure GetShowName(ShowCode: Code[20]): Text
var
        TelevisionShow: Record "Television Show";
begin
        if ShowCode <> '' then begin
            TelevisionShow.Get(ShowCode);
            exit(TelevisionShow.Name);
        end;
end;

local procedure MakeTvdbUrl(ShowName: Text) Url: Text
var
        UrlBase: Label 'https://www.thetvdb.com/search?q=';
begin
        if ShowName <> '' then begin
            ShowName := ConvertStr(DelChr(ShowName, '<>',
            ' '), ' ', '+');
            Url := UrlBase + ShowName;
        end;
end;
```

In a nutshell, we're grabbing the first show marked as the favorite for the customer, and then using a JSON object to pass the television show name and a URL to the control add-in. If the customer doesn't have a favorite, then we're just passing a standard text string. Nothing too complicated, right?

5. Now that we have all of our logic in place, we need to add the control add-in to the page. Add the following code to the `area(Content)` section in order to display the control add-in:

```
usercontrol(TelevisionControlAddIn; TelevisionControlAddIn)
{
        ApplicationArea = All;
        Visible = true;

        trigger ControlReady()
        begin
            GetFavoriteTelevisionShow();
        end;
}
```

Notice that the trigger name, ControlReady, is the same as the event name that we defined in the control add-in in step 2. This is how the triggers on the AL page get linked to the events in the control add-in.

6. The ControlReady event ensures that the control add-in is updated when it first opens, but we also need to make sure that if the user is scrolling through customer records without closing and reopening the page, everything is updated when the customer records change. Add the following code after the layout section to do this:

```
trigger OnAfterGetRecord()
begin
    GetFavoriteTelevisionShow();
end;
```

7. At this point, we've defined our control add-in and we've added it to a FactBox so that we can see it, so the last step is to add the FactBox to Customer Card.

    In **Explorer**, click on the Customer Card Extension.al file and in the **Editor,** add following code after the addlast(General) section:

```
addfirst(FactBoxes)
{
    part("Television Control AddIn Fctbx"; "Television Control
    AddIn Fctbx")
    {
        Caption = 'Favorite Television Show';
        ApplicationArea = All;
        SubPageLink = "No." = field ("No.");
    }
}
```

8. Now, we can try it out! Press *F5* to build and publish your application. When your browser opens and you log in to your sandbox, perform the following steps:
    1. Go to **Customer List** and select any customer to open **CUSTOMER CARD**.
    2. At the top-right, you should see your new FactBox. It displays the name of the customer's favorite television show and a button, similar to this:

If you scroll through the records in **CUSTOMER CARD**, then you will see that the add-in gets updated every time the customer record changes.

How it works...

When you define your add-in control, you can use straight-up JavaScript as I did here, or you can use jQuery or Angular, depending on what your needs are and what the business requirements are.

When you define the control add-in in AL, you can set which scripts are part of the add-in. You have the option of using local scripts (like the ones in your AL project) or you can reference external scripts, including ones that are online, by providing a URL.

You can also define a special script in the control add-in in order to identify what script is executed, not only when the control add-in starts, but also if you need any specific scripts to fire when the add-in is refreshed or recreated.

Passing data to and from a control add-in is easily done by using JSON objects. Of course, you can also pass individual pieces of information using simple variable types. If you need to pass complex data structures, then using the built-in JSON types makes things quite easy!

Linking procedures and events that are contained within the add-in to ones in your AL code is done by simply making sure that they have the same name in the add-in and in the AL code. In this recipe, we created a `ControlReady` event and a `SetTelevisionShow` procedure in both the JavaScript add-in and in the AL add-in. Simply using the same names creates a link.

See also

Here are some articles you can read on Microsoft Docs about control add-ins:

- **Control add-in object:** `https://docs.microsoft.com/en-us/dynamics365/business-central/dev-itpro/developer/devenv-control-addin-object`
- **Control add-in style guide:** `https://docs.microsoft.com/en-us/dynamics365/business-central/dev-itpro/developer/devenv-control-addin-style`

The style guide is particularly useful for ensuring that the add-ins you create match the look and feel of Business Central, not like the one we created here in this recipe (ha!).

Dependencies

At this point, we've built new functionality and we've extended some existing Business Central base platform features, but what if we need to modify another extension, or what if we want to create multiple applications that all share a common set of functions?

In order to reference entities and functions that are in another Business Central application, we need to create a dependency on that application. This recipe will show you how to create a dependency between two Business Central applications.

Getting ready

We're going to take a bit of a break from our Television Show application for just a moment.

For this recipe, you need to get the `ch3-dependencies-start.zip` file from the `ch3/2-dependencies` folder in the GitHub repository.

Extract this ZIP file to any folder that you have access to on your local machine.

For the purposes of this recipe, I'll refer to the dependent application as the `Parent`, and the application that is being depended on as the `Child`.

How to do it...

1. In Visual Studio Code, select **File | Open Workspace**. Browse to the folder extracted from the ZIP file you downloaded and open the `ch3-dependencies.code-workspace` file.

   A Visual Studio Code workspace can contain multiple projects. In our case, the workspace contains two different AL projects:

   - `Parent`
   - `Child`

2. We need to connect these two projects to our development sandbox.

   If you've been working along with this book, you can copy the `launch.json` file from any of your completed recipe projects and place it in the `.vscode` folders for each project (there's a folder for both the `Child` and `Parent` projects, so make sure you copy the file to both).

   If you don't already have a `launch.json` file from a previous recipe in this book, then you'll need to go back to `Chapter 1`, *Let's Get the Basics Out of the Way*, and set up a development sandbox. Once you have done that, you can configure a new `launch.json` file to connect to the sandbox environment.

3. We now need to download the symbols for these new projects. Because the projects are separate, we have to download the symbols for each project separately.

   When working in a workspace, the context in which Visual Studio Code operates is based on which project you have selected:

   1. In **Explorer**, click on the `Parent Page.al` file within the `Parent` folder and press *Ctrl + Shift + P* to open **Command Palette**.
   2. Type in or select **AL: Download Symbols**.
   3. Once the symbols have been downloaded for the `Parent` project, click on the `Child Table.al` file under the `Child` folder in **Explorer.**
   4. Press *Ctrl + Shift + P* to open the **Command Palette** and type in or select **AL: Download Symbols.**

   We've now downloaded the symbol files for both of our projects!

4. Let's compile our projects.

   In **Explorer**, select the `Child Table.al` file and press *Ctrl + Shift + B* to build the project. In the **Output** window, you should see a message like this:

   ```
   Success: The package is created.
   ```

   In **Explorer,** select the `Parent Page.al` file and press *Ctrl + Shift + B* to build the project. You will notice an error like this:

   ```
   error AL0185: Table 'Child Table' is missing
   ```

5. If you look at the contents of the `Parent Page.al` file, you will see a reference to `Child Table`, but that reference is highlighted with a compiler error.

This is because the `Parent` project does not know about the existence of the `Child` project, so any references to it cannot be resolved. In order to tell the `Parent` project about the `Child` one, we must create a dependency from the `Parent` to the `Child`.

In **Explorer**, select the `app.json` file under the `Parent` folder and update the `dependencies` property as follows:

```
"dependencies": [
    {
        "appId": "c5c7fc1e-a0c4-4e16-b4eb-f1b4db2b34c9",
        "name": "AL Child Project",
        "publisher": "Default publisher",
        "version": "1.0.0.0"
    }
],
```

The values that you enter in the `dependencies` property are found in the `app.json` file of the app you are adding the dependency for, and can also be found on the **Extension Management** page in Business Central.

6. Now that we have told the `Parent` project about the `Child` project, we need to download the symbols for the `Child` project into the `Parent` project. We need to do this so that we can reference the entities and functions within the `Child` project.

We need to first publish the `Child` project to the development sandbox:

1. Select the `Child Table.al` file and press *F5* to build and publish the `Child` project. You can just close your browser when it launches.
2. After the `Child` project has been published, select the `Parent Page.al` file and press *Ctrl + Shift + P* to open the **Command Palette**.
3. Type in or select **AL: Download Symbols**.

If you've published earlier projects from this book to your development sandbox, you'll need to uninstall and unpublish those before you can publish either of these new projects.

Once the symbols have been downloaded to the `Parent` project, you should notice that you have a `symbols` file for the `Child` application that you previously published, similar to this:

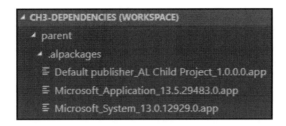

7. Now, let's build the `Parent` project again.

   Select `Parent Page.al` and press *F5* to build and publish the project to your sandbox. This time, it should work and your browser should launch successfully!

   The reference to the `Child` table in `Parent Page.al` can now be resolved because the `Parent` project now knows about, and has the symbols for, the `Child` project.

8. If you plan on continuing with the recipes in this book, then you will need to uninstall and unpublish both the `Child` and `Parent` applications from your development sandbox. You can do that from the **Extension Management** page.

How it works...

In order to access the entities (such as tables and pages) and functions in a Business Central application, you need to have the **symbols** for that application. Remember that the `symbol` file is what contains the metadata about those entities so that Visual Studio Code knows what is accessible.

You get the symbols by installing the application to your development sandbox and then using Visual Studio Code to download them to your AL project. After you have obtained the symbols, you need to tell your application to use them, and that's done by creating a dependency entry in the `app.json` file of your AL project.

When you have done all of this, you will be able to extend entities and use any available functions in another application.

 You only need to define a dependency when your application is directly accessing an entity or function within another application.

There's more...

While dependencies provide a mechanism for directly extending or using other applications, they do come with some challenges that you need to be aware of.

Since the version number is part of the dependency entry, any time that the version number of the dependent application changes, you must update all the applications that have the dependency in order to reference the new version. This could prove to be cumbersome if you create a lot of dependencies between your applications.

Also, consider dependencies from a software release standpoint. If you're creating a collection of parent applications that all reference a common child application, then any time that you update the library application, you will need to update all the applications that reference it, regardless of whether you changed those applications or not. I'm not saying this is a bad model, but be careful what you put into the child application, because you don't want to be constantly updating all your applications because of frequent changes to the dependencies.

The following example illustrates a rather complex scenario where multiple applications have multiple dependencies. Technically speaking, it all works fine, but as I said, managing dependencies like this will prove to be quite challenging:

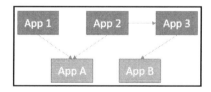

Looking at the preceding example, consider the following scenarios:

- An update to **App A** means that **App 1** and **App 2** need to also be updated.
- An update to **App B** means an update to **App 3** is required, which in turn means an update to **App 2** is required.

As you can see, if you're not careful, you can get yourself into a spiderweb of dependencies, so take care in how you architect your dependent applications.

Translations

Being able to provide your application in multiple languages is an absolute must if you want to release your application in other countries. Luckily for us, the AL language fully supports multi-language capabilities and even provides us with some tools to automate some of this.

This recipe will show you how to generate translation information that can be used to add additional languages to your application.

Getting ready

You're going to need an AL project to work on that's connected to a development sandbox. We will continue to build on the Television Show project that we worked with in Chapter 1, *Let's Get the Basics Out of the Way* and Chapter 2, *Customizing What's Already There*. If you have not completed those chapters, you can download the project from the GitHub link at the start of this chapter.

How to do it...

1. Open your AL project's folder in Visual Studio Code.
2. The first thing we need to do is enable the translation feature in our project. In **Explorer**, select the `app.json` file and in **Editor** add the following property:

   ```
   "features": ["TranslationFile"]
   ```

3. Once the `TranslationFile` feature has been enabled, when you build the project, the compiler automatically creates an **XML Localization Interchange File Format (XLIFF)** translation file for you.

   Press *Ctrl + Shift + B* to build your application.

Once the application has been built, in **Explorer**, notice that there is a new folder named `Translations`, and in that folder, there an XLIFF file (with an extension of `.xlf`) containing the translations:

4. When you look at the XLIFF file that was generated, you can see that both the source and target language properties are set to `en-US`, which is the default language for Business Central. See line number 3 in the following screenshot:

```
ALProject1.g.xlf ×
1  <?xml version="1.0" encoding="utf-8"?>
2  <xliff version="1.2" xmlns="urn:oasis:names:tc:xliff:document:1.2" xmlns:xsi="http://www.w3.org/2001/XMLSchema-instance" xsi:schemaLocation="urn:oasis:
3    <file datatype="xml" source-language="en-US" target-language="en-US" original="ALProject1">
4      <body>
5        <group id="body">
6          <trans-unit id="Table 2502664837 - Field 4190130733 - Property 2879900210" size-unit="char" translate="yes" xml:space="preserve">
7            <source>Customer No.</source>
8            <note from="Developer" annotates="general" priority="2"></note>
9            <note from="Xliff Generator" annotates="general" priority="3">Table Customer Television Show - Field Customer No. - Property Caption</note>
10         </trans-unit>
11         <trans-unit id="Table 2502664837 - Field 2025947974 - Property 2879900210" size-unit="char" translate="yes" xml:space="preserve">
12           <source>Television Show Code</source>
13           <note from="Developer" annotates="general" priority="2"></note>
14           <note from="Xliff Generator" annotates="general" priority="3">Table Customer Television Show - Field Television Show Code - Property Caption</note>
15         </trans-unit>
16         <trans-unit id="Table 2502664837 - Field 2640982432 - Property 2879900210" size-unit="char" translate="yes" xml:space="preserve">
17           <source>Favorite</source>
18           <note from="Developer" annotates="general" priority="2"></note>
19           <note from="Xliff Generator" annotates="general" priority="3">Table Customer Television Show - Field Favorite - Property Caption</note>
```

This file, which is automatically regenerated every time you build your AL project, serves as the basis for performing translations. It does not do any translations itself.

Because this file is automatically regenerated each time you build your project, you should not make any edits directly to this file or else they will be lost.

5. In order to create a file that provides us with another language, we need to create a new XLIFF file for the new language. Let's start by making a copy of the original file:

1. In **Explorer**, right-click on the XLIFF file and choose **Copy**.

2. Now, right-click on the `Translations` folder and select **Paste**.

3. Right-click the new file and rename it to `ALProject1.fr-CA.xlf`.

Each language that you want to provide with your application requires a separate XLIFF file. While the name of the file doesn't actually matter, the recommended standard is to use the `<extensionname>.<language>.xlf` format.

6. Now, let's update the `ALProject1.fr-CA.xlf` translation file to provide the translation. In **Explorer**, select `ALProject1.fr-CA.xlf`, and in **Editor**, set the following property on line number 3:

```
target-language="fr-CA"
```

Search for the following section in the file:

```
<trans-unit id="Table 2502664837 - Field 2025947974 - Property
2879900210" size-unit="char" translate="yes"
xml:space="preserve">
  <source>Television Show Code</source>
  <note from="Developer" annotates="general"
  priority="2"></note>
  <note from="Xliff Generator" annotates="general"
  priority="3">Table Customer Television Show - Field
  Television Show Code - Property Caption</note>
</trans-unit>
```

Notice in the previous section that the source text is `Television Show Code` and it relates to the caption of the field in the `Customer Television Show` table.

Modify the section and add the `target` property, as follows:

```
<trans-unit id="Table 2502664837 - Field 2025947974 - Property
2879900210" size-unit="char" translate="yes"
xml:space="preserve">
  <source>Television Show Code</source>
  <target>Code de la télévision</target>
  <note from="Developer" annotates="general"
  priority="2"></note>
  <note from="Xliff Generator" annotates="general"
  priority="3">Table Customer Television Show - Field
  Television Show Code - Property Caption</note>
</trans-unit>
```

7. We've now made the translation, so let's check it out. Press *F5* to build and publish your application:

    1. In **My Settings**, change your language to **French (Canada).**

    2. Go to any **Customer Card** entry and then to the **Customer Television Shows** page.

The page should look similar to the following, with the `Translated` field:

 Depending on how you created your development sandbox, you may not be able to change your language to **French (Canada)**. If you cannot do this, then go back and update the XLIFF file to a language you can access and try the process again.

How it works...

When you enable the `TranslationFile` feature in your AL project, an XLIFF file is automatically created for you when the project is built. XLIFF is a standardized format based on XML that is used to hold translation information for consumption in software applications.

When the application is built, and the base XLIFF file is generated, if there is already an existing file, then it gets overwritten. The XLIFF file serves as the base to perform all translations, but it does not actually provide any translations itself. It should simply be used as the starting point for creating new translations. As it always represents the current state of the project, you can also use this file to identify updates that need to be merged to your existing translation files. This needs to be done periodically as you make changes to your application after you've already created some translations.

You can control some aspects of the translation by utilizing a few AL code property attributes for things such as field captions and labels. When you create a caption or label, you are able to tell the system if a translation should not be allowed, or if there is a maximum length for the translated text. You do that by using the `Locked` and `MaxLength` attributes, as follows:

```
NoFavoriteShowErr: Label 'You need to define a favorite television show for
Customer %1.', Locked = true, MaxLength = 250;
```

If you do not specify the `Locked` property, then it is assumed to be `false`, which means that a translation is allowed.

There's more...

Obviously, what we did was a manual translation, but we know that it's not a realistic approach to take when your application is of a considerable size. There is another way... well, a couple of ways actually!

Because AL projects use a standard XLIFF translation file, there are services and tools out there that can perform automated translations of those files. Are they perfect? Probably not, but at least they can provide you with a basis and maybe get you 80% of the way there.

A couple of examples of such tools that I've blogged about before are **Microsoft Dynamics Lifecycle Services** and the **Multilingual App Toolkit Editor**. The service is for partners only; however, the application toolkit can be used by anyone, partner or not.

You can read more about those tools here:

- *Microsoft Dynamics Lifecycle Services*: `https://navbitsbytes.com/2018/03/06/al-extensions-translate-your-solution-using-microsoft-dynamics-lifecycle-services/`
- *Multilingual App Toolkit Editor*: `https://navbitsbytes.com/2018/04/27/al-extensions-translate-your-solution-with-the-multilingual-app-toolkit-editor/`

As I said though, we're using standard XLIFF files, so the previous solutions are not the only ones that are available. There are a load of paid and open source tools available online for automatically and manually working with translation files.

See also

You can read more about working with translations on the Microsoft Docs website here: `https://docs.microsoft.com/en-us/dynamics365/business-central/dev-itpro/developer/devenv-work-with-translation-files`.

Adding new manual setups

Creating a great experience for your customers should always be on your mind when creating any application. Providing an easy-to-use environment adds a load of value to your application. One of the challenges that can arise in ERP software as large as Business Central is having a lot of setups to do, and knowing where all those setups are can be challenging for customers, especially if they are new to Business Central.

This recipe will show you how you can make your setups available in a central location so that customers can easily find them.

Getting ready

You're going to need an AL project to work on that's connected to a development sandbox. We will continue to build on the `Television Show` project that we have been working on throughout this book. You can download that from the GitHub link at the start of this chapter.

Even if you have already been working on the `Television Show` project, you're still going to need to grab a few files from GitHub for this recipe. Get the following files from `ch3/4-manual-setups` and copy them into your AL project's folder:

- `Television Show Setup.al`
- `Television Show Setup Card.al`

How to do it...

1. Open your AL project in Visual Studio Code.
2. In **Explorer**, create a new file named `Register Manual Setups.al`. In **Editor**, create a new `codeunit` object:

```
codeunit 50105 "Register Manual Setups"
{
}
```

3. In Business Central, the handling of manual setups is done using what's referred to as a **discovery pattern**. When the page that contains all the manual setups loads, it fires an event that looks to see which manual setup pages should be loaded and then loads them. That makes it extremely easy for you to add your setup to the manual setup area!

   To do this, we need to add a subscriber to our new `codeunit` object:

```
[EventSubscriber(ObjectType::Table, Database::"Business Setup",
'OnRegisterBusinessSetup', '', false, false)]
local procedure OnRegisterBusinessSetup(var TempBusinessSetup:
Record "Business Setup")
var
    TelevisionShowSetupNameTxt: Label 'Television Show Setup';
    TelevisionShowSetupDescriptionTxt: Label 'Set up television
    show application.';
    KeyWordsTxt: Label 'television, show, tv, setup';
begin
    TempBusinessSetup.InsertExtensionBusinessSetup(
      TempBusinessSetup, TelevisionShowSetupNameTxt,
      TelevisionShowSetupDescriptionTxt, KeyWordsTxt,
      TempBusinessSetup.Area::Sales,
      PAGE::"Television Show Setup Card", 'ALProject1');
end;
```

   Now, let's check it out! Press *F5* to build and publish your application:

   1. Switch to the **Business Manager** role center if you're not already on it. You can do that in **My Settings**.
   2. In the Business Manager role center, choose **Setup & Extensions.**
   3. Choose **Manual Setup.**
   4. Press **Search.**
   5. Type in `television` and press **Enter.**

You should see the **Television Show Setup** entry, as follows:

From here, you can click on **Name** and go to the **Manual Setup** page. Note that our **Manual Setup** page is empty as this is only to demonstrate how to add the setup to the **Manual Setup** area.

 Note that since we added some additional keywords, when you perform the **Search** function, you can enter in any of those keywords and the setup page should be found. This makes it easier for your users to find things when they may refer to things by different names.

How it works...

The **Manual Setup** area uses a discovery pattern to make it easy to extend and add new setups. When the user accesses the **Manual Setup** area, an event is fired that looks for all the setups that are subscribed to it and loads them into the **Manual Setup** page. This means that any Business Central applications can add their setups to this area, so users can find all the setups in the same place.

There's more...

At the time of writing this book, the **Manual Setup** area is only available from the Business Manager role center. One thing that you may want to consider is making it available on other role centers that your users will be assigned to. This might mean adding the area to new role centers that you create, or extending the base ones to include it.

Assisted Setup wizards

Having a setup page allows customers to configure the system to work the way they want it to, but what if the setup requires more than just populating a few fields and turning a few options on or off? What if the customer can easily create data based on their desired setup?

This is where we can make use of assisted setups in Business Central. These setups typically take the user through a wizard in order to provide information to the system so that configuration and setups can be done automatically for the user. This recipe will show you how to create a simple **Assisted Setup** wizard and make it available to the user.

Getting ready

You're going to need an AL project to work on that is connected to a development sandbox. We will continue to build on the `Television Show` project that we have been working on throughout this book. You can download that from the GitHub link at the start of this chapter.

Even if you have already been working on the `Television Show` project, you're still going to need to grab a few files from GitHub for this recipe. Get the `Load Television Shows.al` file from `ch3/5-assisted-setup-wizards` and copy it into your AL project folder.

How to do it...

1. Open your AL project in Visual Studio Code.
2. In **Explorer**, create a new file named `Setup Television Shows Wizard.al` and use **Editor** to create a new empty page object as follows:

```
page 50107 "Load Television Shows Wizard"
{
    Caption = 'Load Television Shows';
    PageType = NavigatePage;

    layout
    {
        area(content)
        {

        }
    }

    actions
    {
        area(processing)
        {

        }
```

```
        }
    }
```

 Wizard pages are defined using the `NavigatePage` page type.

3. Following the standards from Microsoft for **Assisted Setup** wizards, we need to add a couple of sections to show the banners on the page. This will give our wizard the same look and feel as the rest of the wizards in Business Central.

Add the following code to the `area(content)` section:

```
group(StandardBanner)
{
    Caption = '';
    Editable = false;
    Visible = TopBannerVisible and not FinishActionEnabled;
    field(MediaResourcesStandard; MediaResourcesStandard."Media
    Reference")
    {
        ApplicationArea = All;
        Editable = false;
        ShowCaption = false;
    }
}
group(FinishedBanner)
{
    Caption = '';
    Editable = false;
    Visible = TopBannerVisible and FinishActionEnabled;
    field(MediaResourcesDone; MediaResourcesDone."Media
    Reference")
    {
        ApplicationArea = All;
        Editable = false;
        ShowCaption = false;
    }
}
```

4. The first page of the wizard is the one that the users will see when they launch the wizard, so let's provide a welcoming message and some instructions as to what they are about to do and why they are doing it.

Add the following code to the `area(content)` section, after the `group(FinishedBanner)` section:

```
group(Step1)
{
    Visible = Step1Visible;
    group(Welcome)
    {
        Caption = 'Welcome to the Television Shows
        application!';
        Visible = Step1Visible;
        group(Welcome1)
        {
            Caption = '';
            InstructionalText = 'This wizard will let you
            select which genre of television shows we
            should load for sample data.';
        }
    }
    group(LetsGo)
    {
        Caption = 'Let''s go!';
        group(LetsGo1)
        {
            Caption = '';
            InstructionalText = 'Press Next to continue.';
        }
    }
}
```

5. The second page in the wizard is where the user should start making decisions that will drive the setup that we're building. In our case, we want them to select what genres of television shows we will load into the system.

Add the following code to the `area(content)` section, after the `group(step1)` section:

```
group(step2)
{
    Caption = '';
    InstructionalText = 'Select the genre(s) of television
    shows you want to load.';
    Visible = Step2Visible;

    field(Genre1Selected; Genre1Selected)
    {
        Caption = 'Comedy';
```

```
                    ApplicationArea = All;
                }
                field(Genre2Selected; Genre2Selected)
                {
                    Caption = 'Drama';
                    ApplicationArea = All;
                }
                field(Genre3Selected; Genre3Selected)
                {
                    Caption = 'Family';
                    ApplicationArea = All;
                }
            }
        }
```

6. Now that we've laid out the different screens within the wizard, we need to add the navigation button logic. There are three buttons that need to be defined for a wizard: **Back**, **Next**, and **Finish**.

   Add the following code to the `area(processing)` section:

```
action(ActionBack)
{
    ApplicationArea = All;
    Caption = 'Back';
    Enabled = BackActionEnabled;
    Image = PreviousRecord;
    InFooterBar = true;
    trigger OnAction();
    begin
        NextStep(true);
    end;
}
action(ActionNext)
{
    ApplicationArea = All;
    Caption = 'Next';
    Enabled = NextActionEnabled;
    Image = NextRecord;
    InFooterBar = true;
    trigger OnAction();
    begin
        NextStep(false);
    end;
}
action(ActionFinish)
{
    ApplicationArea = All;
    Caption = 'Finish';
```

```
            Enabled = FinishActionEnabled;
            Image = Approve;
            InFooterBar = true;
            trigger OnAction();
            begin
                FinishAction();
            end;
    }
```

7. The screens are done. The buttons are done. Now... the logic.

   Add the following trigger code after the `actions` section:

   ```
   trigger OnInit();
   begin
       LoadTopBanners();
   end;

   trigger OnOpenPage();
   begin
       Step := Step::Start;
       EnableControls();
   end;
   ```

8. We need to make use of a lot of variables in order to manage the logic within the page. Add the following variables after the `trigger` code:

   ```
   var
       MediaRepositoryDone: Record "Media Repository";
       MediaRepositoryStandard: Record "Media Repository";
       MediaResourcesDone: Record "Media Resources";
       MediaResourcesStandard: Record "Media Resources";
       Step: Option Start,Finish;
       BackActionEnabled: Boolean;
       FinishActionEnabled: Boolean;
       NextActionEnabled: Boolean;
       Step1Visible: Boolean;
       Step2Visible: Boolean;
       TopBannerVisible: Boolean;
       Genre1Selected: Boolean;
       Genre2Selected: Boolean;
       Genre3Selected: Boolean;
   ```

9. Now, we need to add a number of small functions to help control the navigation within the wizard page, in order to show and hide the correct elements as the user navigates forward (and backward!) through the steps.

Add the following functions after the `variables` section:

```
local procedure EnableControls();
begin
    ResetControls();

    case Step of
        Step::Start:
            ShowStep1;
        Step::Finish:
            ShowStep2;
    end;
end;

local procedure FinishAction();
begin
    TestGenresSelected();
    LoadTelevisionShows();
    CurrPage.Close();
end;

local procedure NextStep(Backwards: Boolean);
begin
    if Backwards then
        Step := Step - 1
    ELSE
        Step := Step + 1;

    EnableControls();
end;

local procedure ShowStep1();
begin
    Step1Visible := true;

    FinishActionEnabled := false;
    BackActionEnabled := false;
end;

local procedure ShowStep2();
begin
    Step2Visible := true;

    NextActionEnabled := false;
    FinishActionEnabled := true;
end;

local procedure ResetControls();
```

```
begin
    FinishActionEnabled := false;
    BackActionEnabled := true;
    NextActionEnabled := true;

    Step1Visible := false;
    Step2Visible := false;
end;
```

10. And now add, the function to load the banners. This pulls icon information from pre-loaded data in Business Central.

Add this code after the previous set of functions:

```
local procedure LoadTopBanners();
begin
    if MediaRepositoryStandard.GET('AssistedSetup-NoText-
    400px.png', FORMAT(CurrentClientType())) AND
        MediaRepositoryDone.GET('AssistedSetupDone-NoText-
        400px.png', FORMAT(CurrentClientType()))
    then
        if MediaResourcesStandard.GET(MediaRepositoryStandard
        ."Media Resources Ref") AND
            MediaResourcesDone.GET(MediaRepositoryDone."Media
            Resources Ref")
        then
            TopBannerVisible := MediaResourcesDone."Media
            Reference".HasValue();
end;
```

11. And finally... a function that ensures that the user has selected at least one genre, and a function to call the routine that loads the television shows.

Add this code after the previous set of functions:

```
local procedure TestGenresSelected()
    var
        NothingSelectedConfirmLbl: Label 'You did not
        select any genres so no data will be loaded.
        Are you sure you want to exit?';
    begin
        if (not Genre1Selected) and (not Genre2Selected)
        and (not Genre3Selected) then
            if not Confirm(NothingSelectedConfirmLbl,
            false) then
                Error('');
    end;
```

```
local procedure LoadTelevisionShows();
var
    LoadTelevisionShows: Codeunit "Load Television Shows";
begin
    LoadTelevisionShows.LoadTelevisionShows(
    Genre1Selected, Genre2Selected, Genre3Selected);
end;
```

12. Okay, we've now defined our **Assisted Setup** wizard page and implemented the logic to load the television shows based on which genres the user selects. Now, we need to make the wizard available to the user.

Similar to the **Manual Setup** area that we touched on in the previous recipe, there is a central place in Business Central from where we can access all the **Assisted Setup** wizards, and just like the Manual Setup area, we can add our new wizard simply by subscribing to an event.

In **Explorer**, create a new file named `Register Assisted Setups.al`, and in **Editor**, create a new `codeunit` object with the following subscriber code:

```
codeunit 50106 "Register Assisted Setups"
{
    [EventSubscriber(ObjectType::Table, Database::"Aggregated
    Assisted Setup", 'OnRegisterAssistedSetup', '', false,
    false)]
    local procedure OnRegisterAssistedSetup(var
    TempAggregatedAssistedSetup: Record "Aggregated
    Assisted Setup" TEMPORARY);
    var
        AssistedSetupRecord: Record "Television Show";
    begin
        TempAggregatedAssistedSetup.AddExtensionAssistedSetup(
            Page::"Load Television Shows Wizard",
            'Load Television Shows', True,
            AssistedSetupRecord.RecordId(),
            GetAssistedSetupStatus(
            TempAggregatedAssistedSetup), '');
    end;
```

When the user accesses the **Assisted Setup** area, our wizard will automatically be loaded into the area along with all the other wizards.

13. One of the features of the **Assisted Setup** area is that it contains a status so that the user knows whether they've performed that particular configuration or not. In order to set and manage the status of our wizard, we need to add one more subscriber. Add the following function to our new `codeunit` object:

```
[EventSubscriber(ObjectType::Table, Database::"Aggregated Assisted
Setup", 'OnUpdateAssistedSetupStatus', '', false, false)]
    local procedure OnUpdateAssistedSetupStatus(var
    TempAggregatedAssistedSetup: Record "Aggregated
    Assisted Setup" TEMPORARY);
    begin
        TempAggregatedAssistedSetup.SetStatus(
        TempAggregatedAssistedSetup, Page::"Load
        Television Shows Wizard",
        GetAssistedSetupStatus(TempAggregatedAssistedSetup));
    end;
```

14. And finally, we need to add a function that will tell the system when the **Assisted Setup** should be considered complete. This logic is likely to be different for each of your **Assisted Setup** wizards, as it depends on what the wizard is responsible for.

    In our scenario, when the television shows have been successfully loaded, we write to `Television Show Setup Table` that the wizard has been completed.

    Add the following function to the `codeunit` object:

```
    local procedure GetAssistedSetupStatus(AggregatedAssistedSetup:
    Record "Aggregated Assisted Setup"): Integer;
    var
        TelevisionShowSetup: Record "Television Show Setup";
    begin
        with AggregatedAssistedSetup do begin
            if TelevisionShowSetup.Get() then begin
                if TelevisionShowSetup."Finished Assisted Setup"
then
                    Status := Status::Completed
                else
                    Status := Status::"Not Completed";
            end else
                Status := Status::"Not Completed";
            exit(Status);
        end;
    end;
```

15. Wow, that's a lot of code, right!? Now, it's finally time to test it! Press *F5* to build and publish your application:

    1. Switch to the **Business Manager** role center if you're not already in it. You can do that in **My Settings.**

    2. In the **Business Manager** role center, choose **Assisted Setup.**

    3. Our new **Load Television Shows** wizard is listed with a **Status** of **Not Completed**:

If you click on the name, then you can launch the wizard and walk through the steps, choosing one or more genres to load:

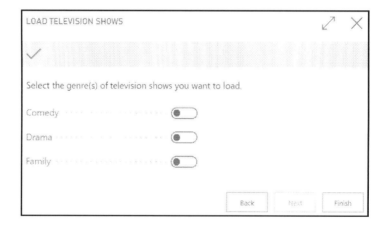

Once you choose the genre(s) and finish the wizard, you can go to the Television Show List to see the shows that have been loaded:

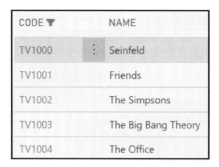

If you look back at the **Assisted Setup** area now, notice that the **Status** is now set to **Complete**, as in the given screenshot:

How it works...

Designing and implementing **Assisted Setup** wizards is, in my mind, one of the most important things to include in your Business Central applications. Since Business Central is an end-to-end ERP solution, it is very large and there is a load of different setups that need to be done. It can certainly be a bit intimidating to even an experienced user, let alone one that is completely new to the system.

If you can give the user a simple and easy-to-follow wizard to do some of the setups for them, then you will raise their user experience to another level. In this recipe, we simply loaded some sample data for the user, but imagine providing a questionnaire experience for the user that, after they fill it out, result in the software being configured across a whole bunch of different areas, and sample data can be provided to give the user a sense of what they can do with the system.

Once you have your **Assisted Setup** created, making it available to the user is easy. A discovery pattern is used to dynamically load all the **Assisted Setup** wizards each time the user interacts with the **Assisted Setup** area, so they are always certain to see the latest list of available wizards.

As you can see in this recipe, there's a lot of boilerplate code needed in an **Assisted Setup** wizard for managing things such as the navigation. Luckily for us, there is an extension you can get from the **Visual Studio Marketplace** named **CRS AL Language Extension**. When you install it, among many other cool features, it loads a set of new snippets, one of which is an **Assisted Setup** wizard page snippet. You can use that to easily create a generic wizard that you can then tailor to your own needs.

Isolated storage

Even though Business Central applications are self-contained and separate from each other, data from one extension can be accessed from another extension. For the most part, this might be perfectly okay, but there may be times when you want to shield data from other applications. For example, if you want to store license information within your application, then you won't necessarily want others to see that information.

This recipe will show you how you can use isolated storage to store and retrieve data that is only available to your application and no others.

Getting ready

You're going to need an AL project to work in that's connected to a development sandbox. We will continue to build on the `Television Show` project that we have been working on throughout this book. You can download that from the GitHub link at the start of this chapter.

Even if you've been following along with the book, you're still going to need to grab the `License Input Dialog.al` file from the `ch3/6-isolated-storage` folder in the GitHub repository and copy it to your AL project.

How to do it...

1. Open your AL project in Visual Studio Code.
2. For the purposes of this recipe, our license will be a simple 10-character string. We need a function that will accept this key, as entered by the user, and put it into our isolated storage so that it is hidden from all other Business Central applications.

In **Explorer**, select the `Television Show Setup Card.al` file, and in **Editor**, add the following function after the `OnOpenPage` trigger. This function will accept a license string and put it in the isolated storage:

```
local procedure SetLicenseInStorage(LicenseText: Text[10])
var
    SuccessMsg: Label 'License successfully stored';
    FailureErr: Label 'License could not be stored';
    MustNotBeBlankErr: Label 'You must provide a valid
    license';
begin
    if LicenseText <> '' then begin
        DeleteExistingLicense();
        if IsolatedStorage.Set(GetLicenseStorageKey(),
        LicenseText, DataScope::Module) then
            Message(SuccessMsg)
        else
            Error(FailureErr);
    end else
        Error(MustNotBeBlankErr);
end;
```

3. Next, we need a function that will retrieve the license from the isolated storage. Add the following function to the page:

```
local procedure GetLicenseFromStorage()
var
    SuccessMsg: Label 'License retrieved: %1';
    FailureErr: Label 'License could not be retrieved';
    LicenseText: Text;
begin
    if IsolatedStorage.Get(GetLicenseStorageKey(),
    DataScope::Module, LicenseText) then
        Message(SuccessMsg, LicenseText)
    else
        Error(FailureErr);
end;
```

4. Now, add a function to delete the existing license that we have stored:

```
local procedure DeleteExistingLicense()
var
    PromptToDeleteMsg: Label 'There is an existing license stored.
    Are you sure you want to replace it?';
begin
    if IsolatedStorage.Contains(GetLicenseStorageKey(),
    DataScope::Module) then
        if Confirm(PromptToDeleteMsg, false) then
```

```
                    IsolatedStorage.Delete(GetLicenseStorageKey(),
                    DataScope::Module);
        end;
```

5. Add a function to return the unique identifier that will be used to find and set the license value in the isolated storage:

```
local procedure GetLicenseStorageKey(): Text
var
    LicenseStorageKey: Label 'LIC';
begin
    exit(LicenseStorageKey);
end;
```

 Each value that you store in isolated storage needs to have a unique identifier associated with it.

6. Now, let's add a couple of actions to the page to test our functions. Add the following code to the page object, after the `layout` section:

```
actions
{
    area(Processing)
    {
        action(SetLicense)
        {
            ApplicationArea = All;

            trigger OnAction()
            var
                LicenseInputDialog: page "License Input Dialog";
            begin
                if LicenseInputDialog.RunModal() = Action::OK then
                    SetLicenseInStorage(
                    LicenseInputDialog.GetLicenseText());
            end;
        }
        action(GetLicense)
        {
            ApplicationArea = All;

            trigger OnAction()
            begin
                GetLicenseFromStorage();
            end;
```

```
            }
        }
    }
```

7. Testing time! Press *F5* to build and publish your application:
    1. Using the  icon, search for the `Television Shows Setup Card` and open it.
    2. Select **Actions | SetLicense.**
    3. Enter any text string into the dialog box.
    4. Press **OK.**

You should receive the following message:

License successfully stored

OK

Now, let's make sure our license was stored correctly. On the **Television Show Setup Card**, choose **Actions | GetLicense.**

You should see a message such as this, showing the license text you entered previously:

License retrieved: TESTLIC123

OK

How it works...

Using isolated storage ensures that the data you put in there is not accessible outside of your application. This is extremely useful when it comes to storing things such as license keys, API keys, and integration connection information.

Entries in isolated storage have a defined scope, which means you can further control how accessible the data is. This is done using the `datascope` parameter, which has the following options:

- `Module`: Available to the entire application
- `Company`: Available to a specific company
- `User`: Available only to a specific user
- `CompanyAndUser`: Available to a specific company and user

Why did we add these functions to a page object instead of a central codeunit?

The answer is rather simple, but easy to overlook. The point of isolated storage is to protect the data that you store there. If you put functions in a codeunit, then you have to make global functions to get/set the data, which means that if another developer creates a dependency on your app, they will be able to access your global functions, and therefore will be able to retrieve (or change!) your sensitive data.

By creating local functions within the object that is interacting with the sensitive data, the functions are not accessible to any other application, even if a direct dependency is created between them.

See also

You can read about isolated storage on the Microsoft Docs website here: `https://docs.` `microsoft.com/en-us/dynamics365/business-central/dev-itpro/developer/devenv-` `isolated-storage`.

Notifications

There are a few ways that you can notify the user of something happening in the system. You can pop up a message to the user and force them to acknowledge it by clicking on it, but this can be very intrusive in the event that you just want to let the user know about something but don't necessarily require them to do anything about it.

Luckily, there is a much less intrusive way to do this: using notifications. This method allows us to provide an onscreen message with some available actions, but the user is not forced to click on it. Think of these as a *hey, by the way, did you know...* type of message to the user. This recipe will show you how to add a notification to `Customer Card` to let the user know that there are no television shows set up for the customer.

Getting ready

You're going to need an AL project to work on that's connected to a development sandbox. We will continue to build on the `Television Show` project that we have been working on throughout this book. You can download that from the GitHub link at the start of this chapter.

How to do it...

1. Open your AL project in Visual Studio Code.
2. In **Explorer**, create a new file named `Customer Card Notification.al`, and in **Editor**, create a new `codeunit` object:

```
codeunit 50108 "Customer Card Notification"
{

}
```

3. In order to make the notification show, we must subscribe to `OnAfterGetRecordEvent` so that our notification will be evaluated when the customer record is retrieved from the database.

   Add the following code to the `codeunit` object to create the subscriber:

```
[EventSubscriber(ObjectType::Page, Page::"Customer Card",
'OnAfterGetRecordEvent', '', false, false)]
local procedure OnAfterGetRecordEvent(var Rec: Record Customer)
begin
    HandleCustomerCardNotification(Rec."No.");
end;
```

4. Now, let's create the function that shows the notification if the customer has no television shows defined:

```
local procedure HandleCustomerCardNotification(CustomerNo:
Code[20])
begin
    if CustomerNo = '' then
        exit;

    if not HasTelevisionEntries(CustomerNo) then
        ShowCustomerCardNotification(CustomerNo);
end;
```

5. We need to add the function to see if the customer has any television shows:

```
local procedure HasTelevisionEntries(CustomerNo: Code[20]): Boolean
var
    CustomerTelevisionShow: Record "Customer Television Show";
begin
    CustomerTelevisionShow.SetRange("Customer No.", CustomerNo);
    exit(not CustomerTelevisionShow.IsEmpty());
end;
```

6. Now, we can add the function that shows the actual notification:

```
local procedure ShowCustomerCardNotification(CustomerNo: Code[20])
var
    CustomerCardNotification: Notification;
    NotificationMsg: Label 'Customer %1 has no television shows.
    Do you want to set some up?';
    ActionYesTxt: Label 'Yes';
begin
    CustomerCardNotification.Message := StrSubstNo(
    NotificationMsg, CustomerNo);
    CustomerCardNotification.Scope :=
NotificationScope::LocalScope;
    CustomerCardNotification.SetData('CustomerNo', CustomerNo);
    CustomerCardNotification.AddAction(ActionYesTxt,
    CODEUNIT::"Customer Card Notification",
    'OpenCustomerTelevisionShows');
    CustomerCardNotification.Send();
end;
```

In the previous example, we define what the message will be to the user using the `Message` notification property. By setting `Scope := NotificationScope::LocalScope`, we're telling the system that the notification will appear on the current page that the user is working on.

`NotificationScope::GlobalScope` is available, but at the time of writing this book, it is not yet supported in Business Central. According to the Microsoft Docs site, it is slated for a future release.

Since we want the user to be able to interact with the notification, we added an action to the notification using the `AddAction` function. When the user clicks on this action within the notification, it will launch a function named `OpenCustomerTelevisionShows` in the `Customer Card Notification` codeunit.

The last piece of information that we add to the notification is the customer number. We need to store this piece of data within the notification itself so that we can use it later to open the list of television shows for the action. We do that by using the SetData function.

You can store multiple pieces of data within the notification simply by assigning a unique identifier to each value.

The last step in this function is to display the notification using the Send function.

7. The final piece of code we need to add to our codeunit is the function that will be called when the user clicks on the notification action that we defined previously.

Add the following code to the codeunit:

```
procedure OpenCustomerTelevisionShows(CustomerCardNotification:
Notification)
var
    CustomerTelevisionShow: Record "Customer Television Show";
    CustomerTelevisionShows: Page "Customer Television Shows";
    CustomerNo: Code[20];
begin
    CustomerNo := CustomerCardNotification.GetData(
    'CustomerNo');
    CustomerTelevisionShow.SetRange(
    "Customer No.", CustomerNo);
    CustomerTelevisionShows.SetTableView(
    CustomerTelevisionShow);
    CustomerTelevisionShows.Run();
end;
```

In the previous function, we use the GetData function to get the customer number from the notification that we previously stored there.

Three things are important to remember when creating actions for notifications:

- The name of the function that the action calls must be the same name that's used in the AddAction function of the notification definition.
- The function that the action calls must be declared as a global function.
- The function must accept an object of the Notification type as a parameter.

8. It's testing time again! Press *F5* to build and publish your application:
   1. Go to **Customer List** and find a customer that does not have any television shows defined.
   2. Click on the customer entry to open the **CUSTOMER CARD** page.

You should see a similar notification to this:

If you repeat the process for a customer that has television shows defined, then you should not see the notification.

How it works...

Notifications provide a non-intrusive way of letting the user know about things in the system. The idea is that you can use these notifications to show things that it might be interesting to let the user know about, but that they don't need to stop what they're doing to address. For example, you'd never show posting errors with a notification because you need the system to stop and for the user to address the issue right away.

Using notifications is also a great way to provide a helping hand to users who might be new to the system. For example, you can provide a notification to the user to view a video or online help article when they visit a specific page, and then hide the notification once the user has acted upon it.

Getting the notification to be displayed is as simple as subscribing to the event at a point where it makes sense to evaluate the notification. It could be when a record is retrieved from the database, when a page opens, or when a user selects a pre-determined combination of data. Once you determine where to evaluate the notification, you then add the logic that will determine whether the notification needs to be shown, which will be unique for each notification.

When writing the logic, be careful when determining whether the notification should be shown or not. Since this logic will fire every time the event happens, we don't want to write logic that will put a performance strain on the system. Try and keep this logic as simple as possible.

See also

You can read about notifications on the Microsoft Docs site here: `https://docs.microsoft.com/en-us/dynamics365/business-central/dev-itpro/developer/devenv-notifications-developing`.

Using the task scheduler

There are times when you would like a routine to run, but perhaps it's a long-running routine, or it's something that will lock up a user from performing other tasks.

The **task scheduler** allows you to create tasks and schedule them to run at a later time. The tasks will execute in a background session, which means they will not lock up a user session. This means that you could build a feature where the user is able to kick off a long-running process, but they don't have to wait around for it to "unlock" their screen. Instead, they can continue and perform other tasks while the long-running one runs.

This recipe will show you how to create a task and add it to the task scheduler to run at a later time.

Getting ready

You're going to need an AL project to work on that's connected to a development sandbox. We will continue to build on the `Television Show` project that we have been working on throughout this book. You can download that from the GitHub link at the start of this chapter.

Even if you have been following along through the book, you're still going to need to grab a couple of files from the `ch3/8-task-scheduler` folder in the GitHub repo. Copy the following files into your AL project:

- `Scheduled Tasks Example.al`
- `Simple Task Result.al`

How to do it...

1. Open your AL project in Visual Studio Code.
2. In **Explorer**, create a new file named A Simple Task.al, and in **Editor**, create a new codeunit object:

```
codeunit 50109 "A Simple Task"
{
}
```

3. We're going to create a very simple function that will just record the date and time that the task is executed. Definitely not fancy, but it'll get the job done!

   Add the following code to the codeunit:

```
trigger OnRun()
begin
    SimpleTaskFunction();
end;

local procedure SimpleTaskFunction()
var
    SimpleTaskResult: Record "Simple Task Result";
begin
    SimpleTaskResult.UpdateWithNewRun();
end;
```

A scheduled task can be configured to run a codeunit, but not a specific function within a codeunit. This is why you will need to create a new codeunit with an onRun() trigger, where you can then define what function(s) you want to run when the task executes.

4. Now, let's add a function to create a new task:

```
procedure AddTaskToScheduler()
begin
    TaskScheduler.CreateTask(Codeunit::"A Simple Task", 0, false,
    '', CurrentDateTime());
end;
```

5. And let's add a function to delete a scheduled task:

```
procedure DeleteTaskFromScheduler(TaskID: Guid)
begin
    TaskScheduler.CancelTask(TaskID);
end;
```

6. A task will not be executed until it is marked as **Ready**. You can set that when the task is created or you can have a separate function to let the user decide when the task is ready.

> For our example, let's create a function to mark the task as ready for processing:

```
procedure SetTaskToReady(TaskId: Guid)
begin
    TaskScheduler.SetTaskReady(TaskId);
end;
```

> Alrighty, we've built our code so let's try it out! Press *F5* to build and publish your application:

1. Use the 🔍 icon and search for `Scheduled Task Example`. Click on it to launch the page.
2. Use the actions on the page to create a few tasks.
3. Note that even if you wait a few minutes, the tasks will not disappear when you select **Actions | Refresh Page**. This is because the tasks are not ready to be processed.
4. Select one of your tasks and choose **Actions | Set Task to Ready**.
5. Press **Actions | Refresh Page**. It may take a few moments but the record you marked as **Ready** will disappear and the result should get updated to reflect when the task was completed, like so:

Process	Open in Excel	Actions	Less options			
Create Task	Set Task to Ready	Delete Task	Refresh Page			

Result

Task last ran: .... 4/30/2019 9:44 PM

ID		RUN CODEUNIT	NOT BEFORE	IS READY
{2b9f9cb3-d163-4bfe-8f79-65ff195e5d24}		50109	4/30/2019 10:00 PM	
{e890e7e2-3497-4114-9872-7207edcfe9cc}	⋮	50109	4/30/2019 10:00 PM	
{2c511d76-a71d-4d63-b3f4-bc225ee4ca10}		50109	4/30/2019 10:00 PM	

You may find you have to wait a few moments for the data to be updated, so you might have to click the button a few times. Remember though, these scheduled tasks don't have a guaranteed start time. They will be executed when the task scheduler is finished with all previous tasks, so small delays like this are to be expected.

How it works...

The task scheduler is used to schedule processes to be executed at a later time. While you cannot control the exact date and time a task will be executed, you can tell the system the earliest date and time that it can be run.

When a task is executed, it will be run in a background session, which means it will not lock up an existing user's interface. This also means that there is no interaction with the process while it is running, so routines that require inputs from a user need to be handled accordingly by using saved setups.

Each task is assigned a unique GUID when it is created, giving you the ability to cancel the task if necessary, before it executes. You can also mark the task as not ready for processing, which will cause the task scheduler to ignore that task until it is marked as ready.

See also

You can read more about the task scheduler on the Microsoft Docs site here: `https://docs.microsoft.com/en-us/dynamics365/business-central/dev-itpro/developer/devenv-task-scheduler`.

.NET interoperability

With all the AL code available to you in Business Central, sometimes you just need something that is not there, and it may already exist in a .NET library. If you are developing for an on-premises customer, you are able to directly use any .NET library within your AL code. This recipe will show you how to do that.

Getting ready

You're going to need an AL project to work on that's connected to a development sandbox. We're taking another break from our Television Show application for this recipe.

Download the `ch3-dotnet-interop-start.zip` file from the `ch3/9-dotnet-interop` folder in the GitHub repository at the beginning of this chapter.

Extract this ZIP file to any folder that you have access to on your local machine.

If you are using a development sandbox hosted in Business Central, or you are using an environment that has been configured as a **Software as a Service (SaaS)** environment, then you will not be able to perform this recipe using either of these systems. You must configure a development sandbox that replicates an on-premises environment since .NET usage is not allowed in SaaS environments.

Refer back to the *Setting up your development sandbox* recipe in `Chapter 1`, *Let's Get the Basics Out of the Way*, for notes on how to set up development sandboxes. You can still use a Docker-based environment, but you need to use an on-premises image instead of a SaaS one.

How to do it...

1. In Visual Studio Code, open the folder containing the `dotnet-interop-start` project that you downloaded from GitHub.
2. The first thing we need to do is configure our project to allow .NET controls to be used in our AL code. In **Explorer**, select `app.json`. In the **Editor** window, add the following property:

```
"target": "Internal"
```

By adding the previous property to your project, your extension will no longer be supported on the Business Central SaaS platform. In other words, you can only use .NET controls in your AL code for on-premises (or possibly private cloud) installations, so be aware of this limitation when designing solutions, in case the on-premises customer has plans to move to the cloud.

3. In **Explorer**, create a new file named `DotNet Package.al`, and in **Editor**, create a new `dotnet` package:

```
dotnet
{

}
```

Notice that `dotnet` is referred to as a package and not an object. This package acts as a container to define all the .NET assemblies and types that you will use in your application.

You can use the `tdotnet` snippet to create a basic `dotnet` package. It is recommended that you define only one package to hold all the .NET assemblies and types that you want to use.

4. Next, we need to define the .NET assembly, and which type within the assembly we will use:

```
assembly(mscorlib)
{
    type(System.Math; MyMathLib) { }
}
```

In the previous example, we're using the `System.Math` class, but we've assigned it an alias of `MyMathLib`. When we make references to it in our AL code, we'll be using the alias.

Initially, the AL compiler only knows about the `mscorlib` assembly. You are able to tell it about other assemblies though, by adding new paths to the `al.assemblyProbingPaths` property in the AL Language extension settings in Visual Studio Code:

AL: Assembly Probing Paths
Sets the list of directory paths where the compiler should search for referenced .NET assemblies.

Edit in settings.json

5. Now, let's create a short example. In this example, we will create a page that allows you to enter a number and a power. We'll use the math library to do the calculation (for example, 3 to the power of 4).

In **Explorer**, create a new file named `DotNet Example Page.al` and in **Editor**, create a new page object:

```
page 50145 "DotNet Example Page"
{
    PageType = ListPlus;
    ApplicationArea = All;
    UsageCategory = Tasks;


}
```

6. Add the `layout` section to the page:

```
layout
{
    area(Content)
    {
        group(Group)
        {
            field(Number; Number)
            {
                Caption = 'Enter the base number:';
                ApplicationArea = All;
            }
            field(Power; Power)
            {
                Caption = 'Enter the power to be applied:';
                ApplicationArea = All;
            }
        }
    }
}
```

7. Add the `actions` section to the page, after the `layout` section:

```
actions
{
    area(Processing)
    {
        action(ActionName)
        {
            ApplicationArea = All;
            Promoted = true;
            PromotedCategory = Process;
```

```
            PromotedIsBig = true;
            Caption = 'Calculate power';

            trigger OnAction()
            var
                MessageTxt: Label '%1 to the power of %2 is %3';
            begin
                Message(MessageTxt, Number, Power,
                CalculatePowerOfNumber(Number, Power));
            end;
        }
    }
}
```

8. Add a couple of global variables for the calculation, after the `actions` section:

```
var
    Number: Decimal;
    Power: Decimal;
```

9. And finally, add the function that will perform the calculation, after the `var` section:

```
local procedure CalculatePowerOfNumber(Number: Decimal; Power:
Decimal): Decimal
var
    Math: DotNet MyMathLib;
begin
    exit(Math.Pow(Number, Power));
end;
```

You can see from the preceding code that to use the .NET library, we must create a `DotNet` variable type and reference the alias name, `MyMathLib`, which we created in the `dotnet` package.

Now, we can try it out! Press *F5* to build and publish your application:

1. Use the 💡 icon and search for **DotNet Example Page**.
2. Click on it to open the page.
3. Enter some numbers and choose **Process | Calculate power.**

You should see a result similar to the following:

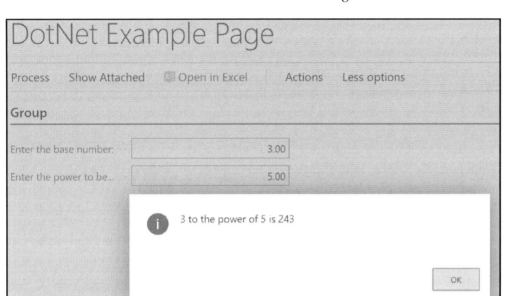

How it works...

Before you can use .NET libraries in your AL code, you must configure the project to allow them, by updating the `target` property in `app.json`. It must be set to internal in order to use .NET variables.

The next step in using .NET libraries is that you need to define a `DotNet` package. This lists the assemblies and types that you will be using. It's recommended that you create only one `DotNet` package and list all the assemblies and types in the single package. By default, you can only reference the `mscorlib` library in the package, but you can configure the AL Language extension to look at other paths for additional assemblies.

Once you define the `DotNet` package, you reference the assembly type by creating a `DotNet` variable and referencing the alias name you defined in the package.

Remember!
You can only make use of .NET variables in on-premises environments. You cannot publish an application to the Business Central cloud platform if it contains .NET variables, so make sure that if you do use them in your on-premises solutions, you are aware that the solutions will not be able to move to the cloud platform as is.

See also

You can read more about .NET interoperability on the Microsoft Docs site here: `https://docs.microsoft.com/en-us/dynamics365/business-central/dev-itpro/developer/devenv-get-started-call-dotnet-from-al`.

Implementing telemetry events

Knowing how your application is being used and how your application is working are two very important things for a Business Central developer. Maybe you've built that super cool feature and it turns out that users don't know it's there, or you've created a routine that takes a lot longer than you ever thought it would.

Using **telemetry** events in your on-premises Business Central application gives you the ability to gather data from your application so that you can analyze it for troubleshooting, performance improvements, and more.

This recipe will show you how to add telemetry events to your Business Central application.

Getting ready

You're going to need an AL project to work on that's connected to a development sandbox. We're taking another break from our Television Show application for this recipe.

Download the `ch3-telemetry-events-start.zip` file from the `ch3/10-telemetry-events` folder in the GitHub repo.

Extract this ZIP file to any folder that you have access to on your local machine.

If you are using a development sandbox hosted in Business Central, or you are using an environment that has been configured as a SaaS environment, you will not be able to perform this recipe using either of these systems. You must configure a development sandbox that replicates an on-premises environment since raising custom telemetry events is not yet allowed in SaaS environments.

Refer back to the *Setting up your development sandbox* recipe from `Chapter 1, Let's Get the Basics Out of the Way,` for notes on how to set up development sandboxes. You can still use a Docker-based environment, but you need to use an on-premises image instead of a SaaS one.

How to do it...

1. Open your AL project in Visual Studio Code.

   The first thing we need to do is configure our project to allow custom telemetry events to be used in our AL code. In **Explorer**, select `app.json`. In the **Editor** window, add the following property:

   ```
   "target": "Internal"
   ```

   By adding the previous property to your project, your extension will no longer be supported on the Business Central SaaS platform. In other words, you can only use custom telemetry events in your AL code for on-premises (or possibly private cloud) installations, so be aware of this limitation when designing solutions in case the on-premises customer has plans to move to the cloud.

2. In **Explorer**, create a new file named `Raise Telemetry Events.al`, and in **Editor**, create a new `codeunit` object:

   ```
   codeunit 50130 "Raise Telemetry Events"
   {

   }
   ```

3. Add a function that will raise the telemetry events:

```
procedure RaiseEvent(Level: Verbosity)
var
    CriticalEventMsg: Label 'A critical event';
    ErrorEventMsg: Label 'A error event';
    WarningEventMsg: Label 'A warning event';
    NormalEventMsg: Label 'A normal event';
    CategoryTxt: Label 'Page Action';
    EventRaiseMsg: Label 'Event raised';
begin
    case Level of
        level::Critical:
            SendTraceTag('TelEx-000', CategoryTxt, Level,
            CriticalEventMsg, DataClassification::CustomerContent);
        level::Error:
            SendTraceTag('TelEx-001', CategoryTxt, Level,
            ErrorEventMsg, DataClassification::CustomerContent);
        level::Warning:
            SendTraceTag('TelEx-002', CategoryTxt, Level,
            WarningEventMsg, DataClassification::CustomerContent);
    end;

    Message(EventRaiseMsg);
end;
```

4. Now, let's try it out! For the purposes of this recipe, I'll assume that you have access to the Event Viewer on the machine where your Business Central Server is located.

Press *F5* to build and publish your application:

1. Using the 💡 icon, search for `Telemetry Example` and click on it to open it.
2. Use the various buttons under **Actions** to log some telemetry events.
3. Open the **Event Viewer** on the Business Central Server machine.
4. Click on **Windows Logs | Application.**

Depending on the events you logged, you should see some entries in the log, such as this example:

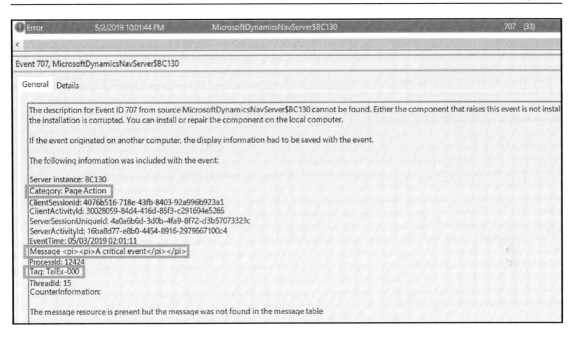

I've highlighted the elements in the previous screenshot that were set using the `SendTraceTag` call in our AL code.

If you are using a container-based sandbox, you have to get the event log in a slightly different way. You can do this by using the `Get-NavContainerEventLog` command-let that is part of `NavContainerHelper`.

Example:
```
Get-NavContainerEventLog –containerName mycontainer
```

How it works...

Raising telemetry events in your on-premises application will allow you to collect data for analysis later. This data could be used to determine how well your application is performing, debugging why a feature is not working as intended, or simply logging how many times a certain function is executed.

When you raise the telemetry event with the `SendTraceTag` function, you need to set a few things:

- **Tag**: A unique identifier for the event
- **Category**: A way to group your events to identify them more easily
- **Verbosity**: The log level (Critical, Warning, or Error)
- **Message**: The text that you want to appear in the event
- **DataClassification**: Identifies the type of data in the event

By setting all of these components, and placing the calls to `SendTraceTag` throughout your AL code, you will be able to capture the data you need to perform your analysis.

When the event is logged, an **Event ID** is assigned to the entry. The Event ID is determined by the combination of the verbosity and data classification properties that you use:

DataClassification	Verbosity	Event ID
`AccountData`, `SystemMetadata`, `EndUserPseudonymousIdentifiers`, `OrganizationIdentifiableInformation`	Critical	700
	Error	701
	Normal	702
	Verbose	704
	Warning	705
`CustomerContent`, `EndUserIdentifiableInformation`	Critical	707
	Error	708
	Normal	709
	Verbose	711
	Warning	712

There's more...

Performing an analysis on your on-premises telemetry data can be done using a variety of tools, including Event Viewer and Performance Monitor.

But what about those cloud customers!?

Even though you cannot (as of writing this book, at least) create custom telemetry events in the Business Central cloud environment, you can still view telemetry information that the cloud environment is configured to log, which includes telemetry events for all of the extensions installed. One such example is as follows:

Timestamp ↓	Level	Opcode Name	Object Type	Object Id	Object Extension Id	Object Extension Info	Function Name
4/30/2019, 9:37:59 PM	4	Stop	Page	50,109	0e8ea749-e...	ALProject1 by Default publisher 1.0.0.0	OnAction
4/30/2019, 9:37:59 PM	4	Start	Page	50,109	0e8ea749-e...	ALProject1 by Default publisher 1.0.0.0	OnAction
4/30/2019, 9:37:58 PM	4	Stop	Page	50,109	0e8ea749-e...	ALProject1 by Default publisher 1.0.0.0	OnAction
4/30/2019, 9:37:58 PM	4	Start	Page	50,109	0e8ea749-e...	ALProject1 by Default publisher 1.0.0.0	OnAction
4/30/2019, 9:37:57 PM	4	Start	Page	50,109	0e8ea749-e...	ALProject1 by Default publisher 1.0.0.0	OnAction
4/30/2019, 9:37:57 PM	4	Stop	Page	50,109	0e8ea749-e...	ALProject1 by Default publisher 1.0.0.0	OnAction
4/30/2019, 9:37:56 PM	4	Stop	CodeUnit	50,109	0e8ea749-e...	ALProject1 by Default publisher 1.0.0.0	OnRun

You do this by using the **Business Central Admin Center**.

You can access the admin center by using the following
URL: `https://businesscentral.dynamics.com/<TenantId>/admin`. Make sure to
replace `<TenantId>` with the appropriate one you want to access.

Once you have logged into the admin center, select **Telemetry** on the left-hand navigation
pane, and then select the environment (**Production** or **SandBox**) that you wish to view the
data for. You can further filter the data to look for a specific moment in time as well!

 You need to be either an administrator within the tenant or a
delegated administrator in order to access the Business Central Admin
Center.

There's more information about the admin center on Microsoft Docs here: `https://docs.`
`microsoft.com/en-us/dynamics365/business-central/dev-itpro/administration/`
`tenant-admin-center`.

See also

You can read more about using telemetry event in your on-premises application on
Microsoft Docs here: `https://docs.microsoft.com/en-us/dynamics365/business-`
`central/dev-itpro/developer/methods-auto/session/session-sendtracetag-method`.

Testing and Debugging - You Just Gotta Do It

4

Building a Business Central application is only one of the responsibilities of a good developer. Testing and debugging that application to ensure high-quality user experience is another—and an extremely important—task that all developers need to do throughout the life of the application.

We're going to cover some topics that will show you how to diagnose issues in your application, as well as steps you can take during the development phase to try and weed out all of those issues before your application gets into the customers' hands.

In this chapter, we'll cover the following recipes:

- Introducing the debugger
- Debugging SQL
- The Automated Testing Toolkit
- Creating a test application
- Creating automated tests
- Testing the UI
- UI handlers
- Creating a test library

Technical requirements

For some of the recipes in this chapter, we're going to build upon the Television Shows application that we started in Chapter 1, *Let's Get the Basics Out of the Way*. If you haven't worked through this book, you really want to consider doing that so you have a good idea of what's going on.

Remember, you need a development sandbox. Chapter 1, *Let's Get the Basics Out of the Way*, covered how to do that if you aren't familiar with the process, so check it out.

Code samples and scripts are available on GitHub. Some of the recipes in this chapter build on previous recipes. You can download the completed recipe code from here: https://github.com/PacktPublishing/Microsoft-Dynamics-365-Business-Central-Cookbook.

Introducing the debugger

Before you can begin to diagnose and fix errors in your application, or simply trace through a process, you're going to need to get familiar with the debugger.

In this recipe, you will learn how to launch the debugger from Visual Studio Code to debug an AL session.

Getting ready

You're going to need an AL project to work in that's connected to a development sandbox. We will continue to build on the Television Show project that we've been working with in the previous chapters. If you have not completed all of the chapters, download the project from the GitHub link at the start of this chapter.

How to do it...

1. Open your project in Visual Studio Code.
2. In **Explorer**, select Television Show.al and in the **Editor**, click on the following line of code and press *F9* to set a breakpoint:

   ```
   if "Last Aired" = 0D then
   ```

This will cause the debugger to stop any time this line of code is executed.

Setting a breakpoint is one way to launch the debugger. You can also set properties in `launch.json` to have the debugger launch when an error occurs or any time a record is updated in the system.

3. Press *F5* to build and deploy the project to your sandbox. Once you log in, follow these steps:

    1. Use the 💡 icon to search for `Television Show List` and click it to open the page.
    2. Select an existing Television Show entry to open it and edit either of the date fields.

Once you validate one of the date fields, you'll notice, in Visual Studio Code, that the debugger has activated and is now sitting on the breakpoint that you set, like this:

```
          2 references
    64        local procedure VerifyDates()
    65        var
    66            FirstAiredDateCannotBeLaterErr: Label '%1 cannot be earlier than %2';
    67        begin
▷   68            if "Last Aired" = 0D then
    69                exit;
    70
    71            if "First Aired" > "Last Aired" then
    72                Error(FirstAiredDateCannotBeLaterErr,
    73                    FieldCaption("Last Aired"),
    74                    FieldCaption("First Aired"));
    75        end;
    76    }
```

You can use the controls on the debugging toolbar to move through the lines of code.

How it works...

Debugging AL code is done via the Visual Studio Code integrated debugger. The AL Language extension makes it possible for the debugger to understand the AL language.

The debugger can be launched in a number of ways:

- **Breakpoints**: The debugger will activate when the first line of code with a breakpoint is executed.
- **On error**: The debugger will activate when an error is thrown in the code execution. This is enabled by setting `"breakOnError": true` in `launch.json`.
- **On record update**: The debugger will activate when a record is updated. This is enabled by setting `"breakOnRecordWrite": true` in `launch.json`.

In Visual Studio Code, when your application has been published in debug mode, you'll notice there is a toolbar at the top of the window, like this:

This is your indicator that the debugger is running. It will be connected to the session that was launched in your web browser.

When you are debugging, you are able to perform the following actions:

- **Pause**: Temporarily stop the debugger.
- **Step over**: Bypass a function in debugging.
- **Step into**: Enter into a function for debugging.
- **Step out**: Finish executing the current function and return you to the calling function.
- **Restart**: Launch a new debugging session without publishing the application.
- **Stop**: Turn the debugger off.

 Code in a Business Central application can only be debugged if you set `"showMyCode": true` in the `app.json` file.

You can hide individual variables and functions from being debugged by using the `[NonDebuggable]` attribute, as follows:

```
[NonDebuggable]
local procedure MyExampleFunction()
begin

end;
```

There's more...

For you keyboard wizards out there, take note of the following shortcuts that are available:

- *F5*: Publish and debug.
- *Ctrl + F5*: Publish without debugging.
- *Ctrl + Shift + F5*: Debug without publishing.
- *Shift + F5*: Stop debugging.
- *F6*: Pause the debugger.
- *F10*: Step over.
- *F11*: Step into.
- *Shift + F11*: Step out.
- *F12*: Go to definition.

See also

Check out the Microsoft Docs article on debugging here: `https://docs.microsoft.com/en-us/dynamics365/business-central/dev-itpro/developer/devenv-debugging`.

Debugging SQL

Typically, when you are debugging your Business Central application, you're doing it to move through the AL code in order to trace data or find a logic error. However, you are also able to use the debugger to analyze the SQL statements that your AL code generates, with the goal of identifying performance problems.

This recipe will show you how to debug SQL statements using the AL language debugger.

Getting ready

You're going to need an AL project to work in that's connected to a development sandbox. We will continue to build on the Television Show project that we've been working with in the previous chapters. If you have not completed all of the chapters, download the project from the GitHub link at the start of this chapter.

If you have been working along, you're still going to need to grab the `Debug SQL Example.al` file from the `ch4/2-debugging-sql` folder in the GitHub repository and place it in your project.

How to do it...

1. Open your AL project in Visual Studio Code.
2. In **Explorer**, select `Debug SQL Example.al`.

    In the **Editor**, click on the following line of code and press *F9* to set a breakpoint:

    ```
    FindRecords();
    ```

3. Press *F5* to deploy and debug the project. When your web browser opens, follow these steps:
    1. Use the 🔍 icon to search for `Debug SQL Example` and click on it to open the page.
    2. Choose **Actions | Find Records**.
    3. On the debugging toolbar in Visual Studio Code, click ⬇ (or press *F11*) to step into the first function.
    4. In the **Debug** pane, follow these steps:
        1. Click **Locals** to expand it.
        2. Click **<Database Statistics>** to expand it.
        3. Click **<Last Executed SQL Statements>** to expand it.
    5. Click **SQL9** to expand it.
4. On the debugger toolbar, click ⬇ to step into the next function.

    As you step through the functions, you will notice that the contents of **SQL9** (and the other SQL headings for that matter) change to reflect the most recent SQL query that was executed, how long it took to execute, and how many rows it retrieved. All great information to know when you are trying to diagnose performance issues!

You can hover your mouse over the `Statement:` line to view the entire SQL statement that was executed.

Here is an example:

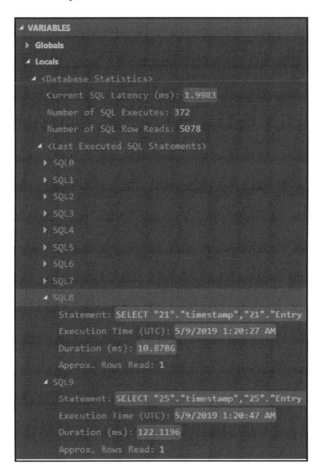

By default, you can see the last 10 SQL statements that were executed. For on-premise installations, you can configure the server to show more or fewer statements.

How it works...

Launching the AL debugger not only allows you to step through the code to debug data and logic flow, but it also lets you view vital SQL information that will help you to diagnose performance-related problems.

As you are debugging, you will be able to see the 10 most recent SQL queries that were executed. For on-premise installations, you can configure the server and set the number of statements you can see.

You are able to view the following information for the recent SQL queries:

- **Statement**: The SQL statement that was generated by the AL code
- **Execution Time**: The time (UTC) at which the statement was executed
- **Duration**: The length of time (milliseconds) it took to execute the query
- **Rows Read**: The number of rows the query processed

In addition to viewing the recent SQL queries, the debugger also shows you some statistics for the current debugging session:

- **SQL Latency**: The time (milliseconds) it takes to execute a SQL statement, which is measured when a breakpoint is hit
- **Number of SQL Executes**: The total number of SQL statements that have been executed in the current debugging session
- **Number of SQL Row Reads**: The number of rows read from the database in the current debugging session

 These statistics are reset at the start of each new debugging session.

See also

You can read more about debugging SQL with the AL debugger on Microsoft Docs here: `https://docs.microsoft.com/en-us/dynamics365/business-central/dev-itpro/developer/devenv-debugging#DebugSQL`.

The Automated Testing Toolkit

The **Automated Testing Toolkit** (**ATT**) provides a mechanism for you to run a suite of automated tests that you can use to ensure that your application is working as intended. Being able to perform regression testing using a static set of tests will give you the ability to see whether a recent change you made has broken a feature or whether an upgrade to a new version of Business Central might break something in your application.

This is an incredibly important step in the development phase since the more tests you perform, the higher the chance that you will find issues before your customers and users do.

This recipe will show you how to use the ATT to run an automated test.

Getting ready

All you're going to need for this one is your development sandbox. However, if you have created your sandbox on the Business Central platform, you're going to have to create a new one using one of the other options.

For this recipe, we will learn about the process of using a Docker container. In order to do this using this type of environment, you're also going to need to make sure that you have NavContainerHelper installed on the machine that is hosting the container. Make sure that you have a valid Business Central development license loaded into the system as well.

Check out the *Setting up your development sandbox* section in `Chapter 1`, *Let's Get the Basics Out of the Way*, for more information on the various ways you can create a development sandbox.

No matter how you create your sandbox, just make sure that you have a few of the standard Microsoft extensions installed.

How to do it...

1. Open **Windows PowerShell** Command Prompt.
2. Type in the following command, replacing `myContainer` with the name of your development sandbox container:

```
Import-TestToolkitToNavContainer -containerName myContainer -
doNotUpdateSymbols -includeTestLibrariesOnly
```

This will import the set of standard testing libraries provided by Microsoft.

We're using the `doNotUpdateSymbols` parameter because the test symbols are actually already in the database that is in the container. All we want to do is install the test CAL objects, but we do not need to update any symbols.

We're using the `includeTestLibrariesOnly` parameter because all we want to load are the libraries that Microsoft provides. Removing this parameter would also import the tests that Microsoft ships, and we do not need those for this recipe.

3. Open the development sandbox with your web browser.

4. Use the 💡 icon to search for `Test Tool` and click the link to open it.

   This is the **Test Tool**. It's a worksheet that lets you pull in any or all of the automated tests that are installed in the database. Out of the box, there are tests built into some of the standard Microsoft applications (such as PayPal, Forecasting, and Yodlee).

5. On the **Test Tool** page, select **Process | Get Test Codeunits | Select Test Codeunits** and press **OK** to view the list of all of the testing codeunits.

6. Select the **Sales Forecast Tests** line. If you don't have that in your system, just choose any other line that looks interesting to you.

   Once you select the line and press **OK**, all of the tests that are contained in that codeunit will be loaded into the **Test Tool**, similar to the following:

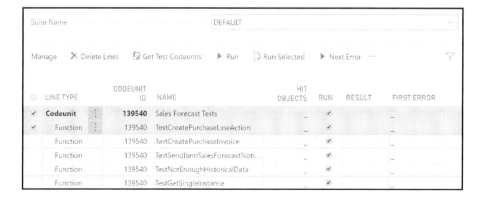

Notice that the results column is empty at the moment.

7. Select **Run | All** and press **OK** to execute the automated tests.
8. Once the tests have been run, you can then use the worksheet to analyze the results of each test. The **Result** column will show you whether the test was a **Success** or a **Failure**. If it failed, then the error will be shown in the **First Error** column, as follows:

LINE TYPE	CODEUNIT ID	NAME	HIT OBJECTS	RUN	RESULT	FIRST ERROR
Codeunit	**139540**	Sales Forecast Tests	...	✓	Failure	Microsoft.Dynamics.Nav.Types.Excepti...
Function	139540	TestCreatePurchaseLineAction	...	✓	Success	...
Function	139540	TestCreatePurchaseInvoice	...	✓	Success	...
Function	139540	TestSendItemSalesForecastNotification...	...	✓	Success	...
Function	139540	TestNotEnoughHistoricalData	...	✓	Success	...
Function	139540	TestGetSingleInstance	...	✓	Failure	Microsoft.Dynamics.Nav.Types.Excepti...
Function	139540	TestGetCredentialsThrowsErrorIfNotValid	...	✓	Success	...
Function	139540	TestMissingApiUriOpenSetup	...	✓	Failure	The value "" can't be evaluated into ty...
Function	139540	TestTimeout	...	✓	Success	...
Function	139540	TestCreatePurchaseOrder	...	✓	Success	...
Function	139540	TestCreateRecurringJobQueueEntry	...	✓	Success	...
Function	139540	TestCreateNonRecurringJobQueueEntry	...	✓	Success	...
Function	139540	TestKeyNeededBeforeScheduledExecuti...	...	✓	Failure	Assert.ExpectedError failed. Expected: ...
Function	139540	TestSetupScheduledExecution	...	✓	Success	...
Function	139540	TestUpdateForecastActionThrowsErrorIf...	...	✓	Failure	Assert.ExpectedError failed. Expected: ...
Function	139540	TestVarianceTooHighMsg	...	✓	Success	...

You can click on each error to view more information about the error and to view the call stack at the point where the error happened.

How it works...

The ATT provides a way for you to run a collection of tests that you can use to test the functionality of your Business Central application.

You can create multiple sets of tests by pulling them into different suites using the Test Tool worksheet. You can choose to pull in all existing tests or you can specify certain ones. Once they've been pulled in, you use the *Test Tool* to run the tests. You can run individual test codeunits or all of them, with the latter option running the tests in a serial fashion.

After the tests have been run, you can analyze the results of each test and drill into the ones that failed in order to identify the error that was triggered by the test and where it occurred in the call stack.

See also

You can read a couple of articles about the ATT on Microsoft Docs here:

- *Application Test Automation*: `https://docs.microsoft.com/en-us/dynamics-nav/application-test-automation`
- *Application Test Toolkit*: `https://docs.microsoft.com/en-us/dynamics365/business-central/dev-itpro/developer/devenv-extension-advanced-example-test#application-test-toolkit`

Creating a test application

Creating tests for your Business Central applications is essential to make sure that they work and perform as you expect and how the customer expects.

When you deliver the application though, you may not want to include the tests with your main application, especially in cases where you may have referenced test libraries that are not part of the main Business Central platform.

This recipe will show you how to create a Business Central application whose purpose is to test another application.

Getting ready

You're going to need an AL project to work in that's connected to a development sandbox. We will continue to build on the Television Shows project that we've been working with in the previous chapters. If you have not completed all of the chapters, download the project from the GitHub link at the start of this chapter.

How to do it...

1. Create a new folder in Windows Explorer to hold your test application. Make sure that this folder is not within the same project folder that contains your `Television Shows` project files.

Copy the following folders and files into the new folder from your
`Television Shows` project folder:

- `.alpackages`
- `.vscode`
- `app.json`

2. In Visual Studio Code, open the new folder. In **Explorer**, select `app.json` and
   update the `"id"` property to a new GUID.

You can use the `new-guid` command in the **Terminal** window to generate
a new GUID.

3. In `app.json`, update the value of the `"name"` property, as follows:

   ```
   "name": "Television Show Test"
   ```

4. Since we're testing our Television Shows application, we need to add a
   dependency to it because our tests need to interact directly with the entities in
   that application.

   In `app.json`, modify the `"dependencies"` property to add a dependency as
   follows:

   ```
   "dependencies": [
       {
           "appId": "",
           "name": "",
           "publisher": "",
           "version": ""
       }
   ]
   ```

You need to open the `app.json` file in your Television Shows project and
get the four values needed for the previous property.

Here is an example of what you should have once you fill in all of the values:

```
"dependencies": [
    {
        "appId": "0e8ea749-edf6-4a29-a396-018ae7aca20a",
```

```
      "name": "ALProject1",
      "publisher": "Default publisher",
      "version": "1.0.0.0"
    }
  ]
```

5. In `app.json`, update the value of the `idRange` property:

```
"idRange": {
  "from": 50150,
  "to": 50199
}
```

6. In order to use the default test libraries that Microsoft supplies, we need to add the following property to `app.json`:

```
"test": "13.0.0.0"
```

7. In **Explorer**, create a new file named `My Test.al` and create a new codeunit object:

```
codeunit 50150 "My Test"
{

}
```

8. Press *Ctrl* + *Shift* + *P* and type in or select **AL: Download symbols**.

9. Once your symbols have been downloaded, the contents of the `.alpackages` folder should look similar to this:

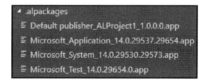

 Note that the names and versions of the files will vary.

That's it! We now have a Business Central test application that we can use to perform tests on our Television Shows application.

How it works...

When you create tests for your application, you can choose to store them within the application, or you can keep them contained to a standalone test application.

Creating a standalone test application allows you to create a separation between what you intend on releasing to your customers, and what you use only internally.

The test application is created in the same fashion that a normal application is created, but there are a few key points to remember:

- The test application needs to have its own unique ID, name, and object range.
- The test application needs a dependency on the application it is testing so that you can directly reference the entities from the test application.
- If you intend on referencing any of the default test libraries from Microsoft, you need to add the `test` property to `app.json`.

There's more...

In this recipe, we created a standalone test application and we opened it in Visual Studio Code as a standalone project. You can also create a multi-root workspace that contains both the test application and the application that it's testing. This makes it much easier to jump between the two projects during the development and testing phases.

You can read more about multi-root workspaces here: `https://code.visualstudio.com/docs/editor/multi-root-workspaces`.

Creating automated tests

Once you create your application and the test application that you'll use to do your testing, you need to create some tests. This recipe will show you how to create a simple automated test.

Getting ready

We will continue to build on the Television Show Test project that we created earlier in this chapter in the *Creating a test application* recipe. If you have not completed that recipe, you can download the project from the GitHub link at the start of this chapter.

You need a development sandbox with the default Microsoft test libraries and test runner installed. If you do not have one, make sure to complete *The Automated Testing Toolkit* recipe earlier in this chapter, and it will walk you through how to set one up. Make sure that you publish your main Television Shows application to your sandbox!

You'll need to install the Television Shows application in your development sandbox. You can also download that project from the GitHub link at the start of this chapter.

How to do it...

1. Open your AL project in Visual Studio Code.
2. In **Explorer**, select `My Test.al`. In the **Editor**, add the `SubType` property to the empty codeunit object in order to define it as a test codeunit:

```
codeunit 50150 "My Test"
{
    SubType = Test;


}
```

Using the `SubType = Test` property allows the *Test Tool* to distinguish this codeunit as one that is used for automated testing.

3. Now, let's add a new test function to the codeunit:

```
[Test]
procedure SuccessTest()
var
    TelevisionShow: Record "Television Show";
    LibraryUtility: Codeunit "Library - Utility";
begin
    TelevisionShow.Init();

    TelevisionShow.Validate(Code,
            LibraryUtility.GenerateRandomCode20(
            TelevisionShow.FieldNo(Code), Database::
            "Television Show"));

    TelevisionShow.Insert(true);
end;
```

This is a simple test that we expect to pass. It just initializes and inserts a new `Television Show` record. The record is created with a random identifier.

4. Let's create another test function:

```
[Test]
procedure FailureTest()
var
    TelevisionShow: Record "Television Show";
    LibraryUtility: Codeunit "Library - Utility";
begin
    TelevisionShow.Get(LibraryUtility
    .GenerateRandomCode20(TelevisionShow.FieldNo(Code),
    Database::"Television Show"));
end;
```

This is a test that we expect to fail. It will try and get a record using a random identifier.

5. Now, let's run our tests! Press *F5* to build and publish your test application in your development sandbox:

   1. Use the 💡 icon to search for *Test Tool* and click the link to open it.
   2. Delete any existing entries in the page or create a new test suite.
   3. Select **Process | Get Test Codeunits | Select Test Codeunits** and press **OK** to view the list of all of the testing codeunits.
   4. Find the **My Test** entry and select it. Click **OK**.
   5. Select **Run | All**.

Once your tests have been run, you should see the following results:

LINE TYPE	NAME	HIT OBJECTS	RUN	RESULT	FIRST ERROR
Codeunit	My Test	_	✔	Failure	The Television Show does not ...
Function	SuccessTest	_	✔	Success	_
Function	FailureTest	_	✔	Failure	The Television Show does not ...

We got a failure, but remember, that's exactly what we expected to happen. This is to simply demonstrate the passing and failing of a test.

> If you want to test a situation where you expect an error to happen, you need to properly handle the failing scenario by using the `asserterror` statement so that the system knows you expect the error to occur.
>
> Read more about that here: `https://docs.microsoft.com/en-us/dynamics365/business-central/dev-itpro/developer/devenv-extension-advanced-example-test#asserterror-statement`.

How it works...

Automated tests are created by first creating a test codeunit. This is done by creating a standard codeunit object and then adding the `SubType = Test` property. This causes the *Test Tool* to pick up the codeunit to be used for automated testing.

Within the test codeunit you can create multiple functions, as you normally would. Only test functions will be shown and executed in the *Test Tool*.

When creating a test function, you must follow these steps:

1. Use the `[Test]` attribute to identify the function as a test. Only these functions will appear and be executed in the *Test Tool*.
2. Create your function as a global function.

There's more...

When you are creating your test functions, it's best practice to use the *Given-When-Then* format:

- **Given**: This is a step that sets up the test. You can have multiple of these.
- **When**: This is a step that describes what is being tested. You should only have one of these.
- **Then**: This is the result being verified by the test. You can have multiple of these.

Here's an example:

- **Given**: This is the Sales Order document page.
- **When**: A user with no approval authority releases the order.
- **Then**: An error is presented to the user, asking them to submit the order for approval.

Check out Microsoft Docs for more information on this: `https://docs.microsoft.com/en-us/dynamics365/business-central/dev-itpro/developer/devenv-extension-advanced-example-test#describing-your-tests`.

See also

You can read more about writing tests on Microsoft Docs here: `https://docs.microsoft.`
`com/en-us/dynamics365/business-central/dev-itpro/developer/devenv-extension-`
`advanced-example-test`.

Testing the UI

In the previous recipe, we created a test using what I refer to as record-based testing. The test was created using records in order to test the business logic. Although this type of test is perfectly acceptable, it does not necessarily recreate the same workflow that a user would take. In order to perform the test in a way that is as close to what a user would do, we need to create our tests slightly differently.

This recipe will show you how to create an automated test using `testpage` objects to more closely mimic the workflow of a user.

Getting ready

We will be continuing to build on the Television Show Test project that we created earlier in this chapter in the *Creating a test application* recipe. If you have not completed that recipe, you can download the project from the GitHub link at the start of this chapter.

You need a development sandbox with the default Microsoft test libraries and test runner installed. If you do not have one, make sure to complete *The Automated Testing Toolkit* recipe earlier in this chapter and it will walk you through how to set one up. Make sure that you publish your main Television Shows application to your sandbox!

You'll need to install the Television Shows application in your development sandbox. You can also download that project from the GitHub link at the start of this chapter.

If you are performing this recipe using a local installation, you need to enable **Page Testability** within the installation wizard here:

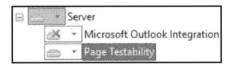

As the **Page Testability** component is not installed by default, make sure that you have installed it.

How to do it...

1. Open your AL project in Visual Studio Code.

2. In **Explorer**, select `My Test.al` and in the editor, add a new test function to the codeunit:

```
[Test]
procedure TestPageTest()
begin

end;
```

3. We're going to recreate the `SuccessTest()` test that we created in the previous recipe, only this time, we will create the test to mimic what the user would actually do in the Business Central client. Thinking about what the user does manually to create a new `Television Show` record, our test needs to do the following:
   1. Open the **Television Show Card** page.
   2. Enter a value into the **Code** field and validate it to create the new record.

   Let's start by creating a few variables that we'll need in our `TestPageTest()` function:

```
TelevisionShow: Record "Television Show";
TelevisionShowCard: TestPage "Television Show Card";
LibraryUtility: Codeunit "Library - Utility";
Assert: Codeunit Assert;
NewShowCode: Code[20];
```

The `testpage` object is a special kind of page object that can only be used in test functions. It allows you to execute pages in a *test mode* where the pages execute like normal pages would, except that there is no UI created. **Test pages** also provide access to some additional page functions that are not normally available.

More information can be found here: `https://docs.microsoft.com/en-us/dynamics365/business-central/dev-itpro/developer/methods-auto/testpage/testpage-data-type`.

4. Now, let's add our test logic (following the previously discussed *Given-When-Then* format, of course!):

```
//GIVEN: Television Show Card
NewShowCode :=
LibraryUtility.GenerateRandomCode20(TelevisionShow.FieldNo(Code),
Database::"Television Show");

//WHEN: user opens Television Show card and creates new record
TelevisionShowCard.OpenNew();
TelevisionShowCard.Code.SetValue(NewShowCode);
TelevisionShowCard.OK().Invoke();

//THEN: the new record is successfully added to the table and
exists once
TelevisionShow.SetRange(Code, NewShowCode);
Assert.RecordCount(TelevisionShow, 1);
```

Okay, we're doing a few things in the previous code:

1. First, we generate a random code to use for the new `Television Show` identifier.
2. Next, we perform the test using the same steps that a user would perform if they were doing it manually:
   1. Open the **Television Show Card** page.
   2. Validate the random identifier value into the **Code** field.
   3. Close the **Television Show Card** page
3. Finally, to test the result, we filter the `Television Show` table directly for the random identifier we generated. We expect to find one record in the table matching that unique identifier.

5. Let's try it out! Press *F5* to build and publish your test application. In your development sandbox, follow these steps:

1. Use the � icon to search for `Test Tool` and click the link to open it.
2. Delete any existing entries in the page or create a new test suite.
3. Select **Process | Get Test Codeunits | Select Test Codeunits** and press **OK** to view the list of all the testing codeunits.
4. Find the *My Test* entry and select it. Click **OK**.
5. Select **Run | All**.

If all goes according to plan, you should see your new test with a success result, like this:

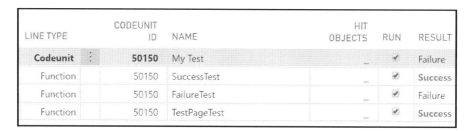

LINE TYPE	CODEUNIT ID	NAME	HIT OBJECTS	RUN	RESULT
Codeunit ⋮	**50150**	My Test	...	✓	Failure
Function	50150	SuccessTest	...	✓	Success
Function	50150	FailureTest	...	✓	Failure
Function	50150	TestPageTest	...	✓	Success

How it works...

By creating your tests using **test pages**, you can more closely mimic the steps that a user would perform if they were doing the steps manually in the Business Central client. This is key to making sure that the interfaces (and logic) respond the way that you intend them to, and that the fields and actions you expect to be on the pages are there.

Before you can execute any tests using **test pages**, you must install the Page Testability component during the installation of your environment.

See also

Check out more about **test pages** on Microsoft Docs here: `https://docs.microsoft.com/en-us/dynamics365/business-central/dev-itpro/developer/devenv-extension-advanced-example-test#test-pages`.

UI handlers

Sometimes, you need to test a process that would normally take input from the user. For example, you write a test to post a sales order, but the posting routine normally pops open a dialog to ask the user whether they want to ship, invoice, or ship and invoice the order. Obviously, in an automated testing scenario, we cannot have the test wait for a user to interact with it.

This is where the UI handlers can be used. They allow us to write a test that has user interaction, and we can write the appropriate data to process that interaction.

This recipe will show you how to handle a confirmation dialog using a UI handler.

Getting ready

We will continue to build on the Television Show Test project that we created earlier in this chapter in the *Creating a test application* recipe. If you have not completed that recipe, you can download the project from the GitHub link at the start of this chapter.

If you have been following along with the previous recipes, you're still going to need to grab a file for this recipe from GitHub at the start of this chapter. Download the UI Handler Test.al file from ch4/7-ui-handlers/televisionShow-test and put it in your Television Show Test project folder.

You need a development sandbox with the default Microsoft test libraries and test runner installed. If you do not have one, make sure to complete *The Automated Testing Toolkit* recipe earlier in this chapter and it will walk you through how to set one up. Make sure that you publish your main Television Shows application to your sandbox!

You'll need to install the Television Shows application in your development sandbox. You can also download that project from the GitHub link at the start of this chapter.

If you are performing this recipe using a local installation, you need to enable **Page Testability** within the installation wizard here:

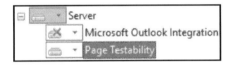

 As the **Page Testability** component is not installed by default, make sure that you have installed it.

How to do it...

1. Open your AL project in Visual Studio Code.
2. In **Explorer**, select My Test.al and in the **Editor**, create a new test function:

```
[Test]
procedure TestConfirmHandler()
var
    UiHandlerTest: TestPage "UI Handler Test";
```

```
begin
    UiHandlerTest.OpenView();
    UiHandlerTest.ConfirmTest.Invoke();
    UiHandlerTest.OK().Invoke();
end;
```

If you deployed this test and ran it as it is right now, you should see the following test result:

What this means is that there is UI interaction happening within your test that is not being handled. Let's fix that!

3. Add the `HandlerFunctions` attribute to your new test function, between the `[Test]` attribute and the function declaration, like this:

```
[Test]
[HandlerFunctions('HandleConfirmDialog')]
procedure TestConfirmHandler()
...
```

This tells the system that we expect to handle some UI and we will do that using a handler function named `HandleConfirmDialog`.

4. Now, let's create the handler function by adding the following code:

```
[ConfirmHandler]
procedure HandleConfirmDialog(Question: Text[1024]; var Reply:
Boolean)
begin
    Reply := true;
end;
```

We used the `ConfirmHandler` attribute to specify that this function is for handling a confirmation dialog.

For this test, all we want to do is mimic the user, selecting **Yes** on the dialog window.

5. Now, let's try out our test. Press *F5* to build and publish the test app. In your development sandbox, follow these steps:

   1. Use the  icon to search for *Test Tool* and click the link to open it.
   2. Delete any existing entries in the page or create a new test suite.
   3. Select **Process | Get Test Codeunits | Select Test Codeunits** and press **OK** to view the list of all of the testing codeunits.
   4. Find the `My Test` entry and select it. Click **OK**.
   5. Select **Run | All**.

Now, the test results for our new test should show as a success:

		☑	Success
TestConfirmHandler	...		

How it works...

UI Handlers allow you to write code in your test to simulate interactions that would normally happen with the user. For example, being able to simulate the user by selecting **Yes** on a dialog box.

You need to tell the system that you expect there to be some sort of UI in your test. You do that by using the `HandlerFunctions` attribute and listing the names of the **UI Handler** functions associated with the test. You can list multiple handler functions for a test.

If you define a **UI Handler** function for a test, but it does not execute during the test, the test will result in an error.

Each type of **UI Handler** function requires a specific signature so that the UI can be handled accordingly. Make use of the Visual Studio Code IntelliSense to remind yourself of what signature to use:

```
procedure HandleConfirmDialog()

The signature of procedure 'HandleConfirmDialog' does not match the signature required
by attribute 'ConfirmHandler'. The expected signature is:
[ConfirmHa  HandleConfirmDialog(Question: Text[1024], var Reply: Boolean). AL(AL0241)
0 references  Quick Fix...  Peek Problem
procedure HandleConfirmDialog()
begin
end;
```

See also

You can read more about the various types of **UI Handlers** on Microsoft Docs here: `https:/` `/docs.microsoft.com/en-us/dynamics365/business-central/dev-itpro/developer/` `devenv-extension-advanced-example-test#ui-handlers`.

Creating a test library

Once you get the hang of writing tests, you're going to want to write a lot of tests, so that you can maximize the test coverage of your application.

When you write a lot of tests, you'll probably notice quickly that you are creating the same data over and over. It's very important for a test to create the data that it needs for the test, or else you run the risk of having too much reliance on the environment that the test is run in.

The best way to tackle this is to make use of test libraries, which allow you to consolidate the common functions used across your tests and create a set of standardized functions so that all of your tests follow the same process flow.

This recipe will show you how to create and make use of a test library.

Getting ready

We will continue to build on the Television Show Test project that we created earlier in this chapter in the *Creating a test application* recipe. If you have not completed that recipe, you can download the project from the GitHub link at the start of this chapter.

You need a development sandbox with the default Microsoft test libraries and test runner installed. If you do not have one, make sure to complete *The Automated Testing Toolkit* earlier in this chapter and it will walk you through how to set one up. Make sure that you publish your main Television Shows application to your sandbox!

You'll need to install the Television Shows application in your development sandbox. You can also download that project from the GitHub link at the start of this chapter.

If you are performing this recipe using a local installation, you need to enable **Page Testability** within the installation wizard here:

 As the **Page Testability** component is not installed by default, make sure that you have installed it.

How to do it...

1. Open your AL project in Visual Studio Code.
2. In **Explorer**, create a new file named `My Test Library.al`. In the **Editor**, create a new codeunit object:

```
codeunit 50151 "My Test Library"
{

}
```

3. Add the following function to the codeunit:

```
procedure CreateTelevisionShow(var TelevisionShow: Record
"Television Show")
var
    LibraryUtility: Codeunit "Library - Utility";
begin
    CLEAR(TelevisionShow);
    TelevisionShow.Validate(Code, LibraryUtility
    .GenerateRandomCode20(TelevisionShow.FieldNo(Code),
    Database::"Television Show"));
    TelevisionShow.VALIDATE(Name, TelevisionShow.Code);
    TelevisionShow.MODIFY(TRUE);
end;
```

4. Add the following function to the codeunit:

```
procedure CreateTelevisionShowCode(): Code[20]
var
    TelevisionShow: Record "Television Show";
begin
    CreateTelevisionShow(TelevisionShow);
    exit(TelevisionShow.Code);
end;
```

5. And finally, add the following function to the codeunit:

```
procedure DeleteTelevisionShow(TelevisionShowCode: Code[20])
var
    TelevisionShow: Record "Television Show";
begin
    TelevisionShow.Get(TelevisionShowCode);
    TelevisionShow.Delete(true);
end;
```

At this point, we've created a library of basic functions to handle the Television Shows application. Now, we have a set of functions that any test can use, and we're certain that any time a `Television Show` record is created or deleted, it will be done the same way.

You can also see that we created two different functions to create a new record. One requires you to pass in an actual `TelevisionShow: Record` variable, but with the other one, you can simply call it and use the return value to identify the new record that was created. Creating standards like this will provide you with more flexibility in writing your tests.

How it works...

Test libraries are simply standard codeunits that contain sets of functions that can be used across all of your tests, in order to create consistent data and processes.

Microsoft provides hundreds of test libraries that provide standard ways to create virtually any type of data, from master records such as customers, vendors, and items to more complex structures such as documents and journals.

Test libraries give you the ability to set the standards for your automated tests. For example, let's assume that you have created a new document entity. What do you test? Well, any time you create a new document entity, it's pretty safe to say that you should have a standard set of tests that you need to create, no matter what the actual functionality of the entity is. I'm talking about things like this:

- Create a document header with *x* lines.
- Create a document line.
- Delete the document header (in turn deletes lines).
- Delete a document line.
- Add a comment to the document header
- Add a comment to the document line

By setting up a standard test library that defines the previous functions, it makes it really easy to ensure that any time you add a new document entity, you also create the same standard tests for it.

If you are really serious about automated testing (why wouldn't you be?), then take a look at **Test-Driven Development (TDD)**. In this approach, you begin building a new feature by creating the tests and then building the feature to meet those test scenarios. Test libraries are a great way of promoting TDD, as the first thing you can do is create your test library and add stubs for all of the standard functions for the entities that your feature needs to interact with.

Check out more information on TDD here: `http://www.agiledata.org/essays/tdd.html`.

See also

I hope you will continue on the path of automated testing. If you do, please take some time to check out the following book, which dives much deeper into the world of Business Central automated testing: `https://www.packtpub.com/business/automated-testing-microsoft-dynamics-365-business-central`.

Old School, Meet New School 5

Up until this point, we've been building a brand new application, but what about all the great CAL solutions that have been created on the Dynamics NAV platform? Sure, you can always re-code them from scratch, but you don't have to. Microsoft has provided a tool that allows us to convert existing CAL objects to new AL-based ones. We'll take a look at what that process looks like, as well as some of the things that need to happen when the conversion is done.

Handling the source code is one step of the conversion from CAL to AL. We'll also explore how to upgrade the data that was held in the old CAL objects. Remember, with a modern development extension platform, the data in any AL table or field no longer resides in the same physical place in the database, so we need a way to move it.

In this chapter, we will cover the following recipes:

- Converting CAL to AL
- Post-conversion cleanup
- Upgrading data from CAL objects

Technical requirements

In this chapter, the recipes are based on a specific type of environment setup using Docker containers. You need to have the following installed and configured:

- `NavContainerHelper`
- Docker containers:
  - AL development sandbox: use `mcr.microsoft.com/businesscentral/sandbox` (use whichever localization you want)
  - Dynamics NAV 2018 development sandbox: Use `microsoft/dynamics-nav:2018-cu16` (yes, we want the worldwide version)

You can refer to the *Option 3 – Sandbox in a local container* section of the first recipe, *Setting up your development sandbox*, in `Chapter 1`, *Let's Get the Basics Out of the Way*, for information on how to set all of this up.

Code samples and scripts are available on GitHub. Some of the recipes in this chapter build on previous recipes. You can download the complete recipe code from here: `https://github.com/PacktPublishing/Microsoft-Dynamics-365-Business-Central-Cookbook`.

Converting CAL to AL

Dynamics NAV is the direct predecessor of Business Central, and I can only assume that if you are working through this chapter, you've created at least one CAL-based solution on the C/SIDE development platform. This recipe will show you how to convert a CAL-based Dynamics NAV solution to an AL-based Business Central application.

Getting ready

You need to download the `ch5-convert-cal-to-al-start.zip` file from the `ch5/1-convert-cal-to-al` folder in the GitHub repository link at the start of this chapter.

Don't forget to make sure your Docker environments are set up and working as outlined at the start of this chapter! Make sure that you have loaded a fully functioning non-demonstration license to your container environments. Demonstration licenses do not let you perform all of the required tasks.

How to do it...

Before we get started, it's important to see what we're converting. Our extremely simple CAL solution consists of two modifications to the **Item Card**:

1. A new field named **My CAL Table Code** is shown after the **Description** field:

A new action named **My CAL Action** is shown after **Save as Template**:

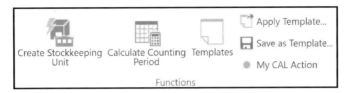

Extract `ch5-convert-cal-to-al-start.zip` to a folder on your machine. You should have the following folders:

- `\modifiedCal`
- `\alProject`

2. Using **NavContainerHelper**, we need to export the original unmodified CAL objects from the Dynamics NAV 2018 container. This gives us a baseline to compare our modified CAL objects to later on.

   Open **PowerShell ISE** in administrator mode, and enter the following code into a new script. Make sure you change the name of the container based on what you have created:

```
$containerName = 'nav2018'
$conversionFolder = 'c:\programdata\navcontainerhelper
\extensions\' + $containerName + '\my\convert'
$originalFolder = Join-Path $conversionFolder "\original"

Export-NavContainerObjects -containerName $containerName -
objectsFolder $originalFolder -filter "" -ExportTo "txt folder
(new syntax)"
```

   Save the script as `1-ExportBaseCalObjects.ps1` and then run it.

3. From the extracted files, import `\modifiedCal\modifiedCalObjects.fob` into your Dynamics NAV 2018 system using the C/SIDE development client:
   1. Select **Tools | Object Designer**.
   2. Select **File | Import...** and select the `\modifiedCal\modifiedCalObjects.fob` file.
   3. Click **Open.**
   4. Click **Yes** to import all the objects.
   5. Select **Later** on the **Synchronize Schema** dialog and click **OK.**
   6. Click **OK** one more time to complete the process.

In **Object Designer**, if you filter on all modified objects, you should see the following:

Type	ID	Name	Modified	Version List
📄	27	Item	✔	NAVW111.00.00.27667
📄	50000	My CAL Table	✔	
🗔	30	Item Card	✔	NAVW111.00.00.24742
🗔	50000	My CAL Table List	✔	

4. Before we can convert CAL objects, we need to get them into a format that the conversion tool can understand. To do that, we need to export them to text. We'll do that with **NavContainerHelper**.

Open **PowerShell ISE** in administrator mode, and enter the following code into a new script. Again, make sure you change the container name accordingly:

```
$containerName = 'nav2018'
$conversionFolder = 'c:\programdata\navcontainerhelper
\extensions\' + $containerName + '\my\convert'
$modifiedFolder = Join-Path $conversionFolder "\modified"

Export-NavContainerObjects -containerName $containerName -
objectsFolder $modifiedFolder -exportTo "txt folder (new
syntax)" -filter "Modified = Yes"
```

Save the script as `2-ExportModifiedCalObjects.ps1` and then run it.

5. Now that we have a folder with all of the unmodified objects, we need to get rid of the ones that our solution didn't modify.

Open **PowerShell ISE** in administrator mode, and enter the following code into a new script. Remember to change the container name accordingly:

```
$containerName = 'nav2018'
$conversionFolder = 'c:\programdata\navcontainerhelper
\extensions\' + $containerName + '\my\convert'
$originalFolder = Join-Path $conversionFolder "\original"
$modifiedFolder = Join-Path $conversionFolder "\modified"
$myOriginalFolder = Join-Path $conversionFolder "\myOriginal"

Create-MyOriginalFolder -originalFolder $originalFolder -
modifiedFolder $modifiedFolder -myoriginalFolder
$myOriginalFolder
```

Save the script as `3-RemoveUnmodifiedCalObjects.ps1` and then run it.

6. We need to determine what changes we made to the original objects. Surprise! There's a `NavContainerHelper` command for that!

   Open **PowerShell ISE** in administrator mode, and enter the following code into a new script. Remember to change the container name accordingly:

```
$containerName = 'nav2018'
$conversionFolder = 'c:\programdata\navcontainerhelper
\extensions\' + $containerName + '\my\convert'
$modifiedFolder = Join-Path $conversionFolder "\modified"
$myOriginalFolder = Join-Path $conversionFolder "\myOriginal"
$deltaFolder = Join-Path $conversionFolder "\delta"

Create-MyDeltaFolder -containerName $containerName -
modifiedFolder $modifiedFolder -myDeltaFolder $deltaFolder -
myOriginalFolder $myOriginalFolder -useNewSyntax
```

   Save the script as `4-CreateCalDeltaFiles.ps1` and then run it.

7. Now that we have our CAL objects in the proper format, we can do the conversion. Once again, we'll use **NavContainerHelper** to do this.

   Open **PowerShell ISE** in administrator mode and create a new script with the following code:

```
$containerName = 'nav2018'
$conversionFolder = 'c:\programdata\navcontainerhelper
\extensions\' + $containerName + '\my\convert'
$deltaFolder = Join-Path $conversionFolder "\delta"
$resultFolder = Join-Path $conversionFolder "\result"

Convert-Txt2Al -containerName $containerName -myAlFolder
$resultFolder -myDeltaFolder $deltaFolder -startId 50000
```

Save the script as `5-ConvertCalDeltaToAl.ps1` and then run it.

You should have the following files in your `result` folder:

8. Now, it is time to create a new AL project where we can put our newly converted AL files:
    1. In Visual Studio Code, open the `alProject` folder that you extracted at the start of this recipe.
    2. Connect the AL project to your AL development sandbox. You can copy and adjust the `launch.json` file from the `Television Show` project or you can refer back to `Chapter 1`, *Let's Get the Basics Out of the Way*, and its first recipe, *Setting up your development sandbox*, for how to do this.
    3. Download the symbols for your new project.
    4. Copy the converted AL files from the `result` folder in step 7 to the `alProject` folder.

You should now have an AL project with the following contents:

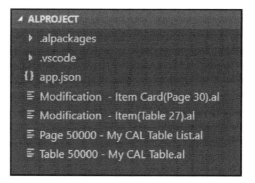

9. Let's try out our new Business Central application! Press *F5* to build and deploy it to your AL development sandbox.

   Go to the **Item List** page, select any item record in order to open the **Item Card**, and look for the following modifications that were converted from the CAL solution:

   - The **My CAL Table Code** field shown after the **Description** field
   - The **My CAL Action** action shown after **Save as Template**

How it works...

There are five steps that need to be done in order to convert CAL objects to AL files:

1. Export all unmodified CAL objects (text format, using a new syntax).
2. Export modified CAL objects (text format, using new syntax).
3. Remove all unmodified objects that have not been modified.
4. Generate delta files based on the unmodified and modified object files (using new syntax).
5. Convert the delta files to AL files.

The delta files are used to identify what changes were made to the original CAL objects, and those changes are brought over to the AL files. The process results in a set of AL files that represent any new objects that were created, and a set of AL files that represent changes made to the base objects. The latter set are converted into page and table extension files.

In the final step of the conversion process, you can set the starting ID number that will be used for any new AL extension files that need to be created. Ideally, you would set this according to either your **Independent Software Vendor** (**ISV**) range or the custom range that the customer has access to. Any CAL object that is converted to a non-extension AL file (such as a table, page, or report), is converted using the object ID from the CAL object.

The actual CAL to AL conversion is done using a tool called `Txt2Al`. This is a command-line tool that evaluates delta files and turns them into AL files. If you dig into the source code behind the `Convert-Txt2Al` command we used in the final step of the conversion process, you'll see that it ends up calling the `Txt2Al` tool.

Although not required, using **NavContainerHelper** provides an easy way to create the environments for both the old (source) and new (destination) versions needed for your conversion. You can use local installations, but the commands that you need to execute will differ, as you are unable to use **NavContainerHelper** without containers. For example, the command to export all base objects to text in the new syntax would be similar to this:

```
finsql.exe Command=ExportToNewSyntax, File=C:\Temp\Objects.txt,
Database="Cronus", ServerName=Localhost
```

Once the conversion has completed, you can simply drop the resulting AL files into an AL project and make adjustments when necessary.

See also

You can read more about performing this process using local installations and commands on Microsoft Docs here: `https://docs.microsoft.com/en-us/dynamics365/business-central/dev-itpro/developer/devenv-txt2al-tool`.

If you are interested in learning more about what other commands **NavContainerHelper** contains, or perhaps what the commands are doing under the hood, check out the GitHub repository for it here: `https://github.com/microsoft/navcontainerhelper`.

There's more...

As with most things in software development, there are multiple ways to perform CAL to AL conversion. Although the recipe that we looked at here is a rather simple set of PowerShell commands, there is a process that consolidates multiple steps. The reason I chose to use this process is that I'm a firm believer in understanding the entire process before you start consolidating and/or automating multiple steps. If you don't have that understanding, you'll have no idea what to do if (but most likely, when...) something goes wrong.

With that being said, `NavContainerHelper` does provide a slightly more streamlined approach to doing the conversion. Although the full explanation and how-to is beyond the scope of this recipe, I recommend that you take a look at the following process, which uses a much more consolidated approach to the five-step process that this recipe showed you:

1. Create your container, but make sure to not use the `-doNotExportObjectsToText` switch:
    - By not specifying the switch, all unmodified objects are exported, which takes the place of performing conversion step 1.

2. Run the `Convert-ModifiedObjectsToAl` command:

  - This performs the same functions that conversion steps 2, 3, 4, and 5 do, as well as copying the resulting AL files to a folder, which would ideally be your AL project folder.

As I said though, it's important to have the foundational knowledge of what is going on in the event that you need to make adjustments or have to deal with any issues that creep up.

You can read more about this conversion process here: `https://freddysblog.com/2019/04/15/c-al-to-al-extension/`.

Post-conversion cleanup

In the previous recipe, we looked at a lovely little CAL solution that provided a complete conversion to AL without leaving any additional work to be done. While I'm certain that there are those kinds of solutions out there in the world, the likelihood of not having to make any post-conversion adjustments is low.

This recipe will show you how to deal with some of the adjustments you will need to make in AL files after converting them from CAL.

Getting ready

In the last recipe, we walked through how to convert CAL objects to AL, so if you've not completed that recipe, you might want to do that so you can understand the process. For this recipe, I'll provide a set of already converted AL files to you. Just download the `ch5-post-conversion-cleanup-start.zip` file from the `ch5/2-post-conversion-cleanup` folder in the GitHub repository link at the start of this chapter.

You also need an AL development sandbox for this recipe. You can reuse the one created for the previous recipe. Just make sure to uninstall the converted CAL application that was published. You do not need the Dynamics NAV 2018 sandbox for this recipe.

How to do it...

1. Extract `ch5-post-conversion-cleanup-start.zip` to a folder on your machine. You should have the `\alCleanupProject` folder.

2. In Visual Studio Code, open the `alCleanUpProject` folder. You need to connect this project to your AL development sandbox. You can reuse the `launch.json` file from the previous recipe or create a new one. You can refer back to *Chapter 1*, *Let's Get the Basics Out of the Way*, and the recipe, *Setting up your development sandbox*, for how to do this. Once the project has been connected, you need to download the symbols.

3. In **Explorer**, select `Modification - Item(Table 27).al` and find the block of code that starts with the following:

   ```
   //Unsupported feature: Code Modification on
   "CheckDocuments(PROCEDURE 23)".
   ```

   This is an example of where a call to a new function, `DoCustomDocumentCheck()`, was added in the middle of the existing `CheckDocuments()` base function. In order to address this, we can move our function call to an event subscriber and then subscribe to the `OnAfterCheckDocuments()` event that is at the end of the base function.

4. In **Explorer**, create a new file named `Item Table Subscribers.al` and enter the following code in **Editor**:

   ```
   codeunit 50000 "Item Table Subscribers"
   {
       [EventSubscriber(ObjectType::Table,
       Database::Item, 'OnAfterCheckDocuments', '', False, False)]
       local procedure OnAfterCheckDocuments(var
       Item: Record Item; var CurrentFieldNo: Integer)
       begin
           Item.DoCustomDocumentCheck(CurrentFieldNo);
       end;
   }
   ```

5. In **Explorer**, select `Modification - Item(Table 27).al` and remove the `local` attribute from the `DoCustomDocumentCheck()` function. Don't worry – this function was intentionally left empty. You can delete the commented block of code for the unsupported feature.

6. In **Explorer**, select `Modification - Item Card(Page 30).al` and find the block of code that starts with the following:

```
//Unsupported feature: Code Modification on "OnOpenPage".
```

This is an example of where code was added to the `OnOpenPage()` trigger of the original page.

Any code modification to a trigger appears as an unsupported feature because it is seen as a modification to the base source code. Since we can access triggers in a page extension object though, this change is actually okay. We can keep our code in the `OnOpenPage()` trigger of the page extension and it will execute after the trigger on the original page executes.

7. In **Editor**, add the following code to the page extension:

```
trigger OnOpenPage()
begin
    MESSAGE('Remember to verify all fields when creating new
items.');
end;
```

You can now delete the commented section of code for the unsupported feature.

8. In **Explorer**, select `Modification - Item Card(Page 30).al` and find the block of code that starts with the following:

```
//Unsupported feature: Code Modification on "ItemsByLocation(Action
68).OnAction".
```

This is an example of where the original page action was changed to launch a custom page instead of the original base one. In this scenario, the easiest course of action is to disable the original action and replace it with our own action that calls the custom page.

9. In **Editor**, add the following code in the `actions` section:

```
modify(ItemsByLocation)
{
    ApplicationArea = Invalid;
    Enabled = false;
    Visible = false;
}
addafter(ItemsByLocation)
{
```

```
action(CustomItemsByLocation)
{
    ApplicationArea = Location;
    Caption = 'Items by Location';
    AccessByPermission = TableData Location = R;
    ToolTip = 'Show a list of items grouped by location.';
    Image = ItemAvailbyLoc;
    trigger OnAction()
    begin
        PAGE.RUN(PAGE::"Custom Items by Location", Rec);
    end;
}
}
```

When you replace existing actions such as this, make sure that you set the actions properties to the same as the original action, so that it looks and feels the same to the user.

Notice that we set `ApplicationArea = Invalid` for the original control. It doesn't matter which `ApplicationArea` value you use but you should use one that won't appear anywhere in the system. This ensures that the control will never be seen by the users, even when performing the personalization feature.

You can delete the commented block of unsupported code.

10. In **Explorer**, select `Page 50000 - Custom Items by Location.al` and find the following block of code:

```
[Scope('Internal')]
```

This is an example of where a base object was copied and then customized. When you convert these objects to AL, there are times when some of the original code/properties don't work within the AL environment because it's now being executed in an extension.

In this example, a function used within the **Items by Location** page was set to `Internal`, which means that the function could not be accessed from an extension. Now that we've copied the page into our extension, we no longer need that property as it actually stops our own extension from accessing the function.

11. To address this, simply delete the following line of code:

```
[Scope('Internal')]
```

12. We've now addressed all the conversion issues. You can use *F5* to build and deploy the application and verify the changes.

How it works...

When we convert from CAL to AL, we move from one development platform to another, and the two are not 100% identical. As a result, there may be some cases where the CAL solution cannot be fully converted.

A few examples of this are as follows:

- The older C/SIDE development client allowed you to do things that the AL platform no longer does.
- Due to the nature of the Business Central AL extension architecture, certain modifications made in CAL are no longer allowed.

When we encounter these scenarios, the conversion tool marks them and, at that point, the only option is for a developer to review and handle them accordingly.

The first thing to do when tackling these things is to ask yourself whether the change is really needed. Enhancements in the platform and the product may dictate that the change is no longer needed. In the event that you need the change in your AL application, you may need to alter it to use the new AL capabilities, or you may simply need to redesign a new solution that works within the boundaries of what a Business Central application can do.

Upgrading data from CAL objects

When you move a customer from a CAL solution to an AL one, you need to handle not only the source code, but also the data that was in any of the old CAL tables and fields. With the AL system architecture, the tables and fields will no longer be in the same place in the database as they were when they were based on CAL. As a result, the data will need to be moved from the CAL tables and fields to the AL ones.

This recipe will show you how you can move data from CAL objects to AL ones.

Getting ready

You need an AL development sandbox for this recipe, but since we're still dealing with CAL objects in this recipe, you need to make sure it's a specific version. The easiest method is to use a Docker container and use the `mcr.microsoft.com/businesscentral/onprem:14.0.29537.0` image to build it.

You also need to download the `ch5-upgrading-data-from-cal-objects-start.zip` file from the `ch5/3-upgrading-data-from-cal-objects` folder in the GitHub repository link at the start of this chapter.

Here is the scenario we're working with:

- A customer has a modified on-premises database that has been upgraded from Dynamics NAV 2018 to Business Central. Their modifications have been merged to the new version. The customer now wants to convert their CAL modifications to AL.
- Their CAL modifications consist of the following tables and fields:
  - A new `Customer Level` table.
  - New fields added to the `Customer` table, including `Level Code` (`Code[20]`, in relation to `Customer Level`) and `Classification` (`Text[10]`).
- In addition to converting their solution to AL, the customer would also like the `Classification` field to now point to a new `Classification` table so that they can perform more consistent reporting and analysis. They also want to change the field from a `Text[10]` field to a `Code[20]` field.

This recipe starts after the following has happened:

- The modified CAL objects have been exported and converted to AL.
- All non-table modifications have been removed from the CAL objects.
- After conversion, the modified CAL objects and fields have been renamed to add `TMP` to the end of each name (for example, `Customer Level TMP`).

 Note that, in the event that you want to use a different image, instead of importing the CAL objects when instructed, you can simply redo the modifications manually, making sure to use the `TMP` naming convention for the table and fields.

How to do it...

1. Extract `ch5-convert-data-from-cal-objects-start.zip` to a folder on your machine. You should have the following folders:

   - `\CalObjects`
   - `\alDataMoveProject`

2. Import all objects in the `CalObjects\modifiedRenamedCalObjects.fob` file with the C/SIDE development client.

   > If you are using a container-based solution, you cannot synchronize the database schema when you import the objects. When you are presented with the **Synchronize Schema** option, you must select **Later**.
   >
   > After the objects have been successfully imported, you need to run the following command in PowerShell, making sure to use the name of your container: `Compile-ObjectsInNavContainer -containerName "<yourContainerName>" -filter Modified=1 - SynchronizeSchemaChanges Yes`.
   >
   > Once you have done this, you will need to update the symbols for this database so that Visual Studio Code picks up the new table and fields. Using **NavContainerHelper**, you can do that by executing the `Generate-SymbolsInNavContainer` command.

3. Open the `alDataMoveProject` folder with Visual Studio Code. Connect this project to your AL development sandbox. You can refer back to the *Setting up your development sandbox* recipe from `Chapter 1`, *Let's Get the Basics Out of the Way*, for guidance on how to do this. Once the project has been connected, you need to download the symbols.

4. Renumber the following AL tables and fields so that they do not overlap with the original CAL ones:

   - `Table 50000 (Customer Level) --> Table 50011`
   - `Field 50000 (Level Code) --> Field 50010`
   - `Field 50001 (Classification) --> Field 50011`

Before you renumber the previous tables and fields, you will notice that they are underlined in red to show that they conflict with the existing CAL entities.

5. In **Explorer,** select `Modification - Customer(Table 18).al` and change the `Classification` field as follows. This way, it now points to the new `Classification` table and is a `Code[20]` value:

```
field(50011; Classification; Code[20])
{
    DataClassification = CustomerContent;
    TableRelation = Classification;
}
```

6. In **Explorer**, create a new file named `Install Application.al`. In **Editor**, create an `Install` codeunit:

```
codeunit 50010 "Install Application"
{
    Subtype = Install;
}
```

 An `Install` codeunit is a special `codeunit` that contains triggers that execute upon the initial installation of the Business Central application, or when the application is re-installed using the same version.

An `Install` codeunit is created by adding the `SubType = Install` attribute as shown in the preceding code snippet.

7. Add a function to move the data from the old `Customer Level` table to the new one:

```
local procedure MoveCustomerLevelData()
var
    OldCustomerLevel: Record "Customer Level TMP";
    NewCustomerLevel: Record "Customer Level";
begin
    if OldCustomerLevel.FindSet() then begin
        repeat
            NewCustomerLevel.Init();
            NewCustomerLevel.TransferFields(OldCustomerLevel);
            NewCustomerLevel.Insert(true);
        until OldCustomerLevel.Next() = 0;

        OldCustomerLevel.DeleteAll();
```

```
        end;
end;
```

Since this table has not changed (with the exception of the table ID) in the AL project, we can simply move all the old entries to the new table.

8. Add a function that moves the data for the Level Code field:

```
local procedure MoveCustomerFields()
var
    Customer: Record Customer;
begin
    if Customer.FindSet() then begin
        repeat
            Customer."Level Code" := Customer."Level Code TMP";
            Customer."Level Code TMP" := '';
            Customer.Modify(true);
        until Customer.Next() = 0;
    end;
end;
```

9. Now, let's add the function to move the data to the Classification field. In addition to moving the data, remember that we need to make sure that the value in this field also exists in the new Classification table:

```
local procedure MoveClassificationField(var Customer: Record
Customer)
var
    Classification: Record Classification;
begin
    if Customer."Classification TMP" = '' then
        exit;

    Customer.Classification := UpperCase(Customer
    ."Classification TMP");
    Customer."Classification TMP" := '';

    if not Classification.Get(Customer.Classification) then begin
        Classification.Init();
        Classification.Code := Customer.Classification;
        Classification.Description := Classification.Code;
        Classification.Insert(true);
    end;
end;
```

Since we already have a function that loops through the `Customer` table to process the `Level Code` field, let's expand it to process the `Classification` field as well:

```
local procedure MoveCustomerFields()
var
    Customer: Record Customer;
begin
    if Customer.FindSet() then begin
        Customer."Level Code" := Customer."Level Code TMP";
        Customer."Level Code TMP" := '';

        MoveClassificationField(Customer);
        Customer.Modify(true);
    end;
end;
```

10. Since all the data we have is company specific, we need to add our function calls to the `OnInstallAppPerCompany()` trigger in the `Install` codeunit. Add the following code to the `Install` codeunit:

```
trigger OnInstallAppPerCompany()
begin
    MoveCustomerLevelData();
    MoveCustomerFields();
end;
```

There you have it! Now, when your application is installed, it will move all the data from the old CAL tables and fields to the new AL ones.

If you want to try out the process yourself, add some data to the old CAL tables and fields, and then build and publish your AL project. When you log in to your AL sandbox, your new AL table and fields should be populated.

How it works...

The architecture of an AL-based system is different from one based on CAL. When a base table is modified in CAL, the new field is created directly in the corresponding SQL table. In AL, that new field is added to a companion SQL table that is related to the original table. When creating tables, instead of the table being alongside the base ones (like in the CAL environment), new AL tables are stored within specially named tables that are directly associated with the application that created them. As a result, existing data in both new tables and new fields needs to be moved when converting from CAL to AL.

The easiest way to move the data is to allow both the CAL and AL modifications to exist in the system at the same time. For this to happen, the object names and numbering needs to be different between the CAL and AL solutions.

As a recommendation, I would do the following:

- Rename the CAL objects and fields to a temporary name, such as by appending TMP to the end of everything. Do this in the C/SIDE environment after you have exported the objects for conversion so that your AL project will have the original names.
- After the AL files are created, renumber the table objects and table extension fields so that they do not overlap with the ones in the CAL solution. This is a far easier task to do within Visual Studio Code than it is in the C/SIDE environment.

When the AL application is installed, logic can be executed to move the data from the pre-existing CAL tables and fields into the new AL ones, while at the same time, you have the option of performing maintenance/updates to the data in order to account for any changes in the AL application.

The final step, of course, is to remove the old CAL modifications by deleting all custom tables and fields. If everything has been converted to AL, then this process just involves reverting all modified objects back to base and deleting any custom objects.

 Don't forget to adjust the customer's license in order to handle any changes in object numbers.

There's more...

While this recipe will work to any solution size, it may not be the right way for you. A CAL solution that contains a large number of custom tables and/or custom fields may require a different approach by moving the data. After all, having to go through all the files to rename and renumber them would take a fair amount of effort and management.

One solution that can work is to move the data using SQL scripting. In this solution, you don't need to have the CAL and AL solutions in a single database, and therefore you aren't required to rename or renumber anything. Another upside is that the data will be moved much faster than doing it using AL code. The potential downside to this type of solution is that it will require some SQL expertise, especially if any data transformation is required.

6
Making Your App Extensible

In this chapter, we'll look at some patterns and other things you can use to make it easier for you to maintain the application for future extensibility.

This is one of my favorite chapters in that once you know this information, you will naturally begin to design your solutions with all of these recipes in mind, thereby raising the bar of the applications you create.

In this chapter, we will cover the following recipes:

- Publishing events in your code
- Enums
- The Discovery design pattern
- The Handled design pattern
- The Variant Façade design pattern
- The Argument Table design pattern

Technical requirements

For this chapter, you will need an AL development sandbox. You can use one that you created previously in this book, but make sure to remove any existing applications that you may have published to it.

If you need help, you can always refer to the *Setting up your development sandbox* recipe in `Chapter 1`, *Let's Get the Basics Out of the Way*, for information on how to set all of this up.

For the recipes in this chapter, we'll be working with a new AL project. Here's an overview of its functionality:

- **Transaction Entry** records are created and then posted to the **Posted Transaction Entry** table.
- New transactions can be created manually in the worksheet, or by using the **Copy Transaction** routine to copy from existing open or posted transaction entries:

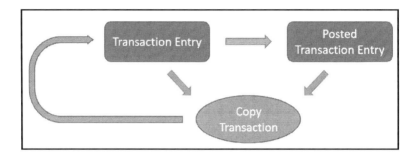

Code samples and scripts are available on GitHub. Some of the recipes in this chapter build on previous recipes. You can download the completed recipe code from `https://github.com/PacktPublishing/Microsoft-Dynamics-365-Business-Central-Cookbook`.

You will need to download `ch6/ch6-start.zip` from the aforementioned GitHub repository in order to perform the recipes in this chapter.

Publishing events in your code

Just as you can extend the Business Central base product with customization, your own solutions can be extended as well by other customers and partners, so that everyone can tailor the solutions they need for their business. In order to provide a solution that can be extended, you'll need to provide events so that key functions and processes can be extended where needed.

This recipe will show you how to add events to your application.

Getting ready

In addition to having your AL development sandbox, make sure you have `ch6-start.zip` downloaded and extracted to a folder on your machine.

How to do it...

1. From the extracted `ch6-start.zip` file, open the `alExtensibleAppProject` folder in Visual Studio Code.

   You need to connect this project to your AL development sandbox. You can reuse the `launch.json` file from the previous recipe or create a new one.

   Once the project has been connected, you need to download the symbols.

2. In **Explorer,** select `Post Transaction.al` and in **Editor**, create a new integration event publisher:

   ```
   [IntegrationEvent(false, false)]
   local procedure OnAfterVerifyTransactionEntry(var TransactionEntry:
   Record "Transaction Entry")
   begin
   end;
   ```

   You can use the `teventint` snippet to quickly create a new integration event publisher.

3. Now, we need to raise that event in our code, so we'll add the call to the new event at the end of the `VerifyTransactionEntry()` function:

   ```
   local procedure VerifyTransactionEntry(var TransactionEntry: Record
   "Transaction Entry")
   begin
       with TransactionEntry do begin
           TestField("Transaction No.");
           TestField("Item No.");
           TestField(Quantity);
           TestField("Unit Cost");
           TestField("Suggested Unit Price");
       end;
       OnAfterVerifyTransactionEntry(TransactionEntry);
   end;
   ```

That's it!

Now that we have an event in place, a customer or another partner can subscribe to it and add additional checks and validations they want to occur during the posting.

How it works...

An event is a specific point in your code which developers can hook into in order to affect functionality. This allows for your application to be customized without modifying the source code, just as you do with the base Business Central application. There are two types of events that you can define in your code:

- **Business:** An event that carries a promise that it will not be changed. Defining business events within your application can be considered the same as defining its API, and as such, there are likely to be ramifications to making changes to its definition.
- **Integration:** It is an event that acts just like business events do, but these events do not have the same promise of not changing.

Defining the event publisher is just the first step. Without raising the event in your code, it will never execute, and therefore, anything subscribed to it will never execute. You raise the event by simply placing a call to the event in your code.

Although events can be raised anywhere in the code, you should take care and think about where you raise them. Adding an event on every other line of code within a function will not provide a good experience for developers and is unlikely to provide for an easier upgrade story. Only put events in places where they are absolutely necessary and where it makes sense. It might be best to err on the side of caution and add fewer events to your application to start with. It's easy to add more events, but once they're published, it becomes more challenging to remove them in cases where customers or partners may have already started using them.

See also

You can read about events, the different types of events, publishing them, and raising them on Microsoft Docs at `https://docs.microsoft.com/en-us/dynamics365/business-central/dev-itpro/developer/devenv-events-in-al`.

Enums

A typical field type used in Dynamics NAV and Business Central development is the option field. While you can define multiple option values for a field, those values are stored within a static string that you cannot modify using a Business Central application. This eliminates any possibility of adding new option values, or changing any of the existing ones.

In AL, there is a new field type called **enum**, or the enumeration type, for those who have developed in other languages. Enums bring with them the ability to extend the list of available values that they contain.

This recipe will show you how to create an `enum` object and link it to a field in a table.

Getting ready

We will continue to build on the `alExtensibleAppProject` project that we started in this chapter. You can download it from the GitHub link at the start of this chapter.

How to do it...

1. In Visual Studio Code, open the `alExtensibleAppProject` folder. In **Explorer**, select `Transaction Entry.al` and add the following field in **Editor**:

```
field(10; Status; Enum "Transaction Status")
{
}
```

2. In Explorer, create a new file named `Transaction Status.al`, and in **Editor**, create a new `enum` object. Let's also add the `New` and `Verified` values to the enum:

```
enum 50000 "Transaction Status"
{
    Extensible = true;

    value(0; New)
    {
        Caption = 'New';
    }
    value(1; Verified)
    {
        Caption = 'Verified';
    }
}
```

You can use the `tenum` snippet to quickly create a new `enum` object.

3. Now, add the new field to the `Transaction Worksheet.al` file, after the **Suggested Unit Price** field:

```
field(Status; Status)
{
    ApplicationArea = All;
}
```

4. Let's add a check to make sure that when the transaction is posted, the **Status** is set to **Verified**.

In **Explorer**, select `Post Transaction.al` and add the check after the **Suggested Unit Price** check, as follows:

```
local procedure VerifyTransactionEntry(var TransactionEntry:
Record "Transaction Entry")
    begin
        with TransactionEntry do begin
            TestField("Transaction No.");
            TestField("Item No.");
            TestField(Quantity);
            TestField("Unit Cost");
            TestField("Suggested Unit Price");
            TestField(Status, Status::Verified);
        end;
        OnAfterVerifyTransactionEntry(TransactionEntry);
    end;
```

As you can see, the syntax for using an enum in code is the same as it is when using an option.

5. And finally, add the following code to the following function to reset the **Status** when an existing transaction is copied to a new one:

```
local procedure CopyFromTransaction(var FromSourceEntryNo: Integer;
var ClearNewTransactionNo: Boolean; var GetNewUnitCost: Boolean)
var
    OldTransaction: Record "Transaction Entry";
    NewTransaction: Record "Transaction Entry";
begin
    OldTransaction.Get(FromSourceEntryNo);
    NewTransaction.Init();
    NewTransaction.TransferFields(OldTransaction, false);
    if ClearNewTransactionNo then
        NewTransaction."Transaction No." := '';
    if GetNewUnitCost then
        NewTransaction.GetLastDirectUnitCost();
```

```
NewTransaction.Status := NewTransaction.Status::New;
NewTransaction.Insert(true);
end;
```

6. Now, use *F5* to build and deploy the application in order to try it out.

Once you're logged in to the sandbox, follow these steps:

1. Use to find the **Transaction Worksheet** page and click on it to open it.
2. Add a new transaction entry.
3. Make sure that **Status** is **New**.
4. Select **Actions | Post Entries**. This should result in the error about **Status** needing to be **Verified**.
5. Change the **Status** field to **Verified**.
6. Repeat step 4 post the entry again. This time it should post without error.

How it works...

An enum is a new object type in the AL development language. It provides developers with a way to define a list of named values. Using an **enum extension** object, the list of values in an enum can be extended by other developers without making modifications to your source code.

You can control whether or not an enum can be extended by using the `Extensible` attribute in the `enum` object.

> If you are going to make an enum extensible, make sure that you handle this in your source code by raising events where necessary in order to handle any additional enum values that might be added.

You can use enums variable types to define the following:

- Table field
- Variables
- Function parameters

You can reuse `enum` objects across multiple entities, meaning you can create a single `enum` object and use it for a table field and a variable.

Both entities will share the same set of enum values, so if the enum is changed or extended, both entities will inherit the change. This could be good or bad, so take care when reusing `enum` object types.

To reiterate, the reason you should use an enum instead of a standard option field is that the enum values can be extended. The list of option values is static and cannot be changed without altering the original source code. In order to add new enum values, a developer creates an `enumextension` object, which then allows them to append new values to the enum values, as follows:

```
enumextension 50000 MyEnumExtension extends "Transaction Status"
{
    value(50000; MyNewValue)
    {
        Caption = 'My New Value';
    }
}
```

See also

You can read all about enums on Microsoft Docs at `https://docs.microsoft.com/en-us/dynamics365/business-central/dev-itpro/developer/devenv-extensible-enums`.

The Discovery design pattern

More often than not, you will design a solution that requires some sort of setup, or contains features that need to be slightly different between customers. While you can try your hardest to design a solution that fits everyone, there is an elegant way that we can build our application to allow for this uniqueness.

By using the Discovery pattern, you can build a solution that will allow your application to remain under control, and yet also be quite dynamic. This pattern provides a way for the data that your application relies on to be extended by customers and other partners, without compromising how your application functions. This means that you can in fact build a single solution for everyone.

This recipe will show you how to use the Discovery pattern in your AL coding.

Getting ready

We will continue to build on the `alExtensibleAppProject` project that we started in this chapter. You can download it from the GitHub link at the start of this chapter. In addition to the project, you will need to download the `ch6-design-pattern-discovery.zip` file from the `ch6/3-design-pattern-discovery` folder.

The scenario we're dealing with here is as follows:

- We've had feedback on our application that some customers wish to execute further functionality after a transaction entry is posted.
- Depending on the transaction, a different process needs to be run.
- We will handle this by allowing the user to specify **Post Transaction Action** on each transaction before posting.

Assuming our application is being used by multiple customers, we need to allow for flexibility in the actions that we make available, and we cannot account for every possibility that a customer may come up with, so we will use the Discovery pattern to allow each customer to use to add their own actions as they see fit.

For the purposes of this recipe, the following has already been done:

- A new `Post Transaction Action` table was created to hold the action entries.
- A new **Post Transaction Action** field was added to the `Transaction Entry` table to allow the user to specify the post-transaction action.
- The posting routine has been updated to process any post-transaction actions.

How to do it...

1. Extract `ch6-design-pattern-discovery.zip` to a folder on your machine and copy/paste the following files into your `alExtensibleAppProject` folder. Make sure to replace the following files with the ones you extracted:
    - `Post Transaction.al`
    - `Transaction Entry.al`
    - `Transaction Worksheet.al`
    - `Post Transaction Action.al`
    - `Handle Post Transaction Action.al`

    Now, open the `alExtensibleAppProject` folder in Visual Studio Code.

2. The first thing we need to do is add an event that can be subscribed to in order to add new post actions.

   In **Explorer**, select `Post Transaction Action.al` and add the following event publisher to the table:

   ```
   [IntegrationEvent(false, false)]
   procedure OnAddPostTransactionAction(var
   TempPostTransactionAction: Record "Post Transaction Action"
   temporary)
   begin
   end;
   ```

   Subscribers to this event will be responsible for adding new entries to the temporary table.

3. Now, let's build the page to display the list of available post actions. Instead of simply displaying the records in the table, we need this page to be dynamic and *discover* any actions that have been added to the system.

   In **Explorer**, create a new file named `Post Transaction Actions.al` and in the **Editor**, create a new list page object, as shown in the following code:

   ```
   page 50004 "Post Transaction Actions"
   {
       PageType = List;
       ApplicationArea = All;
       UsageCategory = Lists;
       SourceTable = "Post Transaction Action";
       SourceTableTemporary = true;
       Editable = false;

       layout
       {
           area(Content)
           {
               repeater(GroupName)
               {
                   field(Code; Code)
                   {
                       ApplicationArea = All;
                   }
                   field(Description; Description)
                   {
                       ApplicationArea = All;
                   }
                   field("Codeunit No."; "Codeunit No.")
   ```

```
                    {
                        ApplicationArea = All;
                    }
                }
            }
        }
    }
```

 Since the page contents will be built dynamically, we need to set the page to not be editable and make the source table temporary. Physical records will never be written to the table.

4. When the page opens, we need to raise the `OnAddPostTransactionAction()` event in order to build the temporary table that the page will display. Add the following code to the page:

```
trigger OnOpenPage()
begin
    OnAddPostTransactionAction(Rec);
end;
```

5. Open the `alExtensibleAppProject` folder in Visual Studio Code. Let's build and deploy the application and confirm the list of available post-transaction actions.

   Press *F5* to build and deploy the app to your AL development sandbox.

   Once you log in, follow these steps:

   1. Use to search for `Transaction Worksheet` and click on the link to open it.
   2. Add a new transaction record.
   3. Scroll to the right side of the line and drill down on the **Post Transaction Action** field.

   You should see an empty list as no actions have been added to the system.

6. For this step, let's now pretend that we're the customer that wants to have a specific post action take place for some transactions.

   We will use the same project for this step, but typically, the customer would do this in their own extension.

   In **Explorer**, create a file named `Add Custom Post Actions.al` and in the **Editor**, create a new `codeunit` object and a subscriber to the `OnAddPostTransactionAction()` event that we created earlier:

```
codeunit 50003 "Add Custom Post Actions"
{
    [EventSubscriber(ObjectType::Table, Database::
    "Post Transaction Action", 'OnAddPostTransactionAction',
    '', false, false)]
    local procedure OnAddPostTransactionAction(
    var TempPostTransactionAction: Record
    "Post Transaction Action")
    begin
        AddCustomPostTransactionActions(
        TempPostTransactionAction);
    end;
}
```

7. Now, add a function to create some new **Post Transaction Action** entries:

```
local procedure AddCustomPostTransactionActions(var
TempPostTransactionAction: Record "Post Transaction Action")
var
    Action1Code: Label 'ACTION1';
    Action1Desc: Label 'Action 1';
    Action2Code: Label 'ACTION2';
    Action2Desc: Label 'Action 2';
begin
    if not TempPostTransactionAction.Get(Action1Code) then begin
        TempPostTransactionAction.Init();
        TempPostTransactionAction.Code := Action1Code;
        TempPostTransactionAction.Description := Action1Desc;
        TempPostTransactionAction."Codeunit No." := 0;
        TempPostTransactionAction.Insert();
    end;
    if not TempPostTransactionAction.Get(Action2Code) then begin
        TempPostTransactionAction.Init();
        TempPostTransactionAction.Code := Action2Code;
        TempPostTransactionAction.Description := Action2Desc;
        TempPostTransactionAction."Codeunit No." := 0;
        TempPostTransactionAction.Insert();
```

```
        end;
    end;
```

8. Now, press *F5* to build and deploy the app to your sandbox.

   Once you log in, follow these steps:

   1. Use 🔍 to search for `Transaction Worksheet` and click on the link to open it.
   2. Add a new transaction record.
   3. Scroll to the right side of the line and drill down on the **Post Transaction Action** field.

   You should now see the two actions that you created with your subscriber.

How it works...

The **Discovery** pattern is a great way to allow your application to *set itself up*. In other words, your application can look for the data it needs by raising an event. Subscribers to that event will then provide the requested data.

This allows for a very dynamic way of extending your application, while still maintaining control over what your application does.

The pattern begins by raising an event in your code at the point where you need the desired data. Typically, you would use a temporary table in the event so that the subscribers can insert their data into it. Once all the subscribers have executed, the resulting data that they provided can then be processed by your application.

Another, maybe more entertaining way of thinking of this pattern is the following conversation between the main application (for example, your application) and three custom applications that are installed in the same system:

```
Main Application: Hey everyone, I need some data for this routine I'm about
to run. Does anyone have it?
Custom Application 1: Yes, here is some data for you.
Custom Application 2: <no reply>
Custom Application 3: I sure do! Here is some data for your routine.
Main Application: Thanks, I'll carry on now and do the routine now!
```

Care should be taken when subscribing to the Discovery pattern event.

You should never assume that you're the only subscriber, so make sure to create unique records by using GUIDs and prefixes that another application won't duplicate, and if that happens, handle it accordingly.

See also

You can read more about the Discovery pattern on the Microsoft Dynamics NAV design patterns wiki at `https://community.dynamics.com/nav/w/designpatterns/271.discovery-event`.

You can see some examples of this pattern in the Business Central base application in the following objects:

- Page 1808 (Assisted setup):
    - `OnRegisterAssistedSetup()`
- Page 1500 (Workflows):
    - `WorkflowSetup.InitWorkflow()`

The Handled design pattern

Often, you will find yourself writing a calculation in your code that you are absolutely certain everyone will want to use to calculate the same way. Well, the reality is that it's not always possible to satisfy everyone. In some cases, a customer may want to inject their own calculation and completely bypass the one you created.

The Handled pattern allows you to build specific points within your application where functionality can be bypassed.

This recipe will show you how to use the Handled pattern within your AL code.

Getting ready

We will continue to build on the `alExtensibleAppProject` project that we started in this chapter. You can download it from the GitHub link at the start of this chapter.

Here's the scenario we're going to...handle (*yes, I know, I did that on purpose*):

- We've gathered feedback from customers that the last direct unit cost is a unique calculation for a number of different customers, so we need to allow each customer to have their own calculation so that it pulls the desired cost into the `Transaction Entry` record.
- If the customer does have their own calculation, then we wouldn't want to perform the standard calculation as it wouldn't be required.

How to do it...

1. Open the `alExtensibleAppProject` folder in Visual Studio Code.
2. In **Explorer**, select `Transaction Entry.al`. In the **Editor**, add a new event publisher to the table:

```
[IntegrationEvent(false, false)]
local procedure OnBeforeGetLastDirectUnitCost(var TransactionEntry:
Record "Transaction Entry"; var IsHandled: Boolean)
begin
end;
```

3. In the `GetLastDirectUnitCost()` function, create a new local variable:

```
IsHandled: Boolean;
```

4. Now, raise the event at the start of the `GetLastDirectUnitCost()` function:

```
OnBeforeGetLastDirectUnitCost(Rec, IsHandled);
```

5. After the call to the event, add logic to exit the function if the subscriber has set `IsHandled` to `true`:

```
if IsHandled then
    exit;
```

Your function should now look like this, with the new code highlighted as follows:

```
procedure GetLastDirectUnitCost()
var
    PurchaseInvLine: Record "Purch. Inv. Line";
    IsHandled: Boolean;
begin
    OnBeforeGetLastDirectUnitCost(Rec, IsHandled);
```

```
if IsHandled then
    exit;
clear("Unit Cost");

if "Item No." = '' then
    exit;

PurchaseInvLine.SetRange(Type, PurchaseInvLine.Type::Item);
PurchaseInvLine.SetRange("No.", "Item No.");
if PurchaseInvLine.FindLast() then
    validate("Unit Cost", PurchaseInvLine."Direct Unit
Cost");
end;
```

It's that easy!

Now, a subscriber can *take over* the function, as well as perform its own calculation and bypass the rest of the logic within the function.

How it works...

The **Handled** pattern allows you to define pieces of code that you will allow a subscriber to bypass. This is done by raising an event before the piece of code, and using a variable parameter that the subscriber can set to notify the application that the rest of the code should be bypassed. If there are no subscribers that set the flag to bypass, then the original code will continue to be executed.

This is extremely useful in the scenarios where you have processes or calculations that may not be a *one-size-fits-all* kind of thing.

Using our recipe example, by subscribing to the `OnBeforeGetLastDirectUnitCost()` event, a developer can perform their own logic to calculate the last direct unit cost, such as, maybe they only want to look at documents from a specific time period. Once the calculation is performed, their logic will set `IsHandled := true` so that the original code will not be executed and overwrite their custom calculation.

Caution!
Care needs to be taken with this pattern. Since you cannot guarantee that the subscriber will actually handle the functionality properly, you need to make sure to verify that any critical data is handled correctly.

You don't want to create a situation where your function is bypassed and it leads to incomplete or incorrect data.

This pattern can also be used in reverse. Instead of using a `Boolean` value to bypass your code, you can use it to ensure that there is an active subscriber to the event that performs some logic.

In this scenario, instead of skipping your code if the flag is not set, you might throw an error (or some other handling).

See also

You can see this pattern in action in the Business Central base application here:

- Table 37 (Sales line):
    - `OnValidateLocationCodeOnBeforeSetShipmentDate()`
    - `OnBeforeUpdateUnitPrice()`
- Table 83 (Item journal line):
    - `OnBeforeRetrieveCosts()`

The Variant Façade design pattern

Have you ever written a function to do something to an open table, and then you had to do the same function for the posted one? Or, maybe you've created a routine to process customer records, and then you've also needed the same function for vendors?

What did you do?

I bet more often than not, you took a copy of that original function and updated/renamed the variables to point to the second table. Now, you're left with two copies of the same function to maintain, and two entry points to the same functionality.

The **Variant Façade** pattern enables you to define a single entry point for your function, allowing it to accept any table record.

This recipe will show you how to use the Variant Façade pattern in your AL code.

Getting ready

We will continue to build on the `alExtensibleAppProject` project that we started in this chapter. You can download it from the GitHub link at the start of this chapter.

The scenario that we'll handle in this recipe is as follows:

- Currently, we have duplicate functions in the `Copy Transaction` routine:
    - `CopyFromPostedTransaction()`
    - `CopyFromTransaction()`
- Both functions create a new `Transaction Entry` record with the only difference being the source table (open versus posted).

We want to clean up this routine to eliminate the duplicate code so that we have a single point of entry into the `Copy Transaction` routine. This will make the routine easier to read and maintain.

How to do it...

1. Open the `alExtensibleAppProject` folder in Visual Studio Code.
2. In **Explorer,** select `Copy Transaction Dialog.al`, and in the **Editor**, add the following new function:

```
local procedure SetFromRecordVariant(var FromRecordVariant:
Variant)
var
    FromTransactionEntry: Record "Transaction Entry";
    FromPostedTransactionEntry: Record "Posted Transaction Entry";
begin
    case FromType of
        FromType::Transaction:
            begin
                FromTransactionEntry.Get(FromTransactionEntryNo);
                FromRecordVariant := FromTransactionEntry;
            end;
        FromType::"Posted Transaction":
            begin
FromPostedTransactionEntry.Get(FromTransactionEntryNo);
                FromRecordVariant := FromPostedTransactionEntry;
            end;
    end;
end;
```

3. Update the `GetCopyTransactionParameters()` function with the following:
   1. Call the new `SetFromRecordVariant()` function.
   2. Replace the `FromSourceType` and `FromSourceNo` parameters with `FromRecordVariant`.

Your function should look like this:

```
procedure GetCopyTransactionParameters(var FromRecordVariant:
Variant; var ClearNewTransactionNo: Boolean; var
GetNewUnitCost: Boolean)
begin
    SetFromRecordVariant(FromRecordVariant);
    ClearNewTransactionNo := ResetNewTransactionNo;
    GetNewUnitCost  := GetUpdatedUnitCost;
end;
```

4. In **Explorer**, select `Copy Transaction.al` and in the **Editor**, delete the following four functions:
   - `CopyTransaction()`
   - `DoCopyTransaction()`
   - `CopyFromTransaction()`
   - `CopyFromPostedTransaction()`

Yeah, I know you have an empty codeunit right now. We'll create a new and improved version of it!

5. Add the `CopyTransaction()` function:

```
procedure CopyTransaction()
var
    CopyTransactionDialog: Page "Copy Transaction Dialog";
    ClearNewTransactionNo: Boolean;
    GetNewUnitCost: Boolean;
    FromRecordVariant: Variant;
begin
    if CopyTransactionDialog.RunModal() = Action::OK then begin
CopyTransactionDialog.GetCopyTransactionParameters(FromRecordVa
riant, ClearNewTransactionNo, GetNewUnitCost);
        DoCopyTransaction(FromRecordVariant,
ClearNewTransactionNo, GetNewUnitCost);
    end;
end;
```

6. Add the `DoCopyTransaction()` function:

```
local procedure DoCopyTransaction(var FromRecordVariant: Variant;
var ClearNewTransactionNo: Boolean; var GetNewUnitCost: Boolean)
var
    FromRecordRef: RecordRef;
    DataTypeMgmt: Codeunit "Data Type Management";
begin
    DataTypeMgmt.GetRecordRef(FromRecordVariant, FromRecordRef);
    CopyFromSourceRecord(FromRecordRef, ClearNewTransactionNo,
GetNewUnitCost);
end;
```

7. Add the `CopyFromSourceRecord()` function:

```
local procedure CopyFromSourceRecord(var FromRecordRef: RecordRef;
var ClearNewTransactionNo: Boolean; var GetNewUnitCost: Boolean)
var
    FromTransactionEntry: Record "Transaction Entry";
    FromPostedTransactionEntry: Record "Posted Transaction Entry";
    NewTransaction: Record "Transaction Entry";
begin
    NewTransaction.Init();
    case FromRecordRef.Number() of
        Database::"Transaction Entry":
            begin
                FromRecordRef.SetTable(FromTransactionEntry);
                NewTransaction.TransferFields(FromTransactionEntry,
false);
            end;
        Database::"Posted Transaction Entry":
            begin
                FromRecordRef.SetTable(FromPostedTransactionEntry);
NewTransaction.TransferFields(FromPostedTransactionEntry, false);
            end;
    end;
    if ClearNewTransactionNo then
        NewTransaction."Transaction No." := '';
    if GetNewUnitCost then
        NewTransaction.GetLastDirectUnitCost();
    NewTransaction.Status := NewTransaction.Status::New;
    NewTransaction.Insert(true);
end;
```

You're done!

You can now deploy your application if you want to try it out. The `CopyTransaction()` function should work just as it did previously in step 5, only now, we have a single set of code to maintain.

How it works...

The **Variant Façade** pattern allows you to define a single point of entry to a function or a set of functions. Using this pattern allows you to pass any type of record into a function as opposed to having to create a function to handle each type.

This pattern works by passing along a combination of `Variant` and `RecordRef` parameters between the functions. This allows for the function signatures to remain completely generic so that you don't need to maintain multiple versions of the same function.

Using this pattern is another way that you can ensure your application is extensible by other developers. Using combinations of variants and events, you can allow your functions and routines to be used for any type of table that may be introduced into the system.

See also

You can read up on the Variant Façade pattern on the Microsoft Dynamics NAV design pattern wiki at `https://community.dynamics.com/nav/w/designpatterns/246.variant-facade`.

The Argument Table design pattern

The final pattern that we'll look at is the **Argument Table** pattern. This pattern allows you to pass multiple parameters to a function, while not having to update the signature of the function in the event that the parameters change over time. It's not unheard of to have to revisit a function after it's been published because a new requirement dictates for another parameter to be added, or for an existing one to be removed.

This recipe will show you how to use the Argument Table pattern to pass parameters between your functions.

Getting ready

We will continue to build on the `alExtensibleAppProject` project that we started in this chapter. You can download it from the GitHub link at the start of this chapter.

The scenario we'll be working with is as follows:

- Currently, there are a number of parameters defined for the `Copy Transaction` routine.
- However, feedback gathered from customers tells us that often, customers need some additional control over what gets copied from a previous transaction.
- Therefore, we will redesign our solution to better allow for parameters to be added in the future.

How to do it...

1. Open the `alExtensibleAppProject` folder in Visual Studio Code.
2. In **Explorer**, create a new file named `Copy Transaction Argument.al` and create the following table object:

```
table 50003 "Copy Transaction Argument"
{
    fields
    {
        field(1; "Reset Transaction No."; Boolean)
        {
        }
        field(2; "Get Updated Unit Cost"; Boolean)
        {
        }
    }
}
```

 There is no primary key defined as we will never physically insert records into this table.

3. In **Explorer**, select `Copy Transaction Dialog.al` and in the **Editor**, add the following new function:

```
local procedure SetArgumentTable(var TempCopyTransactionArgument:
Record "Copy Transaction Argument" temporary)
begin
    TempCopyTransactionArgument."Get Updated Unit
    Cost" := GetUpdatedUnitCost;
    TempCopyTransactionArgument."Reset Transaction
    No." := ResetNewTransactionNo;
end;
```

4. Replace the existing `GetCopyTransactionParameters()` function with the following one:

```
procedure GetCopyTransactionParameters(var FromRecordVariant:
Variant; var TempCopyTransactionArgument: Record "Copy Transaction
Argument" temporary)
begin
    SetFromRecordVariant(FromRecordVariant);
    SetArgumentTable(TempCopyTransactionArgument);
end;
```

5. Replace the existing `CopyTransaction()` function with the following one:

```
procedure CopyTransaction()
var
    CopyTransactionDialog: Page "Copy Transaction Dialog";
    FromRecordVariant: Variant;
    TempCopyTransactionArgument: Record
    "Copy Transaction Argument" temporary;
begin
    if CopyTransactionDialog.RunModal() = Action::OK then begin
        CopyTransactionDialog.GetCopyTransactionParameters(
        FromRecordVariant, TempCopyTransactionArgument);
        DoCopyTransaction(FromRecordVariant,
        TempCopyTransactionArgument);
    end;
end;
```

6. Replace the existing `DoCopyTransaction()` function with the following one:

```
local procedure DoCopyTransaction(var FromRecordVariant: Variant;
var TempCopyTransactionArgument: Record "Copy Transaction Argument"
temporary)
var
    FromRecordRef: RecordRef;
    DataTypeMgmt: Codeunit "Data Type Management";
begin
    DataTypeMgmt.GetRecordRef(FromRecordVariant, FromRecordRef);
    CopyFromSourceRecord(FromRecordRef,
    TempCopyTransactionArgument);
end;
```

7. Replace the `CopyFromSourceRecord()` function with the following one:

```
local procedure CopyFromSourceRecord(var FromRecordRef: RecordRef;
var TempCopyTransactionArgument: Record "Copy Transaction Argument"
temporary)
var
    FromTransactionEntry: Record "Transaction Entry";
    FromPostedTransactionEntry: Record "Posted Transaction Entry";
    NewTransaction: Record "Transaction Entry";
begin
    NewTransaction.Init();
    case FromRecordRef.Number() of
        Database::"Transaction Entry":
            begin
                FromRecordRef.SetTable(FromTransactionEntry);
                NewTransaction.TransferFields(FromTransactionEntry,
false);
            end;
        Database::"Posted Transaction Entry":
            begin
                FromRecordRef.SetTable(FromPostedTransactionEntry);
                NewTransaction.TransferFields(
                FromPostedTransactionEntry, false);
            end;
    end;
    if TempCopyTransactionArgument."Reset Transaction No." then
        NewTransaction."Transaction No." := '';
    if TempCopyTransactionArgument."Get Updated Unit Cost" then
        NewTransaction.GetLastDirectUnitCost();
    NewTransaction.Status := NewTransaction.Status::New;
    OnBeforeInsertNewTransactionEntry(
    NewTransaction, TempCopyTransactionArgument);
    NewTransaction.Insert(true);
end;
```

8. Now, create a new event:

```
[IntegrationEvent(false, false)]
local procedure OnBeforeInsertNewTransactionEntry(var
NewTransaction: Record "Transaction Entry"; var
TempCopyTransactionArgument: Record "Copy Transaction Argument"
temporary)
begin
end;
```

This event will let other developers subscribe and process any new arguments that they add to the Copy Transaction Argument table.

Now we've created a set of functions that we can pass parameters through and we'll never need to update the signatures to handle any updates to the parameters.

How it works...

The **Argument Table** pattern allows you to pass multiple parameters through your functions without having to define each parameter in the signature of the functions. This allows you to easily modify the set of parameters in the future, without having to refactor your function calls.

This pattern is implemented by creating a table to hold the parameter values. You can define any type of field as required by the parameter. You do not need to define any keys since no physical entries will be created in the table.

Using a combination of this pattern and events, you can build a solution that will allow the parameters of your routine to be extended (via a table extension on the Argument Table pattern) and the logic of those new parameters to be implemented (by using an event at the place you use the parameters).

In our recipe example, in order for a developer to add a new parameter that's used in the Copy Transaction routine, all they'd have to do is the following:

1. Extend the Copy Transaction Argument table to add a new field for the new parameter.
2. Subscribe to the OnBeforeInsertNewTransactionEntry() event and write logic that to handle the new parameter.

See also

You can read more about the Argument Table pattern on the Microsoft Dynamics NAV design patterns wiki at `https://community.dynamics.com/nav/w/designpatterns/245.argument-table`.

Business Central for All 7

Alright, now we're getting into one of my favorite sections of the book! In this chapter, we're going to take a look at some of the ways that we can interact with Business Central from *outside* of Business Central. First, we'll look at how web services can be published in Business Central, which is critical for surfacing data to external applications and services. Next, we'll move on to one of the newest platforms available in Business Central, the Business Central API. This is a new RESTful web service platform that will allow you to consume and create data in Business Central using standard API calls.

Moving on from the API, we get into the Power Platform. This super cool collection of Microsoft online services and applications puts a lot of...power...into your hands.

Once we finish with Power Platform, we'll look at Azure Functions. They provide us with a way to deploy serverless .NET applications to the cloud so that we can consume them in our Business Central applications. This is very important for those that need to leverage .NET libraries in the online Business Central environments.

In this chapter, we will cover the following recipes:

- Consuming external web services
- Publishing your own web service
- Enabling basic authentication
- Business Central API – exploring with Postman
- Business Central API – retrieving data
- Business Central API – creating data
- Business Central API – publishing a custom endpoint
- Power Platform – using Microsoft Power BI
- Power Platform – using Microsoft Flow
- Power Platform – using Microsoft PowerApps
- Consuming Azure Functions

Technical requirements

For this chapter, you will need an AL development sandbox. It is recommended that you use an online Business Central sandbox for these recipes and, as such, the recipes in this chapter assume that setup. If you need help, then you can always refer to the *Setting up your development sandbox* recipe in `Chapter 1`, *Let's Get the Basics Out of the Way*, for information on how to set all of this up.

Code samples and scripts are available on GitHub. Some of the recipes in this chapter build on previous recipes. You can download the completed recipe code from `https://github.com/PacktPublishing/Microsoft-Dynamics-365-Business-Central-Cookbook`.

We're going to work with our old friend, the `Television Show` project, but I've made a few updates that we'll need for this chapter, so even if you've worked through all of the previous recipes to build the project, you need to download `ch7/ch7-start.zip` from the aforementioned GitHub repository. This file contains an updated `Television Show` project that you will need to use for the recipes in this chapter.

Extract the contents of `ch7-start.zip` and use them to overwrite the previous `Television Show` project files that you created.

Consuming external web services

One new feature that is native to the AL programming language is the ability to make web requests. Using new variable types, it's incredibly easy to connect to external endpoints to push and pull data between an external system and your Business Central application.

This recipe will show you how to connect to a RESTful API in order to retrieve JSON-formatted data.

Getting ready

You need to have your AL development sandbox ready to go. I'll mention it again, but it's recommended that you use a Business Central online sandbox for the recipes in this chapter. Any of the additional deployment types may require further setup and configuration that are beyond the scope of the recipe.

Make sure that you've downloaded `ch7-start.zip` and have extracted the contents to your machine, overwriting your existing `Television Show` project.

In this recipe, we're working with the scenario of achieving the ability to download episodic information about the episodes of a given television show.

To achieve this, we'll connect to a free API provided by TV Maze (`https://www.tvmaze.com/api`), and download the information to a new table named `Television Show Episode`. The information will be accessible from `Television Show Card`.

For the purposes of this recipe, the new objects have been created and hooked up. The only thing left to do is to create the function to connect to the API and download the television show episode data.

How to do it...

1. In Visual Studio Code, open the `televisionShow` folder that you extracted from `ch7-start.zip`.

2. In **Explorer**, select `Download Episode Information.al`.

3. In the `DownloadEpisodes()` function, add the following local variables:

```
Client: HttpClient;
ResponseMessage: HttpResponseMessage;
JsonArray: JsonArray;
JsonToken: JsonToken;
JsonObject: JsonObject;
JsonContentText: Text;
Url: Text;
MissingIdErr: Label 'You must populate the %1 before you can
download episodes.';
RequestErr: Label 'An error occurred when trying to get the
episodes:\\%1:\\%2';
WrongFormatErr: Label 'The response is not formatted correctly.';
Counter: Integer;
```

4. In the `DownloadEpisodes()` function, add the following logic to perform the following functions:
- Connect to the RESTful API.
- Download the JSON-formatted episode information.
- Parse the JSON data and create entries in the `Television Show Episode` table:

```
If TelevisionShow."TVMaze ID" = 0 then
    Error(MissingIdErr, TelevisionShow.FieldCaption("TVMaze
    ID"));
Url := 'http://api.tvmaze.com/shows/' +
Format(TelevisionShow."TVMaze ID") + '/episodes';
Client.Get(Url, ResponseMessage);
if not ResponseMessage.IsSuccessStatusCode() then
    Error(RequestErr, ResponseMessage.HttpStatusCode,
    ResponseMessage.ReasonPhrase);
ResponseMessage.Content().ReadAs(JsonContentText);
if not JsonArray.ReadFrom(JsonContentText) then
    Error(WrongFormatErr);
for Counter := 0 to JsonArray.Count() - 1 do begin
    JsonArray.Get(Counter, JsonToken);
    JsonObject := JsonToken.AsObject();
    CreateTelevisionShowEpisodeEntry(TelevisionShow,
    JsonObject)
end;
```

5. Add a new function named `CreateTelevisionShowEpisodeEntry()`, as shown in the following code. This function will take the data from the JSON response and use it to populate the corresponding `Television Show Episode` fields:

```
local procedure CreateTelevisionShowEpisodeEntry(TelevisionShow:
Record "Television Show"; JsonObject: JsonObject)
var
    TelevisionShowEpisode: Record "Television Show Episode";
    JsonToken: JsonToken;
begin
    TelevisionShowEpisode.Init();
    TelevisionShowEpisode."Television Show Code" :=
    TelevisionShow.Code;
    GetJsonToken(JsonObject, 'id', JsonToken);
    TelevisionShowEpisode."Episode ID" :=
    JsonToken.AsValue().AsInteger();
    GetJsonToken(JsonObject, 'name', JsonToken);
    TelevisionShowEpisode.Name :=
    CopyStr(JsonToken.AsValue().AsText(), 1,
```

```
    MaxStrLen(TelevisionShowEpisode.Name));
    GetJsonToken(JsonObject, 'season', JsonToken);
    TelevisionShowEpisode."Season No." :=
    JsonToken.AsValue().AsInteger();
    GetJsonToken(JsonObject, 'number', JsonToken);
    TelevisionShowEpisode."Episode No." :=
    JsonToken.AsValue().AsInteger();
    GetJsonToken(JsonObject, 'airdate', JsonToken);
    TelevisionShowEpisode."Air Date" :=
    JsonToken.AsValue().AsDate();
    GetJsonToken(JsonObject, 'summary', JsonToken);
    TelevisionShowEpisode.Summary :=
    CopyStr(JsonToken.AsValue().AsText(), 1,
    MaxStrLen(TelevisionShowEpisode.Summary));
    TelevisionShowEpisode.Insert();
end;
```

6. Let's create a small helper function that will try and get the requested key from the JSON data:

```
local procedure GetJsonToken(JsonObject: JsonObject; KeyText: Text;
var JsonToken: JsonToken)
var
    CannotFindKeyErr: Label 'Cannot find the following key: %1';
begin
    if not JsonObject.Get(KeyText, JsonToken) then
        error(CannotFindKeyErr, KeyText);
end;
```

7. Now, we can try out our application. Press *F5* to build and deploy it to your AL sandbox. Once you log in, follow these steps:
    1. Use the 💡 icon, search for `Assisted Setup`, and click the link to open the page.
    2. Click the **Load Television Shows** link.
    3. Click **Next.**
    4. Turn on all the genre options.
    5. Click **Finish.**
    6. Use the 💡 icon to search for `Television Show List` and click the link to open the page.
    7. Click on any of the entries to open the `Television Show Card`.
    8. Click **Actions | Download Episode Information**. You may be prompted to allow the external connection. Click **Always Allow** or **Allow Once** per your discretion, and click **OK**.

Once the data has been downloaded, you should see the following message:

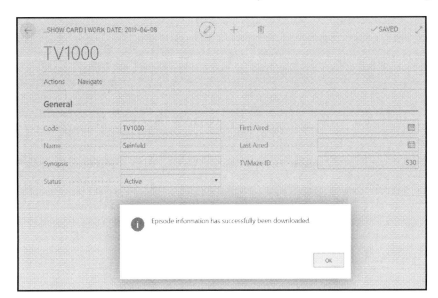

8. Now, let's see the data that was downloaded. On `Television Show Card`, select **Navigate | Episodes** to view the episode information for the television show.

How it works...

The new variable types in the AL language provide native support for making web requests and processing the resulting data. This allows us to easily connect to external web services in order to pass data to, or get data from, them.

The request to the web service is done by using the `HttpClient` variable type. The response from that request is returned into a `HttpResponseMessage` type where it can be parsed in order to determine whether the request was successful or not.

A successful request then allows us to parse the data (in our recipe, this is JSON-formatted data) using a combination of `JsonArray`, `JsonToken`, and `JsonObject` variable types. The combination and logic at this point is dependent on the structure of the data. For example, you may not require the `JsonArray` variable type if the response does not contain arrays.

Once the data is parsed, we just need to convert it to the correct data type and store it in the appropriate table fields

See also

In addition to having native support for handling JSON-formatted data, the AL language also provides support for parsing XML-formatted data!

Check out the Microsoft Docs page to read more about all the HTTP, JSON, and XML variable types that are available to Business Central developers, available at `https://docs.microsoft.com/en-us/dynamics365/business-central/dev-itpro/developer/devenv-restapi-overview`.

Publishing your own web service

Flipping the page and looking at the other side of the integration story, what about external systems that want to connect to a Business Central system? Luckily for us, the AL development platform provides an easy way to surface new web services so they're available to be consumed from outside the Business Central environment.

This recipe will show you how to create and publish a new web service.

Getting ready

You need to have your AL development sandbox ready to go. It's recommended that you use a Business Central online sandbox for the recipes in this chapter, since other deployment types may require further setup and configuration that are beyond the scope of this recipe.

We will continue to build on the `Television Show` project that we used in the previous recipe, *Consuming external web services*. You can download that from the GitHub link at the start of this chapter if you haven't already worked through it.

How to do it...

1. Open your `televisionShow` folder in Visual Studio Code.
2. In **Explorer**, create a new file named `webServices.xml`.

3. Add the following XML code to the file:

```xml
<?xml version="1.0" encoding="UTF-8"?>
<ExportedData>
    <TenantWebServiceCollection>
        <TenantWebService>
            <ObjectType>Page</ObjectType>
            <ServiceName>televisionshows</ServiceName>
            <ObjectID>50100</ObjectID>
            <Published>true</Published>
        </TenantWebService>
    </TenantWebServiceCollection>
</ExportedData>
```

You can use the `twebservices` snippet to create the basic structure for the web services file.

4. Add another `TenantWebService` block to the XML code:

```xml
<TenantWebService>
    <ObjectType>Page</ObjectType>
    <ServiceName>tvshowepisodes</ServiceName>
    <ObjectID>50111</ObjectID>
    <Published>true</Published>
</TenantWebService>
```

You can use the `twebservice` snippet to create the basic structure for a web service. You can add multiple web services to a single file.

5. Now, build and publish your application using *F5* and log in to your development sandbox.

6. In your development sandbox, use the 🔍 icon to search for `Web Services` and click the link to open the page.

   Filter the list of available web services by applying a filter of **tv*** to the **Service Name** field, and you should see the web services that we added in our application:

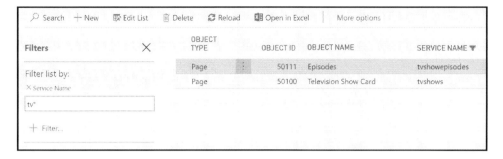

These web services are now ready to be consumed from an external application!

How it works...

Creating a new web service is as simple as filling out an entry on the **Web Services** page.

The following table shows what object types can be published as either SOAP or OData web services:

Object Type	SOAP	OData
Page	Yes	Yes
Codeunit	Yes	No
Query	No	Yes

Entries in the Web Services page can either be created manually or automatically using a Business Central application. In the application, a specially formatted XML file is created that lists the objects you would like to create as a web service. When the application is installed, the web services listed in the XML file(s) will be created in the Web Services page in Business Central.

 The web service XML file can exist anywhere in your AL project, and the compiler will find it and recognize what it is for based on its contents. You can choose to have multiple web service files in your project, or simply stick with a single file.

You can choose to have the web service(s) published by default, or simply have them be available to use but not actually published. The latter means the web services need to be enabled by a user or via business logic before they can be consumed.

See also

You can read more about publishing web services on Microsoft Docs at `https://docs.microsoft.com/en-us/dynamics365/business-central/dev-itpro/webservices/publish-web-service`.

Enabling basic authentication

When connecting to Business Central through a web service, you need to be authenticated before you can access the data and business logic.

This recipe will show you how to configure your system so that you can connect to it from an external application using basic authentication.

> Be aware that while basic authentication is perfectly acceptable for development purposes, it should not be used in a live environment. For live systems, you should use **Azure Active Directory** (**AAD**) or OAuth 2.0 authentication.
>
> You can find a link for setting up AAD at the end of this recipe.

Getting ready

There is no AL coding in this recipe, but you still need to have your AL development sandbox ready to go. This recipe is built around you using a Business Central online sandbox.

We will use the Business Central API as our means of testing the authentication.

How to do it...

1. In your web browser, log in to your AL development sandbox.
2. Using the ⚙ icon, search for `Users` and click on the link to open the page.
3. Select the user that you are logged in as to open the **User Card**.
4. Expand the **Web Service Access** group.

5. Let's create a new web service key:
    1. In the **Web Service Access Key** field, click the **...** button.
    2. Click **Yes** on the prompt.
    3. Select a **Key Expiration Date** or enable the **Key Never Expires** field.
    4. Click **OK**.

6. Now, double-click on the generated key to select the whole value, and copy/paste it to Notepad for later use.

> The **Web Service Access Key** will be used in place of the user's password when we authenticate to the API.

7. Open a new tab in your web browser. In the address bar, enter the following URL:

```
https://api.businesscentral.dynamics.com/v1.0/<tenant
name>/sandbox/api/v1.0
```

Replace `<tenant name>` with the name of your Azure domain in which you created the Business Central sandbox. For example, if your Azure domain is `myazuresub.onmicrosoft.com`, then you would use the following URL:

```
https://api.businesscentral.dynamics.com/v1.0/myazuresub.onmicr
osoft.com/sandbox/api/v1.0
```

> At the time of writing this book, the current version of the Business Central API is 1.0. You may need to adjust the previous URL in the event that there is a newer version.

8. When prompted, enter the following authentication information:

Username:	The **User Name** of the user you created the web services key for in Step 3
Password:	The **Web Services Access Key** value you generated in step 5

Once authenticated, you should see the raw JSON output that lists the entities that are available in the Business Central API.

How it works...

Setting up basic authentication allows you to perform development tasks against the Business Central API.

Basic authentication is enabled by first creating a **Web Services Access Key** for a given user. The key can be configured with an expiration date, or it can be set to never expire.

Listing the entities that are available in the Business Central API is done by connecting to the following URL:

```
https://api.businesscentral.dynamics.com/v1.0/<tenant
name>/sandbox/api/v1.0
```

When authenticating to the service, you need to pass the **User Name** and **Web Service Access Key** (as the password) for the user. You do not pass the user's real password.

There's more...

For development systems, it's fine to make use of basic authentication; however, in a live environment, it should not be used. Instead, you should use **Azure Active Directory** (**AAD**) authentication.

You can find information on how to set up AAD on Microsoft Docs at `https://docs.microsoft.com/en-us/dynamics365/business-central/dev-itpro/developer/devenv-develop-connect-apps#setting-up-azure-active-directory-(aad)-based-authentication`.

See also

You can read more about setting up basic authentication on Microsoft Docs at `https://docs.microsoft.com/en-us/dynamics365/business-central/dev-itpro/developer/devenv-develop-connect-apps#setting-up-basic-authentication`.

The Business Central API – exploring with Postman

Now that you can authenticate to the Business Central API, I bet you're wondering what you can do with it!

As the API is simply a standard RESTful API, we can use some industry-standard tools to navigate through the API to see what's available.

This recipe will show you how to use Postman to take a look at what's available in the Business Central API.

Getting ready

You need to have your AL development sandbox for this recipe. Once again, this recipe is built around you using a Business Central online sandbox.

You're also going to need to install the Postman application. You can grab that from `https://www.getpostman.com/downloads`.

You must complete the *Enabling basic authentication* recipe, which is found earlier in this chapter, in order to set up your system to authenticate properly.

How to do it...

1. In Postman, create a new (`GET`) request.
2. Enter the following **request URL**:

   ```
   https://api.businesscentral.dynamics.com/v1.0/<tenant
   name>/sandbox/api/v1.0
   ```

   Replace `<tenant name>` with the name of your Azure domain in which you created the Business Central sandbox. For example, if your Azure domain is `myazuresub.onmicrosoft.com`, then you would use the following URL:

   ```
   https://api.businesscentral.dynamics.com/v1.0/myazuresub.onmicr
   osoft.com/sandbox/api/v1.0
   ```

At the time of writing this book, the current version of the Business Central API is 1.0. You may need to adjust the previous URL in the event that there is a newer version.

3. Click the **Auth** tab and enter the following information:

Type	Basic Auth
Username:	The **User Name** of the user you created the web services key for
Password:	The **Web Services Access Key** you generated

4. Click **Send** to view the request results. You should now see the list of available entities in the API. The results in Postman can be formatted in `Pretty` mode so that they're more readable.

5. Update the request URL to add `/companies` at the end, as shown by this example:

```
https://api.businesscentral.dynamics.com/v1.0/<tenant
name>/sandbox/api/v1.0/companies
```

6. Click **Send**. Now, you'll see the list of companies that are in your sandbox tenant!

How it works...

Standard tools, such as Postman, can be used to navigate the Business Central API in order to discover what is available and to test requests.

After you configure your sandbox for basic authentication, you just need to enter a valid API URL and your basic authentication information, and then submit the request.

From there, you can view the results of the request in readable JSON format.

You can use Postman to perform any testing of the API prior to ensure your request is formatted properly, and to ensure the data that is returned is what you expect.

If you are creating a non-AL Connect App to integrate with Business Central, then you can use Postman to generate your request in a variety of programming languages, such as C# and JavaScript.

There's more...

While basic authentication is fine for development, you should use AAD authentication in a live environment.

You can read more about using Postman with AAD authentication on Microsoft Docs at `https://docs.microsoft.com/en-us/dynamics365/business-central/dev-itpro/developer/devenv-develop-connect-apps#exploring-the-apis-with-postman-and-aad-authentication`.

See also

You can read more about using Postman with basic authentication on Microsoft Docs at `https://docs.microsoft.com/en-us/dynamics365/business-central/dev-itpro/developer/devenv-develop-connect-apps#exploring-the-apis-with-postman-and-basic-authentication`.

Postman is a very robust product used for API development. There's a very good collection of documents with additional information on all of its features available at `https://learning.getpostman.com`.

The Business Central API – retrieving data

What does integration consist of? Well, you're either going to be pushing data from an external system into Business Central or pulling the data out of Business Central for use in another system. Simple, right?

This recipe will show you how to get data out of Business Central using the API.

Getting ready

You need to have your AL development sandbox for this recipe. Once again, this recipe is built around you using a Business Central online sandbox.

You must complete the *Enabling basic authentication* recipe earlier in this chapter in order to set up your system to authenticate properly. Make sure that you have noted the Username and Web Services Access Key as you'll need those in this recipe.

While you can access the API from any platform that supports web requests, we'll use **PowerShell ISE** for this recipe, so make sure that you have access to that on your machine.

How to do it...

1. Open PowerShell ISE.
2. The first thing that we need to do is determine the ID of the company in our sandbox that we want to pull the data from.

   Create a new PowerShell script and add the following:

   ```
   $username = '<replace with your userName>'
   $webServicesKey = '<replace with your web services key'
   $azureDomain = 'replace with your Azure domain'
   ```

   Make sure to update the previous code with your specific information from your development sandbox.

3. Now, add the following code to create the credentials we need to pass with the web request:

   ```
   $credentials = "$($username):$($webServicesKey)"
   $encodedCredentials =
   [System.Convert]::ToBase64String([System.Text.Encoding]::ASCII.GetB
   ytes($credentials))
   $headers = @{ Authorization = "Basic $encodedCredentials" }
   ```

4. Add the following code to process the web request:

   ```
   $url = 'https://api.businesscentral.dynamics.com/v1.0/' +
   $azureDomain + '/sandbox/api/v1.0/companies'
   Invoke-RestMethod -Uri $url -Method GET -Headers $headers |
   ConvertTo-Json
   ```

   Save the script as 1-GetCompanies.ps1.

5. Now, run the script and you should see output similar to the following screenshot:

```
Invoke-RestMethod -Uri $url -Method GET -Headers $headers | ConvertTo-
{
    "@odata.context":  "https://api.businesscentral.dynamics.com/v1.0/
    "value":  [
        {
            "id":  "36cd1cf7-7cd2-4ac9-9345-0a6fc3ab7ba2",
            "systemVersion":  "32630",
            "name":  "CRONUS Canada, Inc.",
            "displayName":  "CRONUS Canada, Inc.",
            "businessProfileId":  ""
        },
        {
            "id":  "23cf5e81-a13f-420a-b102-83d688b4aba3",
            "systemVersion":  "32630",
            "name":  "My Company",
            "displayName":  "",
            "businessProfileId":  ""
        }
    ]
}
```

6. In your results, choose the company from which you want to pull data from and note down the corresponding **id** value for later.
7. Now that we know which company we want to get the data from, let's pull the list of items.

   Create a new PowerShell script and add the following lines of code to it:

   ```
   $username = '<replace with your userName>'
   $webServicesKey = '<replace with your web services key'
   $azureDomain = 'replace with your Azure domain'
   $companyId = '<replace with the company id from Step 6'
   ```

8. Add the following code to create the credentials we need to use:

   ```
   $credentials = "$($username):$($webServicesKey)"
   $encodedCredentials =
   [System.Convert]::ToBase64String([System.Text.Encoding]::ASCII.GetB
   ytes($credentials))
   $headers = @{ Authorization = "Basic $encodedCredentials" }
   ```

9. Add the following code to retrieve the item list and iterate through it:

   ```
   $url = 'https://api.businesscentral.dynamics.com/v1.0/' +
   $azureDomain + '/sandbox/api/v1.0/companies(' + $companyId +
   ')/items'
   ```

```
$jsonObject = Invoke-RestMethod -Uri $url -Method GET -Headers
$headers | ConvertTo-Json | ConvertFrom-Json

foreach ($item in $jsonObject.value){
    Write-Host "$($item.number) - $($item.displayName)"
}
```

Save the script as `2-GetItems.ps1`.

10. Run the script and you should see a list of items, as follows:

```
1928-S - AMSTERDAM Lamp
1920-S - ANTWERP Conference Table
1900-S - PARIS Guest Chair, black
1964-S - TOKYO Guest Chair, blue
1936-S - BERLIN Guest Chair, yellow
1965-W - Conference Bundle 2-8
1908-S - LONDON Swivel Chair, blue
1972-S - MUNICH Swivel Chair, yellow
1896-S - ATHENS Desk
1968-S - MEXICO Swivel Chair, black
1988-S - SEOUL Guest Chair, red
1960-S - ROME Guest Chair, green
1906-S - ATHENS Mobile Pedestal
1969-W - Conference Package 1
1996-S - ATLANTA Whiteboard, base
1929-W - Conference Bundle 1-8
1953-W - Guest Section 1
2000-S - SYDNEY Swivel Chair, green
1980-S - MOSCOW Swivel Chair, red
1925-W - Conference Bundle 1-6
```

How it works...

By sending a GET request to the Business Central API, you can retrieve any data that is available from any company within your environment.

As with all requests against the API, you need to be authenticated. During the development phase, you can use basic authentication, and make sure to include the username and the web services access keys in order to be authenticated properly.

Remember, in a live environment, you should use AAD for your authentication method.

In order to retrieve data from the correct company, you need to know the ID of the company, which you can retrieve by calling GET <endpoint>/companies.

Once you have that ID, you need to append it to your requests like this: GET <endpoint>/companies(<id>)/items.

This is no different than any other RESTful API in that when your request has been processed, the results are returned and you can then format and process it as you require.

There's more...

In this recipe, we retrieved the entire list of items from our company. However, you can also make use of standard REST API filtering syntax in order to pull back only the data you desire. This avoids having to pull a load of data that you don't need.

For our item list example, sending a filtered request could look something like this:

```
GET endpoint/companies(<id>)/items?$filter=itemCategoryCode eq 'TABLE'
```

You can read more about filtering guidelines at https://github.com/Microsoft/api-guidelines/blob/master/Guidelines.md#97-filtering.

In addition to filtering your GET requests, you also have the ability to use **delta links** in your requests. These allow you to only retrieve the changes that have been made to the entity since the initial API call was made.

In order to use delta links, when you make the initial GET request, you need to pass odata.track-changes in the header of the request. By doing this, you can retrieve the delta link from the result.

Once you have the delta link, you can use that in any subsequent call to find out what has changed for the given entity. That's done by passing the deltaToken in the request like this:

```
GET endpoint/companies(<id>)/items?deltaToken=<deltaLink>
```

You can read more about using delta links on Microsoft Docs at https://docs.microsoft.com/en-us/dynamics365/business-central/dev-itpro/developer/devenv-connect-apps-delta.

See also

You can read more about working with the Business Central API on Microsoft Docs here: `https://docs.microsoft.com/en-us/dynamics365/business-central/dev-itpro/developer/devenv-develop-connect-apps`.

The Business Central API – creating data

As the previous recipe took us through reading data from the API, it's only fair that we now create some.

This recipe will show you how to create data using the Business Central API.

Getting ready

You need to have your AL development sandbox for this recipe. Once again, this recipe is built around you using a Business Central online sandbox.

You must complete the *Enabling basic authentication* recipe earlier in this chapter, in order to set up your system to authenticate properly. Make sure you have noted the username and web services keys as you'll need those in this recipe.

While you can access the API from any platform that supports web requests, we'll use **PowerShell ISE** for this recipe, so make sure that you have access to that on your machine.

How to do it...

1. We need to know the ID of the company we are going to create the data for. If you have completed the previous recipe (*Business Central API – retrieving data*), then you may already have this information.

   If you do not have this information, then download the `ch7/5-api-retrieving-data/scripts/1-GetCompanies.ps1` script from the GitHub and run it. Note the ID of the company you want to create the data for.

2. Open PowerShell ISE.

3. Create a new script and add the following code:

```
$username = '<replace with your userName>'
$webServicesKey = '<replace with your web services key'
$azureDomain = '<replace with your Azure domain>'
$companyId = '<replace with the company id from Step 1>'
```

> Make sure to update the previous code with your specific information from your development sandbox.

4. Now, add the following code to create the credentials we need to pass with the web request:

```
$credentials = "$($username):$($webServicesKey)"
$encodedCredentials =
[System.Convert]::ToBase64String([System.Text.Encoding]::ASCII.GetB
ytes($credentials))
$headers = @{ Authorization = "Basic $encodedCredentials" }
```

5. We're going to create a simple item record. Add the code that will populate a few of the fields and make the request:

```
$url = 'https://api.businesscentral.dynamics.com/v1.0/' +
$azureDomain + '/sandbox/api/v1.0/companies(' + $companyId +
')/items'

$params = @{"displayName"="My Api item";
    "itemCategoryCode"="MISC";
    "type"="Inventory";
}

Invoke-RestMethod -Uri $url -Method POST -Headers $headers -Body
($params|ConvertTo-Json) -ContentType "application/json"
```

> Save the script as `1-CreateItem.ps1`.

6. Now, run the script. If all goes well, then your item will be created and you should see a response similar to the following screenshot:

```
@odata.etag          : W/"JzQOOzd4RVQzWk5NMDZsTGZTbFFsLOJkY1N6eUZzTjM2dE4OMU5kZnFseXlWdEO9MTswMDsn"
id                   : 6546983c-6fe0-4050-a44d-a4cdd00f3e03
number               : 1002
displayName          : My Api item
type                 : Inventory
itemCategoryId       : 8404c4b1-a4cc-4e37-8103-f558c30d0c5e
itemCategoryCode     : MISC
blocked              : False
baseUnitOfMeasureId  : d254d8f7-ac6c-44a0-8299-4c34df434d68
gtin                 :
inventory            : 0
unitPrice            : 0
priceIncludesTax     : False
unitCost             : 0
taxGroupId           : d0cf0351-2b88-419f-96c5-ff36618762e4
taxGroupCode         : TAXABLE
lastModifiedDateTime : 2019-06-14T01:56:44.63Z
baseUnitOfMeasure    : @{code=PCS; displayName=Piece; symbol=; unitConversion=}
```

Note the **number**. You can look up that item through your web browser in your sandbox in order to verify that it has, in fact, been created.

How it works...

To create data using the Business Central API, you create and send a POST request.

You need to be authenticated when making any sort of request against the API. During the development phase, you can use basic authentication and include the username and the web services access keys in order to be authenticated properly.

Remember, in a live environment, you should use AAD for your authentication method.

When creating data, you need to make sure you create it in the correct company. To do that, you need to know the ID of the company, which you can retrieve by calling GET `<endpoint>/companies`.

Once you have that ID, you need to append it to your requests, like this: POST `<endpoint>/companies(<id>)/items`.

The field values within the body of your request. Each value you pass will be validated to make sure the data is valid.

When your POST request is completed, the result will contain the record that was created. Any business logic that executes when a record is created and validated will be executed as normal. Any errors in validation will be returned in the request result.

There's more...

Not only can you create new records, but you can easily update existing records by sending a PATCH request.

When a record is created or retrieved using the API, one of the values that you will have is the **id**. This is a unique identifier for that specific record across the entire database. No two records across the whole database will have the same **id** value.

When issuing a PATCH request, you need to use the ID in order to tell the API which records to update.

An example of a PATCH request could look like this:

```
PATCH endpoint/companies(<id>)/items(<id>) Content-type: application/json
```

You can read more about the PATCH request on Microsoft Docs at https://docs.microsoft.com/en-us/dynamics-nav/api-reference/v1.0/api/dynamics_item_update.

See also

You can read more about working with the Business Central API on Microsoft Docs at https://docs.microsoft.com/en-us/dynamics365/business-central/dev-itpro/developer/devenv-develop-connect-apps.

The Business Central API – publishing a custom endpoint

Now that we know how to read data from the Business Central API, and also how to create data using the Business Central API, what if we want to extend the Business Central API to include new entities that we've added with our Business Central applications?

Well, luckily for us, we can do that!

This recipe will show you how to create and publish a custom endpoint in the Business Central API.

Getting ready

You need to have your AL development sandbox for this recipe. Once again, this recipe is built around you using a Business Central online sandbox.

You must complete the *Enabling basic authentication* recipe covered earlier in this chapter in order to set up your system to authenticate properly. Make sure you have noted the username and web services keys as you'll need those in this recipe.

We will continue to build on the `TelevisionShowProject` project that we used in the *Publishing your own web service* recipe earlier in this chapter. You can download that from the GitHub link at the start of this chapter if you haven't already worked through it.

How to do it...

1. Open the `televisionShow` folder in Visual Studio Code.
2. In **Explorer**, create a new file name `Television Show Api.al`. In **Editor**, create a new API page, as follows:

```
page 50112 "Televison Show API"
{
    PageType = API;
    Caption = 'tvshows';
    APIPublisher = 'mypublisher';
    APIGroup = 'tvshowproject';
    APIVersion = 'v1.0';
    EntityName = 'televisionshow';
    EntitySetName = 'televisionshows';
    SourceTable = "Television Show";
    DelayedInsert = true;

    layout
    {
        area(Content)
        {
            repeater(GroupName)
            {
            }
        }
    }
```

```
        }
    }
```

You can use the `tpage, Page of type API` snippet to create the basic API page structure.

3. Add the following fields to the repeater section of the new page:

```
field(Code; Code)
{
    ApplicationArea = all;
}
field(Name; Name)
{
    ApplicationArea = All;
}
field(Status; Status)
{
    ApplicationArea = All;
}
field(Synopsis; Synopsis)
{
    ApplicationArea = All;
}
```

4. Now, press *F5* to build and publish the application to your development sandbox.
5. Once the application has been published, with your web browser, go to the following URL and take note of the **id** of the company in which you have created some `Television Show` entries. You'll need it in a moment:

```
https://api.businesscentral.dynamics.com/v1.0/<tenant
name>/sandbox/api/v1.0/companies
```

Replace <tenant name> with the name of your Azure domain in which you created the Business Central sandbox. For example, if your Azure domain is `myazuresub.onmicrosoft.com`, then you would use the following URL:

```
https://api.businesscentral.dynamics.com/v1.0/myazuresub.onmicr
osoft.com/sandbox/api/v1.0/companies
```

Log in using the username and web services access keys that you created in the *Enabling basic authentication* recipe earlier in this chapter.

6. Now, with your web browser, go to the following URL:

```
https://api.businesscentral.dynamics.com/v1.0/<tenant
name>/sandbox/api/mypublisher/tvshowproject/v1.0
/companies(<id>)/televisionshows
```

Make sure to replace `<tenant name>` and `<id>` with the appropriate values.

Log in using the username and web services access key that you created in the *Enabling basic authentication* recipe earlier in this chapter. If you have some `Television Show` entries in your system, then you should see something similar to this:

[{"@odata.etag":"W/\"JzQ0O2p0Sm1oanQyTTQ0WXFnWHFCaw5kL3dmTkhtbTVSRXRia3hFczkxOEpwdFk9MTswMDsn\"","Code":"TV1000","Name":"Seinfeld","Status":"Active","Synopsis":""},
{"@odata.etag":"W/\"JzQ0O2F0MEU1Y0RoMXZQL0xabzdEUENLSXV3Y1lE4UDJOa3FjbXY3wWR4dkRBS1k9MTswMDsn\"","Code":"TV1001","Name":"Friends","Status":"Active","Synopsis":""},
{"@odata.etag":"W/\"JzQ0O2NLc0ZxTFJSe1pPUE9jTD10bDVUa2M1YThiQ21MN2ZiaFM1QWR2TjRNc2c9MTswMDsn\"","Code":"TV1002","Name":"The Simpsons","Status":"Active","Synopsis":""},
{"@odata.etag":"W/\"JzQ0O0JjVHFjaUpaN2pzTDg1V1VGYUhaQnZIR0YwaTRWbENJb1NoVmJ5VXdVQlE9MTswMDsn\"","Code":"TV1003","Name":"The Big Bang Theory","Status":"Active","Synopsis":""},
{"@odata.etag":"W/\"JzQ0O3RyMHVQY1JQb3pOc0RVMXM1TEVnNndpSUs5LyszSm5rawJtZEptVV1mZTQ9MTswMDsn\"","Code":"TV1004","Name":"The Office","Status":"Active","Synopsis":""},
{"@odata.etag":"W/\"JzQ0O3ZXVytwN0RZdE1aZHZpVDN3Mj1lUGlSZ1pXNVlLa0Vyd2lGaDB2UjU3VUk9MTswMDsn\"","Code":"TV2000","Name":"The Wire","Status":"Active","Synopsis":""},
{"@odata.etag":"W/\"JzQ0O3p1RzVOdjFvckZnZ2ppT0U3MXdPZkRyQj1GMU04VFZkdU9xUDVBOEtHS1E9MTswMDsn\"","Code":"TV2001","Name":"The Sopranos","Status":"Active","Synopsis":""},
{"@odata.etag":"W/\"JzQ0OzNlY3FpOE40cXVTWVB5dFRtQjhka0UwdXQxOGlucldzRzdmSEtBMko2cGs9MTswMDsn\"","Code":"TV2002","Name":"Mad Men","Status":"Active","Synopsis":""},
{"@odata.etag":"W/\"JzQ0O2JYc1BVL3MyW1NBUUxDbVhyM0s4aVJ0wkQwcm5xZUQ5YUkwcVpvUkdyZDg9MTswMDsn\"","Code":"TV2003","Name":"Deadwood","Status":"Active","Synopsis":""},
{"@odata.etag":"W/\"JzQ0O2g2bUZseVErRy9vNUtjVG1DMjFoMEtNcHQ1bEVONDNpMFAwZ2d1Nnhz1A09MTswMDsn\"","Code":"TV2004","Name":"Breaking Bad","Status":"Active","Synopsis":""},
{"@odata.etag":"W/\"JzQ0O3lrRTFKQwRXZ1FTRkhxYVBQMDFSbGpPWlVISDZYeHFCL0hjS1FwOW1sk1U9MTswMDsn\"","Code":"TV3000","Name":"Full House","Status":"Active","Synopsis":""},
{"@odata.etag":"W/\"JzQ0O5Jb0ExT3ZJM1BEbV1NeE5ykwm9FR1dqajZkT21CbW1MdW5ySXVHVEEwS1U9MTswMDsn\"","Code":"TV3001","Name":"The Andy Griffith Show","Status":"Active","Synopsis":""},
{"@odata.etag":"W/\"JzQ0O1ppNk8zNEtLM1NJWXVId0xPbi9ONUJQUmVLVVhkNEZMY0JnUDZmU0d0NUE9MTswMDsn\"","Code":"TV3002","Name":"The Wonder Years","Status":"Active","Synopsis":""},
{"@odata.etag":"W/\"JzQ0O2x0U2RkKzR2WmRHT05naytZSHBDe1dnd1ZBVGRFRzJNTCt1OWZQQTJPK0E9MTswMDsn\"","Code":"TV3003","Name":"Peppa Pig","Status":"Active","Synopsis":""},
{"@odata.etag":"W/\"JzQ0O1NvUWd2T1YzTHIyaExMRDBROWFTREpQZWt2RXpWkkJRTG82VmRLZHh1N009MTswMDsn\"","Code":"TV3004","Name":"Looney Toons","Status":"Active","Synopsis":""}]}

If you have not yet created any `Television Show` entries in your system, then refer to the *Assisted setup wizards* recipe in `Chapter 3`, *Let's Go Beyond*, to see how to run a wizard to load some default television shows.

How it works...

Custom API objects can be created in order to add custom endpoints to the Business Central API. This allows you to not only surface custom data that you've added, but also to create customized views of all the data in the system.

The following object types can be exposed as API endpoints:

- Page
- Query

Creating the new endpoints is as easy as defining the page/query in your AL project as you normally would, and then defining a few specific properties:

Property	Value
PageType/QueryType	The API
APIPublisher	The name of the app publisher
APIGroup	The name of the group the endpoint is in
APIVersion	The version of the API the endpoint is exposed in
EntityName	The singular name of the entity the endpoint exposes
EntitySetName	The plural name of the entity the endpoint exposes

Once the preceding properties are set, you define the fields that are part of the API object as you normally would, given the object type.

To access your custom endpoint, you would use the following URL structure:

```
endpoint/<apipublisher>/<apigroup>/<apiversion>/companies(<id>)/<entitysetn
ame>
```

See also

You can read more about publishing API pages on Microsoft Docs at `https://docs.microsoft.com/en-us/dynamics365/business-central/dev-itpro/developer/devenv-api-pagetype`.

The API query object is available at `https://docs.microsoft.com/en-us/dynamics365/business-central/dev-itpro/developer/devenv-api-querytype`.

Power Platform – using Microsoft Power BI

Microsoft Power BI is part of the Microsoft Power Platform, a collection of integrated solutions that are designed to improve business productivity. With Power BI, you can turn your data into incredibly rich visualizations, which makes analyzing the data a much more interactive experience.

This recipe will show you how to connect Power BI to your Business Central system to retrieve data.

Getting ready

You need to have your AL development sandbox for this recipe. Once again, this recipe is built around you using a Business Central online sandbox.

You must complete the *Enabling basic authentication* recipe earlier in this chapter in order to set up your system to authenticate properly. Make sure you have noted the username and web services keys as you'll need those in this recipe.

We will take a break from AL coding for now; however, you will need to have Power BI Desktop installed on your machine in order to complete this recipe. You can download it from `https://powerbi.microsoft.com/en-us/desktop`.

Note that you do not need to obtain a Power BI Pro account in order to complete this recipe.

How to do it...

1. Log in to your development sandbox with your web browser.
2. Use the ⚙ icon, search for `Web Services`, and click the link to open the page.
3. Let's publish a web service so we can see customer data in Power BI:
    1. Click the `+ New` action button.
    2. In the list, in the new row, enter the following information:
        - **Object Type:** `Page`
        - **Object ID:** `22`
        - **Service Name:** `customersdemo`
        - **Published:** `Yes` (place a check mark in this column)
    3. Click the `⟳ Reload` action button.
    4. Click the `🔍 Search` action button and search for `customersdemo`:
        - You only see the entry that we created in the list.

5. Select the entry in the list and copy/paste the value into the **OData URL** column to Notepad for later.

- Do not grab the **OData V4 URL** value!

6. Close the `Web Services` page.

Remember that you can also publish web services with your Business Central application automatically to save your users' time! See the *Publishing your own web service* recipe earlier in this chapter for information on how to do it.

4. Open Power BI Desktop.
5. Let's get connected to the web service that we published in Business Central:

    1. On the welcome screen, select Get data.
    2. Select **All | OData Feed**.
    3. Click **Connect**.
    4. In the **OData feed** dialog, make sure that **Basic** is selected, and paste in the **OData URL** you copied from Business Central:

    5. Click **OK**.
    6. Click **Basic**.

7. Fill in the following fields:

- **User name**: Your development sandbox username.
- **Password**: The web services access key you generated for the user in the *Enabling basic authentication* recipe earlier in this chapter:

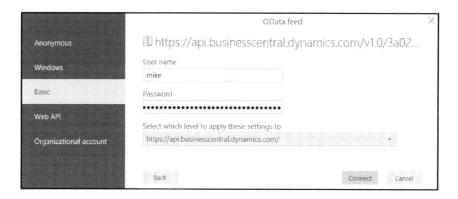

8. Click **Connect**.
9. Click **Load**.

6. Now that we have made the connection to Business Central, Power BI has downloaded the contents of the web service we published. However, some of the data types have not been correctly identified for all fields.

We'll fix that up for a few of the fields:

1. In the left sidebar of Power BI Desktop, select the **Data** ( ) icon.
2. Find and select the **Sales_LCY** column.
3. Select **Modelling | Formatting | Data type: Decimal Number**.
4. Click **Yes** on the confirmation dialog.
5. Repeat steps 2-4 for the **Balance_Due_LCY** column.

Once you have told Power BI what type of data is in the columns, any time that the data is refreshed, it will enforce those rules.

7. Now, let's build a simple visualization of the customer data:

    1. Click the **Report** (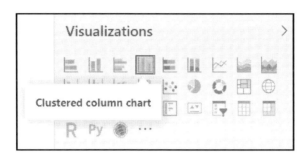) icon in the left sidebar in Power BI Desktop.

    2. Select **Home | New Visual**.

    3. With your new visualization selected, on the right side of the Power BI Desktop window, select the **Clustered column chart** type:

    4. With the visualization selected, on the right side of the Power BI Desktop window, drag and drop the **Axis: Name** and **Value: Sales_LCY**, **Balance_Due_LCY** fields into the appropriate sections:

5. Select your visualization and drag the edge out to make it larger. It should look similar to the following:

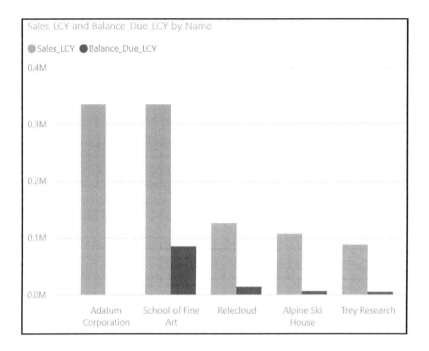

That's it! You've created a Power BI visualization using the customer data from your Business Central sandbox!

How it works...

Power BI is a robust and powerful analytics tool that can be connected to your Business Central system. By publishing OData feeds from Business Central, Power BI can consume them and pull the data into its analytics engine. These data feeds can be manually created by the end users, or they can be automatically published on the installation of a Business Central application.

When the data is pulled into Power BI, it can be manipulated and transformed so that it is in the right format and structure called for by your reporting requirements.

Once the data has been imported into Power BI, it becomes an offline data source, meaning that the data inside of Power BI needs to be refreshed in order to stay current. This is done in Power BI Desktop using the **Refresh** button on the **Home** tab.

There's more...

As I've mentioned, Power BI is very rich with features that go well beyond what this recipe covered. Using Power BI Desktop is probably the most basic usage you can do with Power BI. However, there is far more you can do in terms of sharing dashboards online to viewing them on a mobile device.

If you are serious about getting into Power BI, then it is important to understand the different features among the Power BI products. While some features are free, others are not.

You can get more information about the Power BI products at `https://powerbi.microsoft.com/en-us/what-is-power-bi`.

See also

You can read more about publishing web services in Business Central on Microsoft Docs at `https://docs.microsoft.com/en-us/dynamics365/business-central/dev-itpro/webservices/publish-web-service`.

Oh, by the way, there's also some great learning materials on using Power BI available at `https://powerbi.microsoft.com/en-us/learning`.

Power Platform – using Microsoft Flow

Microsoft Flow is a part of the Power Platform. Flow is a workflow engine that lets you automate processes and tasks in a multitude of different applications. By using Flow, you can use events that occur in Business Central to trigger an event to happen outside of Business Central. For example, how about sending a welcome email to the customer when you ship them their first order?

This recipe will show you how to use Flow to connect to events within Business Central.

Getting ready

Well, I was going to put in the regular stuff here about using an online sandbox and setting up basic authentication. However, for Flow, this will not work; at least not at the moment that I write this recipe. Right now, the only way to connect Flow to Business Central is to use an online Business Central production environment; in other words, not a sandbox environment, and not a container-based or local installation.

In order to obtain a production environment, you can sign up for a trial at `https://trials.dynamics.com`.

Use your work email to sign up for the trial. There is no obligation to carry on once the trial expires, and it will allow you to complete this recipe.

By the time you are reading this, you may be able to connect Flow to an online sandbox environment, so if that is possible, then you can simply use the same one that you've been using for the previous recipes in this book.

The other thing that you will need for this recipe is to be signed up for Flow. You can sign up for free at `https://flow.microsoft.com`.

The scenario we will be tackling in this recipe is as follows:

- As an end user, any time that a customer is blocked from sending shipments, I want the system to send me an email so that I can follow up with the customer to resolve the situation.

How to do it...

1. In your web browser, navigate to the page at `https://flow.microsoft.com` and log in with your Flow account credentials.
2. On the left side, click **Connectors.**
3. In the search box, search for `business central` and select the **Business Central** connector:

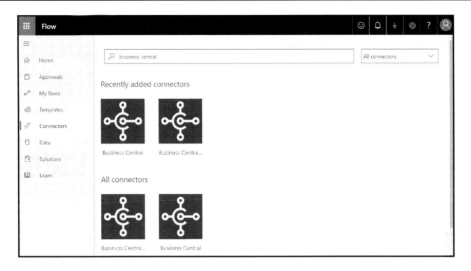

4. Select the **When a record is modified** trigger:

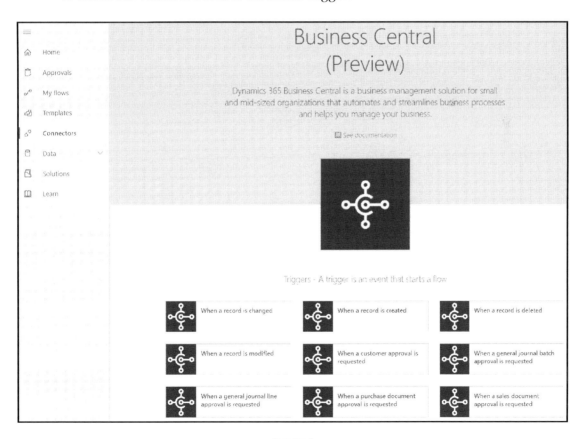

5. In the first workflow step, the following:

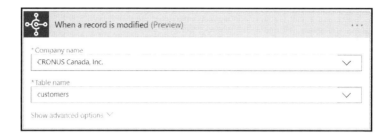

 The exact name of the CRONUS company may differ based on your geographical region.

6. Click **New step**:

7. Select **All | Control**, and choose the **Condition** action:

8. Now, let's configure the condition:
   1. In the **Choose a value** box, select the **blocked** field.
   2. Set the condition criteria field to **is equal to.**
   3. Set the value field to **Ship**:

9. Scroll down to the **If yes** section in the workflow and click **Add an action**:

10. In the **Choose an action** section, select **All | Send me an email notification**:

11. Populate the **Send me an email notification** section, as shown in the following screenshot:

12. At the bottom of your workflow, click **Save**.

13. Now, we can test our workflow. At the top of your workflow, click 🧪 Test .

14. Select **I'll perform the trigger action**, and click **Test**:

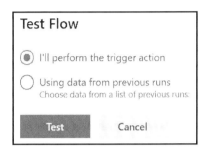

15. In another browser tab (don't close the Flow one!), log in to your Business Central environment and follow these steps:

    1. Navigate to the **Customer List**.

    2. Select a customer to open the **Customer Card**.

    3. Change the **Blocked** field to **Ship**.

    4. Close the **Customer Card**.

16. Switch back to the Flow tab in your web browser and you should see a message similar to the following screenshot:

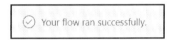

17. Check the email account you used to sign in to Flow. You should have received an email similar to the following:

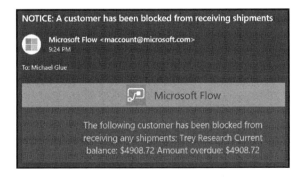

Of course, your email will be based on the customer you decided to block.

How it works...

Microsoft Flow is an online workflow engine that can be used to automate tasks across various applications and services. A Microsoft Flow workflow is built using a combination of triggers and actions. A single workflow can combine triggers and actions across different applications.

With Microsoft Flow, you are not limited to automating Microsoft applications. There are a wide variety of application connectors in Microsoft Flow. Some require a premium plan, as shown in the following examples:

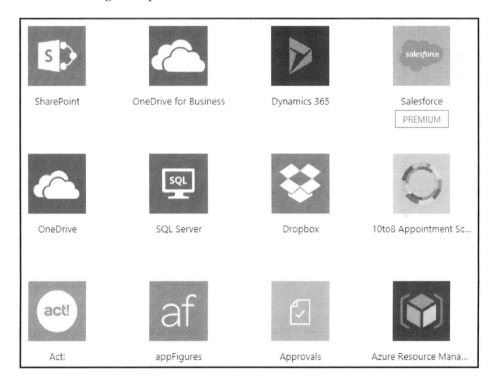

You begin by creating a Flow connector to your Business Central environment. This allows you to access entities within Business Central and create workflows based on a predetermined set of triggers.

There are a number of triggers available for Business Central, including, but not limited to, the following:

- When a customer/vendor approval is requested
- When a record is created/modified/deleted
- When a sales/purchase document approval is requested
- When an item approval is requested

There are also a number of actions available for the Business Central connector:

- Create/modify/delete a record.
- Get a record.
- Get a list of tables.

Within your workflow, you also have the ability to build in conditional logic controls and processing controls such as loops, switches, and terminates. You are also able to create data-driven triggers and actions, based on the data available from Business Central.

The workflow will execute on a frequency that's based on the Microsoft Flow plan that you're subscribed to.

There's more...

With Microsoft Flow, there are multiple types of plans that you can purchase, as well as a free one!

The different plans affect the following aspects of Microsoft Flow:

- How many executions of Flow you can perform per user, per month
- How often the Flows can be executed (for example, every *x* minutes)
- Access to certain connectors

In all cases, an unlimited number of Flows can be created.

Customers that purchase a license to any Dynamics 365 product, including Business Central, also get a license to Microsoft Flow included. The type of Flow license depends on the product and type of Dynamics 365 license they buy.

For more information, check out the Microsoft Flow pricing page at `https://flow.microsoft.com/en-us/pricing`.

See also

You can read more about the Business Central Flow Connector and what triggers and actions are available on Microsoft Docs at https://docs.microsoft.com/en-us/ connectors/dynamicssmbsaas.

There is a collection of learning materials for Microsoft Flow that can be accessed from https://docs.microsoft.com/en-us/flow.

Power Platform – using Microsoft PowerApps

Microsoft PowerApps, another component of Power Platform, is a collection of services, connectors, and data platforms that allow users to build rich custom business applications. PowerApps applications are created in a simple-to-use designer, which allows non-developer users to easily create solutions to meet their needs. The applications that are created can be run in a web browser, or even on a mobile device via the PowerApps mobile app. Developers can take things a bit further by introducing more advanced business logic to their applications.

This recipe will show you how to create a basic PowerApps application to view data from Business Central.

Getting ready

To connect PowerApps to Business Central, you need to have one of the following environments set up:

- A Business Central online production environment (for example, not a sandbox)
- A Business Central on-premises environment

For the purposes of this recipe, however, I will assume you are using an online Business Central environment. If you worked through the previous *Power Platform – using Flow* recipe, then you can reuse that environment, otherwise, you can sign up for a trial at https://trials.dynamics.com.

Use your work email to sign up for the trial. There is no obligation to carry on once the trial expires, and it will allow you complete this recipe.

By the time you are reading this, you may be able to connect PowerApps to an online sandbox environment, so if that's possible, then you can use the same one that you've been using for the previous recipes in this book.

The other thing that you will need for this recipe is to be signed up for PowerApps. Again, if you've already worked through the previous *Power Platform – using Flow* recipe, then you can use the same account for this recipe, otherwise, you can sign up for free at `https://powerapps.microsoft.com`.

How to do it...

1. In your web browser, navigate to `https://powerapps.microsoft.com` and log in with your PowerApps account credentials.
2. First, we need to create a connection between PowerApps and our Business Central environment.

    On the left-hand menu, click **Data | Connections**.

 If you have already completed the previous *Power Platform – using Flow* recipe, then you can jump to step 7 if you're using the same account, since any connections that you create are shared between Flow and PowerApps.

3. At the top of your screen, select **New connection:**

4. In the search box, search for `business central`, and select the **Business Central** button (not the on-premises one!):

5. In the dialog, click **Create**.

6. When prompted, log in with your PowerApps account information to finalize the creation of the connection.

7. On the left-hand menu, select **Apps**:

8. At the top of your screen, select **Create an app | Canvas**:

This will open up the PowerApps Studio in a new tab in your web browser.

9. In the PowerApps Studio tab, select **Phone layout** under **Blank app**:

10. Press **Skip** on the welcome message.

11. In the center of the screen, click **connect to data**.

12. In the **Data** tab, select the **Business Central** connection:

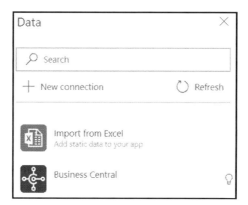

13. Select the CRONUS company that is in your environment:

 The exact name of the CRONUS company in your environment may be different depending on your geographical region.

14. Place a check mark beside the **customers** entity:

15. Click **Connect**.
16. Close the **Data** tab.

17. In the top menu, click the **Insert** tab, and then select **Gallery | Vertical**:

18. Click on the gallery you just inserted, and on the right side, in the gallery **Properties**, next to **Items**, select **customers** as the data source:

 Note that as soon as you select the data source, the data in the gallery control will be updated to show real data from your Business Central environment.

19. In the gallery properties, set the **Layout** property to **Title, subtitle, and body**.

20. In the gallery properties, click on the **Edit** link next to **Fields**, and set the following values:

Your application should now look similar to this:

21. At the top of the screen, click on the **Insert** tab and select **Forms | Display**:

22. With the new form control selected, drag and resize it so that it fills the bottom half of the application window:

23. With the form control selected, in the right-hand menu, select **Advanced** and set the following properties:

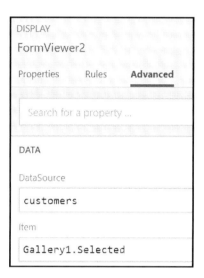

 This connects the new form control to the data source we created earlier, and it tells the form to display the same record that is selected in the gallery control. This will let us show more details for the selected record.

24. With the form control selected, in the right-hand menu, select **Properties,** and then click **Edit fields**:

25. In the **Fields** tab, click **Add field** and select the **balance, overdueAmount,** and **email** fields.

26. Click **Add**.

27. Change the **Control type** of the **email** field to **View email**:

28. Close the **Fields** tab.

29. Press *F5* to try out your new PowerApps application. Notice that when you select a customer record in the upper half of the screen, the details at the bottom are also updated accordingly:

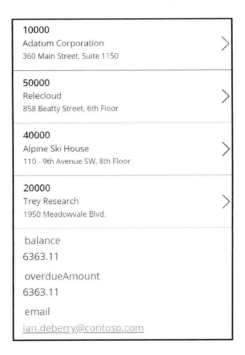

You can also use the ▷ button at the top of the screen to run your application.

30. To save your application, select **File** | **Save** within the PowerApps Studio tab.

That's it! I know this is an extremely simple example, but with a bit more effort in formatting and perhaps adding some more screens to the application, it would be quite easy to turn this into a solid application.

How it works...

Microsoft PowerApps is a collection of online services and controls that allow users to build their own applications to suit their business needs. Applications are built using the PowerApps Studio, which is an intuitive drag-and-drop environment that makes it possible for non-developers to easily create solutions.

PowerApps applications can be consumed directly in a web browser, and on mobile devices, they can be run via the Microsoft PowerApps mobile app, which is free to download from the relevant device store.

In order to create a PowerApps application for Business Central, you first need to create a connection. At the time of writing this book, you can create a connection to an online Business Central (non-sandbox) environment or to an on-premises one. As with the other Power Platform solutions, you are not limited to just one data source in PowerApps. By creating multiple connections, you can combine data from multiple systems into a single PowerApps application!

Once the connection is in place, PowerApps has access to the web services that are published within that environment, meaning any custom web services you publish will also be available.

With PowerApps Studio, you can create a new application from one of the existing templates or start from a blank one; the choice is yours. From there, you can perform tasks such as dragging new controls, moving around existing ones, and adding new screens until the application performs the tasks you need it to.

In addition to being able to use data-bound controls, you can also add other types of controls, including ones that are able to make use of device hardware. Examples of such controls are as follows:

- Images
- Barcode scanners
- Power BI
- Charts

- Audio/video
- Microphones
- PDF Viewer

Once your application has been created, you can save it for yourself, or share it among other users in your organization.

There's more...

Similar to the other Power Platform components, there are multiple plans available when purchasing PowerApps. You can find out more information about the pricing and what's included in each plan at `https://powerapps.microsoft.com/en-us/pricing`.

One very important data source that can be leveraged with PowerApps (and all other Power Platform solutions) is the **Common Data Service** (**CDS**). The CDS is built from the **Common Data Model**, which is a collection of standard business entities that have been created to standardize data across business applications:

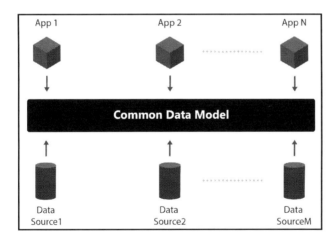

By using the CDS, you can build solutions off of a single data source that is fed from a number of different applications, instead of having to make connections and transforming the data from each one individually.

You can read more about the CDS and the Common Data Model at `https://powerapps.microsoft.com/en-us/common-data-service`.

See also

You can read more about what you can do with PowerApps on Microsoft Docs at `https://docs.microsoft.com/en-us/powerapps/index`.

Consuming Azure Functions

Back in the *.Net Interoperability* recipe in `Chapter 3`, *Let's Go Beyond*, I mentioned a few times that using .NET controls in an online Business Central environment is not allowed. So, what do you do if your solution requires .NET and there's no other way to do what you need to do?

Azure Functions is a serverless application that's published in Azure and that can be called from your Business Central application. This is where you can put your .NET DLLs and logic, which will then let you use .NET in your online Business Central systems.

This recipe will show you how to publish an Azure Function and call it from a Business Central application.

Getting ready

You're going to need a few things in order to do this recipe:

1. An active Azure subscription in which you have permission to create Azure Functions. You can sign up for a free trial at `https://azure.microsoft.com/en-us/free`.
2. A Business Central online sandbox. You can use a previous environment that you've created in previous recipes, as long as it is not a production one. You can also refer back to the *Setting up your development sandbox* recipe in `Chapter 1`, *Let's Get the Basics Out of the Way*, for instructions on how to set up a new one. If you use a previously created sandbox, then make sure to uninstall any other applications that you installed using this book.
3. Download the `ch7/11-consume-azure-function/ch7-consume-azure-function-start.zip` file from GitHub (use the link at the start of this chapter) and extract it to your local machine.

In the first part of this recipe, we'll focus on creating and publishing Azure Function, and in the second part, we'll consume it using a Business Central application. For the AL portion, you'll just need to create the function to call the Azure Function. I've already provided you with the logic to run the function from `Customer Card`.

How to do it...

1. In your web browser, go to `https://portal.azure.com` and log in using the account you set up your Azure subscription with:

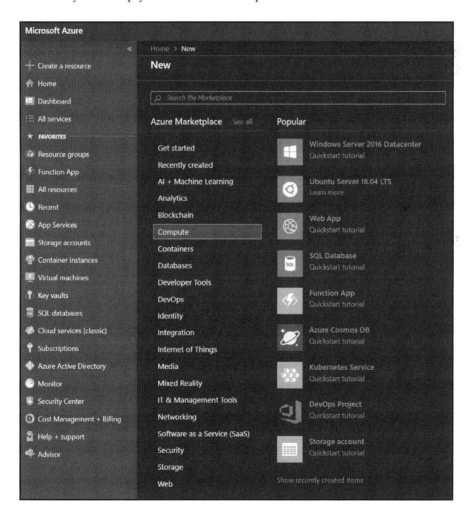

2. Select **Create a Resource**.
3. Select **Compute | Function App**.
4. Configure the **Function App** settings, as shown in the following screenshot:

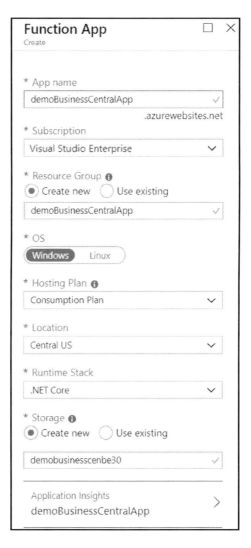

 Note that your subscription name may be different based on your subscription setup. You can also set a location that better suits you based on your geographical location.

5. Click **Create** to create and deploy your Function App. You can use the  icon at the top of the screen to monitor the deployment progress:

After a few minutes, the process will complete and you'll see a message similar to the following:

6. In the deployment notification, click **Go to resource**.
7. Click the + button next to **Functions** to add a new function to your app:

8. Select **In-portal**:

9. Press **Continue**.
10. Select **Webhook + API**:

11. Click **Create**.
12. Replace the sample code with the following, which accepts a name and returns a simple message:

```
#r "Newtonsoft.Json"

using System.Net;
using Microsoft.AspNetCore.Mvc;
using Microsoft.Extensions.Primitives;
using Newtonsoft.Json;

public static async Task<IActionResult> Run(HttpRequest req,
ILogger log)
{
 log.LogInformation("Demo Business Central function processed a
request.");

 string name = req.Query["name"];

 return name != null
 ? (ActionResult)new OkObjectResult($"Hello, {name}")
 : new BadRequestObjectResult("Please pass a name in the query");
}
```

13. At the top of the screen, press **</> Get function URL**:

14. Select **default (Function key)** and press **Copy**:

15. Paste the URL into Notepad for later.
16. In Visual Studio Code, open up the `azureFunctionProject` folder that you extracted from `ch7-consume-azure-function-start.zip`.
17. You need to connect this project to your AL development sandbox. You can reuse the `launch.json` file from the previous recipe or create a new one.

    Once the project has been connected, you need to download the symbols.

18. In **Explorer**, select `Call Azure Function.al`. In **Editor**, add the following local variables to the `CallAzureFunctionDemo()` function:

```
Client: HttpClient;
ResponseMessage: HttpResponseMessage;
AzureFunctionAppBaseUrl: Label '<replace with your Azure Function
App url>';
FullUrl: Text;
RequestErr: Label 'An error occurred when calling the Azure
Function:\\%1:\\%2';
```

19. Update the value of the `AzureFunctionAppBaseUrl` variable to be the URL that you copied and pasted to Notepad in step 15.
20. Add the following line of code in the `CallAzureFunctionDemo()` function:

```
FullUrl := AzureFunctionAppBaseUrl + '&name=' + CustomerName;

Client.Get(FullUrl, ResponseMessage);

if not ResponseMessage.IsSuccessStatusCode() then
    Error(RequestErr, ResponseMessage.HttpStatusCode,
    ResponseMessage.ReasonPhrase);

ResponseMessage.Content().ReadAs(ResponseText);
```

The previous code does a few things:

1. It appends the required `name` parameter to Azure Functions request URL along with the customer name.
2. It executes the web request.
3. It looks at the web request response to ensure an error did not happen.
4. It stores the response message content so it gets returned to the calling function.

21. Now, let's try it out! Press *F5* to build and publish your AL project to your sandbox.
22. Once you log in to your sandbox, follow these steps:
    1. Navigate to the `Customers` list.
    2. Select any customer to open `Customer Card`.
    3. Select **Actions** | **Functions** | **Call Azure Function.**
    4. If prompted, select either **Always Allow** or **Allow Once** depending on your preference, and press **OK**.

You should see the hello message returned by Azure Functions.

How it works...

Consuming an Azure Function from a Business Central application provides you with a way to perform some advanced algorithms and processing that require the use of .NET libraries.

The first step is to create an Azure Function App that contains the required business logic. Within that application, you can create one or more functions that can accept and return simple data types, or they can make use of complex types using a JSON or XML request.

Once your Azure Function App is deployed, you need to grab the function URL. Each function that you publish within Azure Functions application will have a unique URL.

You can use the function URL to make a web request from your Business Central application. Once again, you can use simple data types or you can make use of complex JSON and XML types. Refer back to the *Consuming external web services* recipe earlier in this chapter to learn about how to make web requests using JSON data types.

If you are going to use Azure Functions in your solution, then you need to be aware of the geographic locations of your customers. Since Azure Function Apps are deployed within a specified region, if you plan on supporting customers in multiple regions, then you may want to consider publishing your Azure Functions application in each region so that your customers can select the one closest to them. This will ensure they get the best performance.

See also

There's some great, easy-to-follow documentation on Azure Functions for Microsoft Docs, available at `https://docs.microsoft.com/en-us/azure/azure-functions`.

To read more about the HTTP, JSON, and XML variable types that are available in AL, look here: `https://docs.microsoft.com/en-us/dynamics365/business-central/dev-itpro/developer/devenv-restapi-overview`.

8
DevOps - Don't Live without It

DevOps, a cool buzzword right? Well yes, but it's also something that you cannot live without, and that you really shouldn't even consider living without.

Azure DevOps is a collection of online development services that allow teams to plan and manage work, manage product quality, manage source code, and build and deploy applications.

Before we get started, though, you might be wondering, *why do I need Azure DevOps?* Well, there are three main points that I like to tell people when they ask me:

1. **It saves time**: Yes, at first, it will appear to be additional *overhead* to your existing processes. But trust me, once you get the hang of things, it becomes second nature, and once you implement things such as build and release pipelines, you'll find that you are not spending as much time performing lengthy manual tasks such as setting up machines and installing software updates.

2. **More agile delivery process**: Once you have Azure DevOps humming along, you'll be able to check your code in, run a set of tests, and produce a build of your application in no time, which means you can produce releasable software more often.

3. **It introduces stability to your development process**: No longer do you have to rely on *that one developer* that knows how to do the build, or knows how to run the automated tests properly. Once the build is scripted and set up in Azure DevOps, your developers can focus on what they do best, and your builds and releases will always be done the same way.

A funny story perhaps, but way back around 2005(ish), when I was first introduced to Azure DevOps (or Team Foundation Server, as it was known back then), I was not a fan. I was of the mind that *I've been doing development for years without it; it will just slow me down*. I pushed hard against implementing it. Well, I lost that battle, but I'm glad I did. It probably only took a year or so before I quickly changed my tune and, since then, there hasn't been a reason in the world that would make me consider not using Azure DevOps. So, the moral of this story is the following: don't worry if you are thinking along the same lines that I was. At first, it is extra work, but please give it a real try for a solid period of time. You will not be sorry!

In this chapter, we will cover the following recipes:

- Creating an Azure DevOps project
- Creating a code repository
- Connecting an AL project to Azure DevOps
- Installing a pipeline agent
- Creating a build pipeline
- Creating a release pipeline
- Enabling branch policies

Technical requirements

For this chapter, you will need an AL development sandbox. You can use any type of sandbox environment that you want. If you need help, then you can always refer to the *Setting up your development sandbox* recipe in `Chapter 1`, *Let's Get the Basics Out of the Way*, for information on how to set it up. If you're going to reuse a sandbox that you used for any previous recipes in this book, then make sure to remove all the previous applications that you installed before proceeding with this chapter.

Code samples and scripts are available on GitHub. Some of the recipes in this chapter build on previous recipes. You can download the completed recipe code from: `https://github.com/PacktPublishing/Microsoft-Dynamics-365-Business-Central-Cookbook`.

Creating an Azure DevOps project

With Azure DevOps, you can create projects. Each project can contain one or more code repositories, and you can structure your projects in whatever way best suits your needs.

The project is where you will do the following:

- Store your code in source control.
- Create and manage work items to track things such as bugs, user stories, and features. While this feature is beyond the scope of the recipes in this chapter, I highly recommend you check out the work item portion of Azure DevOps.

This recipe will show you how to create an Azure DevOps project.

Getting ready

Before you can create an Azure DevOps project, you—of course—need to be able to access Azure DevOps.

Luckily for us, you can use Azure DevOps for free, and you can continue to use it for free until you add more than five full users to the system.

To sign up for an Azure DevOps account, go to: `https://azure.microsoft.com/services/devops`.

You can create your Azure DevOps account by using either a personal or a work/school email address.

How to do it...

1. In your web browser, navigate to `https://dev.azure.com` and log in with your Azure DevOps account.
2. On the Azure DevOps main screen, click **Create new project** in the top-right corner.

3. Enter `televisionShow` for the **Project name**, and then select **Private**:

4. Click **Advanced**, and then select the following options:

5. Click **Create**. In a few moments, you will be taken to your project's main screen, which will look similar to the following screenshot:

Can you believe it? That's it! So easy!

How it works...

Before you can start tracking work or doing any sort of source code control, you need to create a project in the Azure DevOps environment.

The project is where all of the following will take place:

- Source code management
- Work management
- Test planning and execution
- Bug tracking
- Development process analysis and insights

You can create an Azure DevOps project for free, which comes with a limit of five basic users. If you need to add more than that, then you will need to purchase additional users. You can read more about adding basic users, and what those users can do, at `https://docs.microsoft.com/en-us/azure/devops/organizations/billing/buy-basic-access-add-users?view=azure-devops`.

You can go beyond the five-user limit by adding more users. There are multiple types of users available:

- **Stakeholder:** These users have limited access to features. You can add an unlimited number of stakeholders for free.
- **Basic:** These users have access to almost all of the features. By default, you can have up to five basic users for free, after which you will need to purchase more.
- **Basic + Test Plan:** These users have access to all the features that a basic user can access, and also, they can access Azure test plans.
- **Visual Studio Subscription:** These are users that have an active Visual Studio or MSDN subscription.

You can see more details about what the preceding user types can access at `https://docs.microsoft.com/en-us/azure/devops/organizations/security/access-levels?view=azure-devops`.

Within an organization, you can create multiple projects. A project can be defined as either private or public. With a private project, every user that needs access to it must be configured with an Azure DevOps license. In a public project, however, users can access it in read-only mode without having a license.

 Public projects are typically what you would use for open source projects.

When you create a new project, if you plan on using it for managing work, then you can define what work item process you are going to use:

- Basic
- Scrum
- Agile
- Capability Maturity Model Integration

You can find more details on the different work item processes at `https://docs.`
`microsoft.com/en-us/azure/devops/boards/work-items/guidance/choose-process?`
`view=azure-devops`.

The work item process that you choose will affect how your team manages work within Azure DevOps, so you may want to try out a few different processes in order to find the one that works best for you.

See also

You can read more about how to configure projects in Azure DevOps at `https://docs.`
`microsoft.com/en-us/azure/devops/organizations/projects/about-projects?view=`
`azure-devops`.

Creating a code repository

A code repository is where you store and manage your source code. In Azure DevOps, this is done using Azure Repos.

Managing your source code in a repository lets you track and manage changes and versions of your source code. Whether or not you are a single developer, or you work in a team, using Azure Repos provides an invaluable set of tools for everyone.

This recipe will show you how to create a source code repository in an Azure DevOps project.

Getting ready

In order to perform this recipe, you need to complete the *Creating an Azure DevOps Project* recipe at the start of this chapter.

How to do it...

1. In your web browser, navigate to `https://dev.azure.com` and log in with your Azure DevOps account.
2. Open the `televisionShow` project.
3. On the left side menu, click **Repos**.

4. Scroll to the bottom of the screen and click **Initialize**:

 Notice that there are other options for creating your code repository. If you have an existing repository on your local machine, then you can upload (push) it to Azure DevOps. Similarly, if you have been working in GitHub, then you can import that repository to Azure DevOps as well.

In a few short moments, your new source code repository will be available:

Can you believe that's it? It only takes a few easy steps to create your own cloud-based source control repository!

How it works...

A code repository is a place where you store your source code. With Azure DevOps, you can create a repository based on two different source code management systems:

1. **Git** is a distributed source control system that allows developers to work in offline copies of the repository, where they can commit their changes as they work. Multiple branches can be created so that the developer can easily and quickly switch between multiple versions of the repository. Eventually, each developer syncs their commits back to the online repository.

2. **Team Foundation Version Control (TFVC)** is a centralized source control system wherein each developer works within a single version of the repository. Branching and maintaining multiple versions of the source code can only be done by using folders within the repository. TFVC allows you to work in two modes:

- **Server workspace mode**: All files are maintained on the server and developers check their changes into the server repository.
- **Local workspace mode**: Developers work on a local copy of the server repository. As the developer completes their code edits, they check those changes back into the server repository.

 When creating an Azure repository, the default source control system is Git. Git is recommended for projects and development teams of all sizes.

A new repository can be created in a number of different ways:

1. Push an existing local repository to Azure DevOps using Git commands, as follows:

```
git remote add origin
https://<yourOrganization>@dev.azure.com/<yourOrganization/<project
Name>/_git/<repoName>
git push -u origin --all
```

2. Import a repository from an existing GitHub or TFVC repository.
3. Initialize a new repository via the Azure DevOps web interface.

You can create one or more repositories within a single Azure DevOps project. The choice is yours.

There's more...

Although both Git and TFVC are source code systems available in Azure DevOps, they are very different to work with.

As I mentioned, the default source code system is Git, and you should be able to use that for almost all of your projects. If you'd like to learn about the differences between Git and TFVC, then you should check out the article on Microsoft Docs at https://docs. microsoft.com/en-us/azure/devops/repos/tfvc/comparison-git-tfvc?view=azure-devops.

If you are currently working within a TFVC repository, then don't fret—there is a way to move to Git if that's what you want to do. There happens to be a tool with which you can migrate from TFVC to Git, and you can read about it and download it from: `https://github.com/git-tfs/git-tfs/blob/master/doc/usecases/migrate_tfs_to_git.md`.

See also

You can read more about Azure Repos on Microsoft Docs at `https://docs.microsoft.com/en-us/azure/devops/repos/get-started/index?view=azure-devops`.

There are a number of good videos and walkthroughs available on Microsoft Docs that will show you what you can do with Azure Repos. Check them out at `https://docs.microsoft.com/en-us/azure/devops/repos/git/index?view=azure-devops`.

Connecting an AL project to Azure DevOps

Now that we've got a code repository, we should probably add some code to it. This recipe will show you how to use Visual Studio Code to upload an AL project to the Azure DevOps code repository.

Getting ready

In order to perform this recipe, you must complete all the previous recipes in this chapter.

If you've been working through this book, then you'll be very familiar with the `Television Show` project. We're going to work on it once again for this recipe, but even if you've worked through all of the previous chapters to build the project, you still need to download `ch8/3-connect-al-project-to-azure-devops-start.zip` from the GitHub link at the start of this chapter, so that you're working from the correct starting point.

Rename any existing `Television Show` project folders and extract the contents of `3-connect-al-project-to-azure-devops-start.zip` to use for this chapter.

In order to use Visual Studio Code to upload our AL project, you're going to need to install **Git**, since we created our code repository based on the Git source control system. This will allow you to interact with the code repository using standard Git commands. You can download and install the latest version from: `https://git-scm.com/download/win`.

How to do it...

1. In your web browser, navigate to `https://dev.azure.com` and log in with your Azure DevOps account.
2. Open the `televisionShow` project.
3. On the left side menu, select **Repos** | **Files**.
4. At the top of the screen, make sure that the `televisionShow` repository is selected:

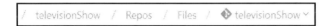

5. In the top-right corner of the screen, select **Clone**.
6. In the **Clone repository** window, copy the HTTPS URL value for the repository:

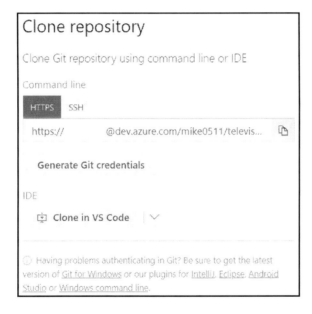

> Example: `https://<yourOrganization>@dev.azure.com/<yourOrganization/televisionShow/_git/televisionShow`

7. Open Visual Studio Code and press *Ctrl* + *Shift* + *P*. Type in and select **Git: Clone** from the menu.
8. Paste in the repository HTTPS URL value that you copied in Step 6 and press *Enter*.

9. Choose a folder where you still store the repository and press **Select Repository Location**. Do not select the folder that you extracted from `3-connect-al-project-to-azure-devops-start.zip`.

Visual Studio Code will create a folder containing the repository name at the location you specify.

10. When prompted, sign in with your Azure DevOps account.

11. After a few moments, you will be presented with the following dialog. Click **Open Repository**:

You should now see your empty code repository, with the exception—of course—of the `README.md` file that we initialized the repository with:

12. Now, let's add our `Television Show` project files to the repository. Copy the contents of the `televisionShow` folder that you extracted from `3-connect-al-project-to-azure-devops-start.zip` and paste it into the root of the code repository folder that Visual Studio Code created. It should look like this:

I deleted the README.md file; you can too if you wish.

I find the best way to perform file tasks such as this is to simply use Windows File Explorer. You can just copy/paste the files and folders from the extracted folders to the repository folder, and then switch back to Visual Studio Code to see the results.

When you drag/drop folders into the Visual Studio Code interface, it will not actually copy the folder contents, but instead, will add the contents to a Visual Studio Code workspace, which is not what we want in this case.

13. Connect the project to your AL development sandbox by either reusing a previous launch.json and placing it in the project, or creating a new one. Once it is connected, download the AL symbols to the project.

14. Now that we have our code in the right folder, we need to commit it and push it to our Azure DevOps repository. In Visual Studio Code, on the left side menu, click the Source Control () icon.

15. In the message box, type in initial checkin and press *Ctrl + Enter*.

This will commit the files to your local Git code repository, but not yet in Azure DevOps.

16. In the bottom-left corner of the Visual Studio Code application window, you will see the following indicator, which tells you that you have one commit that is pending to be pushed to your Azure DevOps repository:

Click the indicator to push the commit up to Azure DevOps.

The other digit of the indicator tells you whether you have any pending commits to pull down from your Azure DevOps repository. Clicking on the indicator does both a push and pull to try and sync everything.

17. In Azure DevOps, navigate to the `televisionShow` repository files. You should now see the files that you pushed from your local machine:

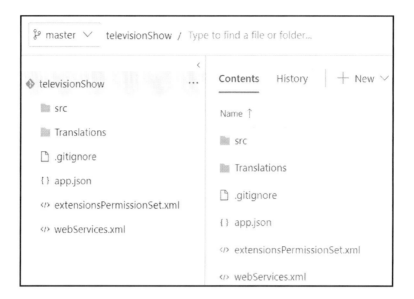

You may have noticed that the `.alPackages` and `.vscode` folders are not in the Azure DevOps repository. This is because of the `.gitignore` file.

You don't typically want to store any of the local configuration or binary files in your repository. With the `.gitignore` file, you can configure Git to ignore specific files and folders so that they are not included in any source control activities.

You can open the `.gitignore` file in Visual Studio Code to check out the contents.

Now, any changes that you make to the `Television Show` project on your local machine can be pushed up to Azure DevOps!

How it works...

When using an Azure DevOps code repository, you need to first clone it to your local machine, as that is where you'll make your code changes and perform all your development tasks. Cloning will create a local copy of that repository and will download any files that currently exist at that time in that repository. You can create branches within your local repository to perform your development.

Once you have the repository cloned, you are free to do your coding and make all the changes you need to make. As you are making changes and testing, you can commit that code to your local repository as much as you want, but it will only exist on your local machine until you push it to Azure DevOps.

You can push your changes to Azure DevOps in a few different ways:

- Use the **Synchronize Changes** button to both push your changes up to Azure DevOps and to pull any changes down from Azure DevOps.
- Use the **Push** menu command in the **Source Control** menu.
- Use the **Git push** command in **Terminal Window**.

As your local repository is an offline copy of the Azure DevOps repository, you need to make sure that you are aware of when it matches the online repository and when it needs to be synchronized.

Making code changes in older versions of the repository will likely lead to merge conflicts that you will have to resolve when you push your changes up to DevOps.

Before beginning any development task, it's a good idea to make sure that your local repository is up to date.

There's more...

If you're going to continue to use Visual Studio and Azure DevOps for your source control management, then you might want to check out the Azure Repos extension for Visual Studio Code. This extension lets you perform more Azure DevOps tasks directly from your Visual Studio Code interface, such as managing work items, managing pull requests, and viewing build history.

Azure Repos is a free extension. You can check it out on the Visual Studio Marketplace at `https://marketplace.visualstudio.com/items?itemName=ms-vsts.team`.

See also

There's a great video that you can watch on the official Business Central YouTube channel regarding source code management with AL projects. Check out the video at `https://youtu.be/os8iOBlWT4E`.

Installing a pipeline agent

So far, we've only performed manual tasks when working with Azure DevOps, but let's get into some of the tasks that Azure DevOps can do for us, namely, building and deploying our Business Central application.

Before we can automate these tasks though, we need to install an **Azure Pipeline Agent**. The agent is responsible for executing build and release pipelines in an environment. This recipe will show you how to install an Azure Pipeline Agent on a local Windows machine.

Getting ready

In order to perform this recipe, you must complete all the previous recipes in this chapter. For this recipe, we'll assume you are going to install the agent on your local Windows machine, so you need to have local administrator rights to the machine.

In order for the pipeline agent to authenticate your Azure DevOps system, you need to provide it with a **Personal Access Token** (**PAT**). You need to create that token before performing the recipe steps. You can do that by following the instructions at `https://docs.microsoft.com/en-us/azure/devops/pipelines/agents/v2-windows?view=azure-devops#authenticate-with-a-personal-access-token-pat`.

When you have created the token, copy and paste it to Notepad for later.

How to do it...

1. In your web browser, navigate to `https://dev.azure.com` and log in with your Azure DevOps account.
2. Open the `televisionShow` project.
3. In the bottom-left corner of the screen, click **Project settings** | **Agent Pools**.
4. In the top-right corner of the screen, click **Add pool**.

5. Select **New**, and populate *televisionShow-local* for the agent pool name:

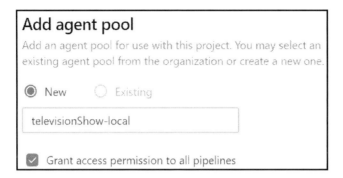

 Make sure to enable **Grant access permission to all pipelines** so that all pipelines can use the new agent pool.

 When pipeline agents are installed, they are assigned to an **agent pool**. This helps you in that you do not have to administer the agents individually. Agent pools can be shared across all the Azure DevOps projects.

6. Click **Create**.

7. In the list of available agent pools, click the one you just created (televisionShow-local):

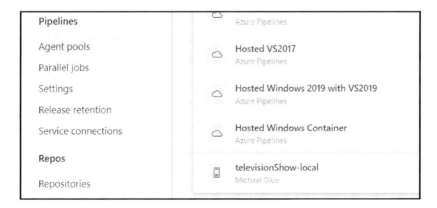

8. Click **New agent**:

9. Make sure that **Windows** | **x64** is selected, and then click **Download**. Save the file (do not open it or rename it) to your default download folder:

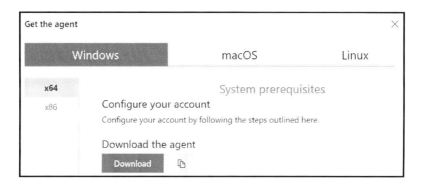

While we're performing this on a Windows machine, notice that there are also agents available for macOS and Linux!

10. Now, we will create the agent on your local machine. Open the PowerShell console.

You must open the PowerShell console in administrator mode.

11. Enter the following command and press **Enter**:

```
cd c:\
```

12. Enter the following command and press **Enter**:

```
mkdir agent ; cd agent
```

13. Enter the following command and press **Enter**:

```
Add-Type -AssemblyName System.IO.Compression.FileSystem ;
[System.IO.Compression.ZipFile]::ExtractToDirectory("$HOME\Download
s\vsts-agent-win-x64-2.153.2.zip", "$PWD")
```

The filename and location should match what you downloaded in **Step 9**. You may need to update the preceding code to reflect that before you can run it.

14. In the PowerShell console window, type in the following command and press **Enter** to configure the pipeline agent:

```
.\config.cmd
```

15. Enter the URL for your Azure DevOps system and press **Enter**; for example, `https://dev.azure.com/<yourOrganization>`.

16. Press **Enter** to accept the **Personal Access Token** (**PAT**) as the authentication method.

17. Enter the token that you generated prior to starting this recipe, and then press **Enter**.

18. Enter the following name for the agent pool, and then press **Enter**:

```
televisionShow-local
```

19. Press **Enter** to accept the default agent name.

20. Press **Enter** to accept the default work folder.

21. Press **Y** to run the agent as a service, and then press **Enter** to move to the next step.

22. Enter in the account that the agent service should run under and press **Enter**.

This account must be a local administrator on the machine!

Upon successful completion, you should see a message similar to this:

```
Service vstsagent.mike0511.televisionShow-local.DESKTOP-MIKE successfully installed
Service vstsagent.mike0511.televisionShow-local.DESKTOP-MIKE successfully set recovery option
Service vstsagent.mike0511.televisionShow-local.DESKTOP-MIKE successfully set to delayed auto start
Service vstsagent.mike0511.televisionShow-local.DESKTOP-MIKE successfully configured
Service vstsagent.mike0511.televisionShow-local.DESKTOP-MIKE started successfully
```

23. Close the PowerShell console.
24. In Azure DevOps, close the **Get the agent** window and click the **Agents** tab. You should now see your new pipeline agent, which is similar to the following:

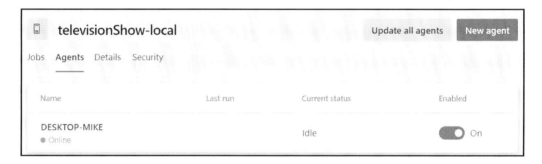

Any time that there is an update in the pipeline agents, you can come to this screen and press **Update all agents** to have all of the agents in the pool updated.

How it works...

The Azure Pipeline Agent is responsible for executing the build and release pipelines that you create in Azure DevOps. In order to create a pipeline agent, you first need to place it in either a new or existing agent pool. An agent pool is a collection of one or more pipeline agents. Using agent pools allows you to organize your pipeline agents and manage them at group level, instead of individually.

Once the agent pool has been created, you can then create the pipeline agent. There are two types of pipeline agents available:

- **Microsoft-hosted agents**: These agents execute and exist solely in the cloud, meaning you do not have to have a machine configured with the agent. Every time a build/release pipeline runs, the agent is created on the fly and is discarded when the pipeline finishes.

- **Self-hosted agents**: These agents require you to set up and configure them on your own. You will need to have either a virtual or physical machine to install these agents on. The agents can be installed in Linux, macOS, and Windows OSes, as well as within Docker containers. These agents remain idle (but running) until a pipeline is executed. When the pipeline finishes, these agents will remain in place, listening for the next pipeline that needs to be executed.

When you configure a pipeline agent, you will have the ability to define capabilities for that agent. In other words, you can tell Azure DevOps what software that particular pipeline agent has access to in their environment. When the pipelines are defined, you can define what the required capabilities are, so that when the pipeline is executed, Azure DevOps can determine which pipeline agent can successfully execute the pipeline. This is helpful in the event that you have to direct your pipeline to a specific pipeline agent.

Self-hosted pipeline agents can be set up to run in two modes:

- **Service mode**: These agents are installed as a service in the OS so that they're always on. You can check the status of these agents on the host machine by using the service manager.
- **Interactive mode**: These agents are installed using auto-login so that they are automatically started whenever the host machine is restarted. When these agents start up, a command-line dialog window will appear and, as long as that window is open, the pipeline agent is running and waiting for the next pipeline to execute.

Installing an interactive pipeline agent with auto-login is a security risk. Be aware of this and only use this type of agent setup when necessary.

See also

You can read more about Azure Pipeline Agents on Microsoft Docs at `https://docs.microsoft.com/en-us/azure/devops/pipelines/agents/agents?view=azure-devops`.

Creating a build pipeline

Automating your application builds is done in Azure DevOps by creating a build pipeline. This pipeline can be manually executed on an ad hoc basis, or it can be configured to be automatically executed when changes are committed to your repositories.

This recipe will show you how to create a build pipeline for an AL project.

Getting ready

In order to perform this recipe, you must complete all the previous recipes in this chapter.

The machine on which you have the pipeline agent installed must have Docker installed and running. You can find instructions on how to do that at the following links. You need to make sure to install the correct edition based on your OS:

- **Windows 10:** `https://store.docker.com/editions/community/docker-ce-desktop-windows`
- **Windows Server:** `https://docs.microsoft.com/en-us/virtualization/windowscontainers/quick-start/quick-start-windows-server`

For some context, we're going to create a build pipeline that does the following:

- Installs NavContainerHelper
- Creates an AL development sandbox container
- Builds an AL app in the repository

We're going to configure the pipeline so that it executes every time a change is committed to the master branch in our repository.

How to do it...

1. In your web browser, navigate to `https://dev.azure.com` and log in with your Azure DevOps account.
2. Open the `televisionShow` project.
3. On the left side menu, select **Pipelines | Builds**.
4. Click **New pipeline**.

5. Click **Azure Repos Git**:

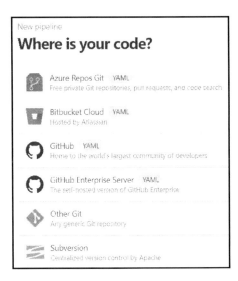

6. Select the **televisionShow** repository.
7. Select **Starter pipeline**. After a few moments, your build pipeline will be created and you will be presented with some sample YAML code.
8. Click **Save and run**.
9. Make sure that **Commit directly to the master branch** is selected and press **Save and run**:

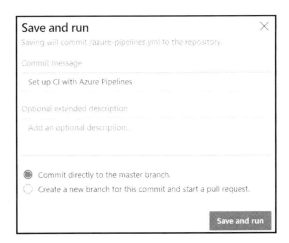

In the next few moments, the sample build pipeline will execute, and if all goes well, then you'll end up with a result like this:

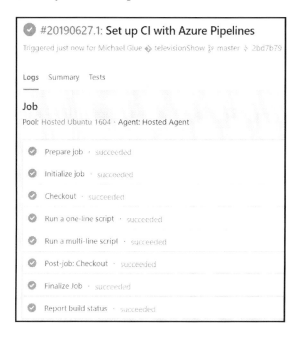

10. In the top-right corner of the screen, click the ⋮ button and select **Edit pipeline**.
11. Clear out all the existing code in the pipeline file.
12. Add the following code to the pipeline:

```
trigger:
  branches:
    include:
    - master

pool:
  name: televisionShow-local

workspace:
  clean: all
```

The preceding code does the following:

- Configures the pipeline to execute using the `master` branch
- Sets the agent pool to the one we created in the **Installing a pipeline agent** recipe earlier in this chapter

- Configures the pipeline to remove all existing files from the pipeline agent's working folders every time the pipeline is executed

13. Add the following code to the pipeline file:

```
variables:
  containerName: build
  containerUserName: admin
  containerPassword: Pass@word1
  imageName: mcr.microsoft.com/businesscentral/sandbox:us
  agentFolder: $env:agentfolder
```

The preceding code does the following:

- Sets the name of the Business Central container that will be created during the pipeline process
- Sets the login and password that will be used to create the Business Central container
- Configures the Docker image that will be used to create the Business Central container
- Sets the folder that will be shared with the Business Central container

Note the `$env:agentFolder` variable used in the preceding code. This is a predefined environment variable that is part of the build pipeline. You can find out what other predefined variables are available at `https://docs.microsoft.com/en-us/azure/devops/pipelines/build/variables?view=azure-devopstabs=yaml`.

14. Add the following code, which adds a task to the pipeline that runs some PowerShell code, in order to install `NavContainerHelper`:

```
steps:
- task: PowerShell@2
  displayName: 'Install NavContainerHelper'
  inputs:
    targetType: inline
    errorActionPreference: stop
    failOnStderr: true
    script:
      Write-Host "Installing NavContainerHelper"
      Install-Module -Name navcontainerhelper -Force
```

For PowerShell tasks in the pipeline, you can choose to code your script inline (for example, directly within the pipeline script) as we did previously, or you can choose to execute an external PowerShell script that can exist within the repository or another location.

15. Now, add some code that contains another PowerShell task. This task will create the Business Central container that we'll use to build our application:

```
- task: PowerShell@2
  displayName: 'Create Build Container'
  inputs:
    targetType: inline
    errorActionPreference: stop
    failOnStderr: true
  script:
    New-NavContainer -containerName $(containerName) `
      -accept_eula `
      -accept_outdated `
      -auth NavUserPassword `
      -Credential (New-Object pscredential $(containerUserName),
        (ConvertTo-SecureString -String $(containerPassword) -
        AsPlainText -Force)) `
      -doNotExportObjectsToText `
      -imageName $(imageName) `
      -alwaysPull `
      -shortcuts None `
      -restart no `
      -updateHosts `
      -useBestContainerOS `
      -assignPremiumPlan `
      -additionalParameters @("--volume
        ""$($env:Agent_HomeDirectory):C:\Agent""")
```

16. Now, add a new task to the pipeline in order to build our AL application:

```
- task: PowerShell@2
  displayName: 'Build AL application'
  inputs:
    targetType: inline
    errorActionPreference: stop
    failOnStderr: true
  script:
    Compile-AppInNavContainer -containerName $(containerName) `
      -credential (New-Object pscredential $(containerUserName),
        (ConvertTo-SecureString -String $(containerPassword) -
        AsPlainText -Force)) `
      -appProjectFolder $env:Build_SourcesDirectory `
```

```
-appOutputFolder $env:Build_StagingDirectory `
-UpdateSymbols `
-AzureDevOps `
-FailOn error | Out-Null
```

17. Add a task to the pipeline to publish the Business Central application once it's been built:

```
- task: PublishBuildArtifacts@1
  inputs:
    pathtoPublish: '$(Build.StagingDirectory)'
    artifactName: televisionShowApp
```

This will allow users to download the application from the completed build, and will also allow you to use the application in a release pipeline.

18. Now, add the final task to remove the container that was created during the pipeline:

```
- task: PowerShell@2
  displayName: 'Remove container'
  condition: always()
  continueOnError: true
  inputs:
    targetType: inline
    failOnStderr: false
  script:
    Remove-NavContainer -containerName $(containerName)
```

Note that we use `condition: always()` to make sure that whether or not the previous pipeline task passes, this task will be executed. This way, we never leave a container running once the pipeline has completed.

19. In the top-right corner of the screen, click **Save**.
20. Make sure that **Commit directly to the master branch** is selected and click **Save**.
21. In the top-right corner of your screen, click **Run**.
22. You will see a message similar to the following that indicates whether the build pipeline has been queued for execution:

Click the build number to view the real-time status of the build:

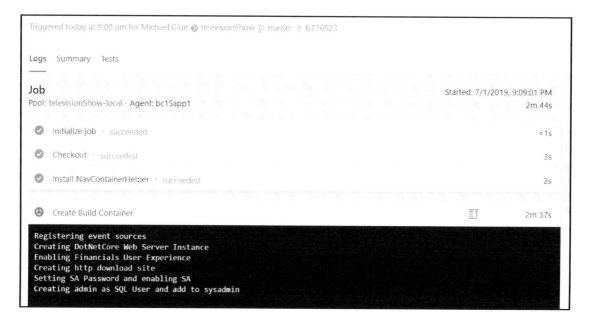

It may take 10 – 20 minutes to execute the build pipeline the first time, depending on the speed of the machine that is executing the build. This is because the Docker image needs to be downloaded. Unless the image is updated and needs to be downloaded again, subsequent runs of the build pipeline will be much shorter.

23. Now, let's make sure that the build is executed when we commit a change to the repository. In Visual Studio Code, open the `televisionShow` folder that you connected to the Azure DevOps repository in the *Connecting an AL project to Azure DevOps* recipe.

24. Press the **Synchronize Changes** button at the bottom-left of the application window.

25. In **Explorer**, select `src/codeunit/Download Episode Information.al`.

26. Find the following code:

```
SuccessMessageTxt: Label 'Episode information has been
downloaded.';
```

Replace the code with this:

```
SuccessMessageTxt: Label 'Episode information has successfully been
downloaded.';
```

27. In the left menu, click  and type `changed success message` in the **Message** box.
28. Press *Ctrl + Enter* to commit the changes to your local repository.
29. Press the **Synchronize Changes** button at the bottom-left corner of the application window to push the changes to Azure DevOps.
30. In your web browser, navigate to Azure DevOps and go to the `televisionShow` project.
31. On the left side menu, select **Pipelines | Build**. You should now see that a new build has been automatically queued:

32. Once the build pipeline completes, you can grab the application that it created by clicking on the **Artifacts** button in the top-right corner of the build results page, and then selecting the name of the artifact, which, in our case, is `televisionShowApp`:

33. Click the **...** to download the Business Central application:

How it works...

By implementing a **build pipeline** to your development process, you can have Azure DevOps automatically produce builds of your application any time that a developer commits changes to the repository.

Automating the build at the time the developer commits their changes is called **Continuous Integration (CI)**. Aside from building the application at the time of commit, you would also typically execute any automated test scenarios that you have for the application. Implementing a CI process ensures that you are building and testing your application at all times, so as to ensure that no broken code gets into your application.

Azure build pipelines are defined using YAML, and are stored as physical files within the code repository. This means that you can maintain source code control on your build pipeline files alongside your application files. You can read more about YAML at `https://yaml.org/spec/1.2/spec.html`.

A build pipeline is structured like this:

The parts of this structure are explained as follows:

- **Stage**: This is a separation between different parts of the build (for example, build, test, deploy). A stage can contain one or more jobs. More information on stages can be found at `https://docs.microsoft.com/en-us/azure/devops/pipelines/process/stages?view=azure-devopstabs=yaml`.

- **Job**: This is a set of steps that is assigned to a pipeline agent. A pipeline that contains multiple jobs can be run in parallel using multiple pipeline agents. A job can contain one or more steps. More information on jobs can be found at `https:/ /docs.microsoft.com/en-us/azure/devops/pipelines/process/phases?view= azure-devopstabs=yaml`.
- **Step (aka task)**: This is the smallest component of the pipeline. A step contains the component of work that the pipeline needs to do. You can find more information on steps from `https://docs.microsoft.com/en-us/azure/devops/ pipelines/process/tasks?view=azure-devopstabs=yaml`, and for a list of the available predefined tasks, look at `https://docs.microsoft.com/en-us/ azure/devops/pipelines/tasks/index?view=azure-devops#build`.

Once your build pipeline has been created, you can define triggers for the pipeline. The **trigger** is what tells the pipeline when to run. There are three types of triggers:

- **Any time that a change is committed**: This is enabled by default when the pipeline is created.
- **Predefined schedule**: For example, running it every weekday at 3:00 a.m.
- **When another build completes**: This allows you to chain together a series of build pipelines.

You can read more about build pipeline triggers at `https://docs.microsoft.com/en-us/ azure/devops/pipelines/build/triggers?view=azure-devopstabs=yaml`.

See also

You can learn more about what you can do with build pipelines at `https://docs. microsoft.com/en-us/azure/devops/pipelines/customize-pipeline?view=azure- devops`.

Creating a release pipeline

Automating the deployment of your applications is done by using a release pipeline. Similar to the build pipeline, a release pipeline can also be manually executed on an ad hoc basis, or it can be configured to be automatically executed.

This recipe will show you how to create a release pipeline for an AL project.

Getting ready

In order to perform this recipe, you must complete all the previous recipes in this chapter.

How to do it...

1. In your web browser, navigate to `https://dev.azure.com` and log in with your Azure DevOps account.
2. Open the `televisionShow` project.
3. On the left menu, select **Pipelines | Releases**.
4. Click **New pipeline**.
5. On the **Select a template** dialog, press **Empty job**:

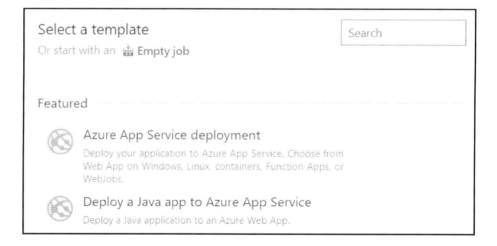

6. On the **Stage** dialog, set **Stage name** to `Create testing environment`. Click the **X** in the top-right corner of the **Stage** dialog to close it.
7. Click **Save** in the top-right corner of the screen.
8. Click **OK**.
9. In the **Artifacts** box, click **Add**:

10. In the **Add an artifact** screen, select **Build**, and set the following values:

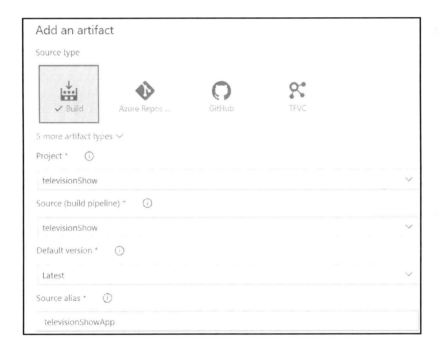

This tells the release pipeline that we want to use the latest build from the *televisionShow* build pipeline as the artifact that we will deploy.

Make sure that the **Source alias** name matches the name of the artifact that you configure in the build pipeline, otherwise the release pipeline will not be able to get the artifact. In the event that your build pipeline produces multiple artifacts, make sure you use the correct one.

11. Click **Add**.

12. In the **Artifacts** box, click the **Continuous deployment trigger** (⚡) icon.

13. Enable **Continuous deployment trigger** and select **Add | The build pipeline's default branch**:

14. Click the **X** to close the **Continuous deployment trigger** screen.

15. Click **Save** in the top-right corner of your screen.

16. Click **OK**.

17. At the top of your screen, select **Tasks | Create testing environment**.

18. Select **Agent job**.

19. On the right side, under **Agent selection**, set **Agent pool** to **televisionShow-local**:

20. Click the + button next to **Agent job**:

21. In the **Add tasks** screen, search for `powershell` and click the **PowerShell** button:

22. Click **Add**.
23. Click the **PowerShell Script** task on the left side.
24. In the **PowerShell** screen on the right side, set the following field values:
    - **Display name**: Create container
    - **Type**: Inline
    - **ErrorActionPreference**: Stop
25. Clear out the existing contents of the **Script** field, and then add the following code:

```
if (Test-NavContainer -containerName $(containerName))
{
 Remove-NavContainer -containerName $(containerName)
}
New-NavContainer -containerName $(containerName) `
 -accept_eula `
 -accept_outdated `
 -auth NavUserPassword `
 -Credential (New-Object pscredential $(containerUserName),
  (ConvertTo-SecureString -String $(containerPassword) -AsPlainText
   -Force)) `
 -doNotExportObjectsToText `
 -imageName $(imageName) `
 -alwaysPull `
 -shortcuts CommonStartMenu `
 -restart always `
 -updateHosts `
 -useBestContainerOS `
 -assignPremiumPlan `
 -additionalParameters @("--volume
  ""$($env:Agent_HomeDirectory):C:\Agent""")
```

This code will check to see whether the deployment container exists, and if it does, it will remove it. After that, it will create a new deployment container.

26. Click the + button next to **Agent job.**
27. In the **Add tasks** screen, search for `powershell` and click the **PowerShell** button.
28. Click **Add.**
29. Click the **PowerShell Script** task on the left side.
30. In the **PowerShell** screen on the right side, set the following field values:
    - **Display name**: Install BC Application
    - **Type**: Inline
    - **ErrorActionPreference**: Stop
31. Now, add some code to install our Business Central application into the container. Clear out the existing contents of the **Script** field, and then add the following code:

```
Get-ChildItem -Path (Join-Path -Path $env:System_ArtifactsDirectory
-ChildPath ($env:Release_PrimaryArtifactSourceAlias +
'\televisionShowApp')) -Filter '*.app' | ForEach-Object {
  Publish-NavContainerApp -containerName $env:containerName
    -appFile $_.FullName -skipVerification -sync -install
}
```

The preceding code looks in the folder where the pipeline downloaded the artifact to. For each Business Central application in that folder (in our case, it's just one), it will install it into the container that was created earlier in the process.

32. At the top of the screen, click **Variables.**
33. Select **Pipeline variables.**
34. Click **Add.**
35. Enter the following values:
    - **Name**: containerName
    - **Value**: release
36. Continue to click **Add** and create the following variables:

Name	Value
containerUserName	admin
containerPassword	Pass@word1
imageName	mcr.microsoft.com/businesscentral/sandbox:us

37. Click **Save** in the top-right corner of your screen.

38. Click **OK**.

39. Now, let's run our release pipeline to make sure that it works. In the top-right corner of your screen, click **Create release**.

40. On the **Create a new release** screen, click the ∨ button and select **Create testing environment**:

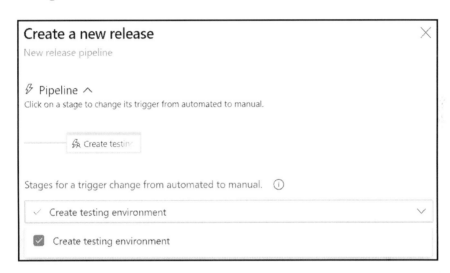

41. At the bottom right of the screen, click **Create**.

42. In the top-right corner of your screen, click **View releases**.

If you don't see the **View releases** button, then check the top-right corner under the **...** button!

43. Here, you can see the release that you created. Click on the release name (for example, **Release-1**) to open it:

44. Hover your mouse over the **Create testing environment** stage, and then click **Deploy**:

45. On the **Create testing environment** screen, click **Deploy**.

Make sure to check out the other information on this screen, as follows:

Commits: Shows you the source code changes that will be included in the release
Work Items: Shows you the associated work items for the release
Artifacts: Shows you what version of the artifact(s) your release will include

46. While the release pipeline is being executed, hover over the **Create testing environment** stage and click the **Logs** button:

You can view the logs of a specific step in the pipeline by clicking on it:

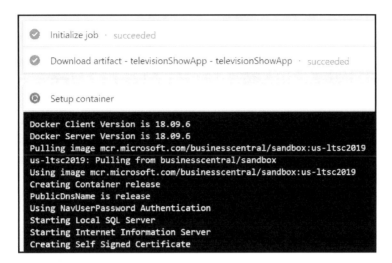

When the release pipeline has completed, the status should look like this:

It may take 10 – 20 minutes to execute the release pipeline the first time, depending on the speed of the machine that is executing it. This is because the Docker image needs to be downloaded. Unless the image is updated and needs to be downloaded again, subsequent runs of the pipeline will be shorter.

47. Now, you can log in to the container that the release pipeline created:
    1. Log in to the machine that you installed the pipeline agent on.
    2. Using a web browser, navigate to the Business Central system (for example, `http://release/NAV`).
    3. Search for `Television` and you should see results for things such as **Television Show List and Episodes**.

If you are not sure what the URL is for the Business Central system, then look in the logs of the release pipeline and click on the setup container step. Look for the **Web Client** value near the end of the log.

How it works...

With a **release pipeline**, Azure DevOps will automatically create environments containing your Business Central applications. This is called **Continuous Delivery** (**CD**) and it helps your development team to deliver software faster, and with lower risk, because you are constantly testing and deploying it.

With a single release pipeline, you can create one or more environments that you can use for the various stages of testing your applications. You can even set up an approval process between each stage so that there needs to be a sign-off in order for the next stage to begin.

You can check out more about the approval process at `https://docs.microsoft.com/en-us/azure/devops/pipelines/release/approvals/?view=azure-devops`.

Aside from deploying the applications, you would also typically execute any automated test scenarios that you have for the application. These tests may be the same ones that you use in the build pipeline, or they can be different; the choice is yours. You might want to do a larger set of tests or perform tests on multiple different combinations of applications during the deployment process in order to simulate the different configurations that your customers might use.

A release pipeline has the following structure:

The parts of this are explained as follows:

- **Artifacts**: This are one or more components that will be deployed by the release pipeline. In our example, the artifact is the Business Central application. The artifacts would typically be the result of a build pipeline.
- **Stage**: This is a separation between different environments that the release will create (for example, development, testing, and production). A stage can contain one or more jobs. More information on stages is can be found at `https://docs.microsoft.com/en-us/azure/devops/pipelines/process/stages?view=azure-devopstabs=yaml`.
- **Job**: This is a set of steps that is assigned to a pipeline agent. A pipeline that contains multiple jobs can be run in parallel using multiple pipeline agents. A job can contain one or more steps. More information on jobs can be found at `https://docs.microsoft.com/en-us/azure/devops/pipelines/process/phases?view=azure-devopstabs=yaml`.
- **Step (aka task)**: This is the smallest component of the pipeline. A step contains the component of work that the pipeline needs to do. You can find more information on steps from `https://docs.microsoft.com/en-us/azure/devops/pipelines/process/tasks?view=azure-devopstabs=yaml`, and for a listing of the available predefined deployment tasks, look at `https://docs.microsoft.com/en-us/azure/devops/pipelines/tasks/index?view=azure-devops#deploy`.

Once your release pipeline has been created, you need to decide when it will run. This is done by setting the triggers. There are two types of triggers:

- **Continuous deployment**: With this trigger, you can choose to have the release pipeline executed upon these events:
    - When the artifact build pipeline completes
    - When a pull request creates a new version of the artifact
- **Scheduled**: The release will run at specific times, for example, running it every weekday at 3:00 a.m.

If you want to read up on what to do with release pipeline triggers, then check out the article on Microsoft Docs at `https://docs.microsoft.com/en-us/azure/devops/pipelines/release/triggers?view=azure-devops`.

See also

Microsoft Docs has some great information on release pipelines here: `https://docs.microsoft.com/en-us/azure/devops/pipelines/release/?view=azure-devops`.

You can also read about CD at `https://docs.microsoft.com/en-us/azure/devops/` `pipelines/get-started/key-pipelines-concepts?view=azure-devops#continuous-` `delivery`.

Enabling branch policies

Now that you've set up your source code repository and the build and release pipelines, you're going to want to set up a number of rules of engagement for when developers are interacting with your source code. These rules are called branch policies and can be used to create a set of standards among the development team, as well as provide some safety for your source code.

This recipe will show you how to configure branch policies within an Azure DevOps repository.

Getting ready

In order to perform this recipe, you must complete all the previous recipes in this chapter.

How to do it...

1. In your web browser, navigate to `https://dev.azure.com` and log in with your Azure DevOps account.
2. Open the `televisionShow` project.
3. On the left side menu, click **Repos | Branches**.
4. Make sure that the **televisionShow** repository is the one that is currently selected:

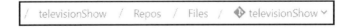

5. Hover your mouse over the **master** branch, and then click the **...** button. Select **Branch policies**:

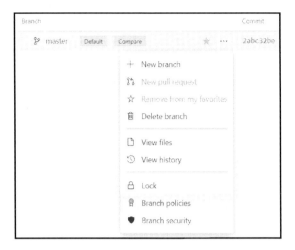

A **branch** is where you commit your code changes. Branches allow you to maintain multiple versions of the source code. The **master** branch is the default branch that is created when a repository is created and should always contain the *production-ready code*. Subsequent branches can be created from a specific point in time along the master branch, or from any other existing branch.

6. In the **Protect this branch** group, configure the **Require a minimum number of reviewers** policy as follows:

Protect this branch
- Setting a Required policy will enforce the use of pull requests when updating the branch
- Setting a Required policy will prevent branch deletion
- Manage permissions for this branch on the Security page

☑ **Require a minimum number of reviewers**
Require approval from a specified number of reviewers on pull requests.

Minimum number of reviewers [1]

☑ Allow users to approve their own changes.

☐ Allow completion even if some reviewers vote "Waiting" or "Reject".

☑ Reset code reviewer votes when there are new changes.

By setting the preceding policy, we have now set up the following rules that will be enforced every time a developer tries to commit code to the master branch:

- A **pull request** must be done in order to commit code changes to the master branch.
- The branch cannot be deleted.
- Before a pull request can be completed, it must be approved by at least one person:
  - Because we're working as a single developer in a demo, we are allowing a developer to approve their own code changes. In a real development environment, you might not want to allow that.
- If a pull request is updated after it has been reviewed, then the approval status will be reset and another approval will need to be done.

 A **pull request** is something that a developer creates when they want to commit changes to a branch. Think of it as the developer *asking* to be allowed to commit the changes. Pull requests can have a review and approval process tied to them in order to enforce certain development standards. When a pull request is completed, the requested changes are committed to the branch.

7. At the top of the screen, click **Save changes**.
8. On the left menu, select **Repos | Branches**. Notice now that the master branch has a new icon displayed on it. The 🎗 icon indicates that there are one or more policies enabled on the branch:

9. Now, let's test everything out.

   In Visual Studio Code, open the televisionShow folder that you connected to the Azure DevOps repository in the *Connecting an AL project to Azure DevOps* recipe.

10. Press the **Synchronize Changes** button at the bottom-left of the application window to make sure our local repository is up to date.

11. In **Explorer**, select `src/codeunit/Check Customer Television Shows.al`.

12. Find the following code:

```
NoFavoriteShowErr: Label 'You need to define a favorite television show for Customer %1.';
```

Replace the preceding code with this code:

```
NoFavoriteShowErr: Label 'There is no favorite television show for Customer %1.';
```

13. On the left side menu, click 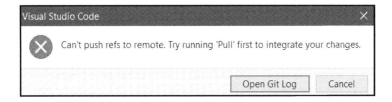 and type `changed error message` in the **Message** box.

14. Press *Ctrl + Enter* to commit the changes to your local repository.

15. Press the **Synchronize Changes** button at the bottom left of the application window to push the changes to Azure DevOps. You should see an error like this:

If you click **Open Git Log,** then you will see that you can no longer push code to the master branch because a pull request is needed. This is because we enabled the branch policy:

```
! [remote rejected] master -> master (TF402455: Pushes to this branch are not permitted; you must use a pull request to update this branch.)
```

16. Click the icon on the left side and then select **Undo Last Commit** under the ... icon:

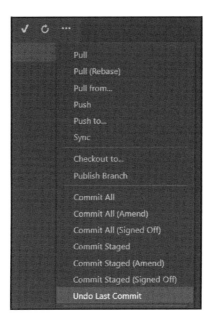

This will undo the commit we just made to our local repository, but the changes will remain in a pending state.

17. Press *Ctrl* + *Shift* + *P*. Type in `Git: Create branch...` and select it from the menu.

18. Type in `minorUpdate` and press *Enter*.

Because we cannot commit our changes to the master branch directly, we need to create another branch that we can commit to, and then we will create a pull request to move the changes from the new branch to the master branch.

19. On the left side menu, click and type `changed error message` in the **Message** box.

20. Press *Ctrl* + *Enter* to commit the changes to your local repository.

21. At the bottom left of the application window, click the  icon to push our new branch (along with our changes) to Azure DevOps. Now the changes will be pushed without any error.

22. In your web browser, navigate to Azure DevOps and go to the `televisionShow` project.

23. On the left side, select **Repos | Branches**.

24. Make sure that the `televisionShow` repository is the active one at the top of your screen.

25. Notice that the **minorUpdate** branch now appears. Hover over the right side of the branch and select **New pull request**:

Mine	All	Stale							
Branch				Commit	Author	Authored Date	Behind | Ahead	Status	Pull Request
master	Default	Compare		eb9d321d	MikeGlue	7/2/2019		✓	
minorUpdate			...	86b9567d	MikeGlue	5 minutes ago	0 | 1		New pull request

26. On the **New Pull Request** screen, click **Create**:

27. Click **Approve**.

Remember we set up the branch policy to require approval from at least one person, and we allowed the developer to approve their own work.

The pull request cannot be completed until it has met the branch policy criteria.

28. Click **Complete**.

29. Click **Complete merge**. The pull request will be completed and should show something similar to the following:

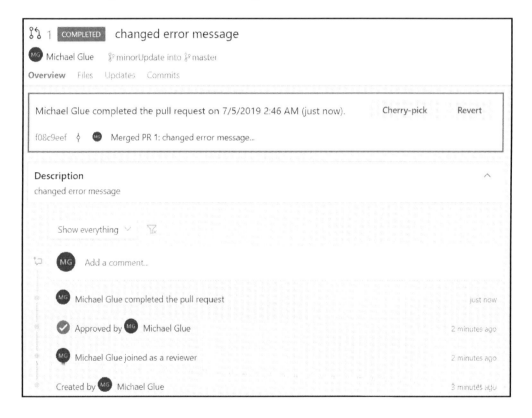

30. On the left menu, select **Repos | Commits**. Notice that the most recent commit is our pull request that we just completed. You can click on it to see that the change was merged into the master branch when we completed the pull request:

Commit	Message
f08c9eef	Merged PR 1: changed error message

31. Clicking on the commit value allows you to see the details of what code was changed:

```
Check Customer Television Shows.al  +1  -1
/src/codeunit/Check Customer Television Shows.al

. . .
  8         local procedure ValidateFavoriteShowExists(CustomerNo: Code[20])
  9         var
 10             CustomerTelevisionShow: Record "Customer Television Show";
 11 -           NoFavoriteShowErr: Label 'You need to define a favorite television show for Customer %1.';
 12         begin
 13             CustomerTelevisionShow.SetRange("Customer No.", CustomerNo);
 14             CustomerTelevisionShow.SetRange(Favorite, true);
. . .
```

```
. . .
  8         local procedure ValidateFavoriteShowExists(CustomerNo: Code[20])
  9         var
 10             CustomerTelevisionShow: Record "Customer Television Show";
 11 +           NoFavoriteShowErr: Label 'There is no favorite television show for Customer %1.';
 12         begin
 13             CustomerTelevisionShow.SetRange("Customer No.", CustomerNo);
 14             CustomerTelevisionShow.SetRange(Favorite, true);
. . .
```

How it works...

Branch policies help to ensure that your source code is safe and that the entire development team is following the same set of standards for managing their code changes.

While policies can be set on any branch in the repository, you will almost always want to ensure that you have configured policies for the master branch, as this is the branch that should, at all times, hold your production-ready code.

As soon as you enable any branch policy, the following rules will be in place for the branch:

- The branch cannot be deleted.
- All commits to the branch must be done by completing a pull request.

A pull request is a request made by a developer to commit changes to a branch. Policies can be set up so that pull requests have to be approved by a certain number of people. Only when the pull request is approved can it be completed, which commits the requested changes to the branch.

There are a number of different branch policies that you configure, such as the following:

- Pull request approvals.
- Pull request comment resolution.
- Code reviewer sign-off.
- Enforcing allowed merge strategies.
- Building validation.
- Enforcing whether all code changes are associated with at least one work item. This ensures that you can trace back to why the code change was executed.

Each branch in a repository can have a different set of policies. Policies can be enabled/disabled/modified at any point in time.

Special Note

Do you remember what else we set up in the previous recipes of this chapter? Well, since we just committed a change to the master branch, the following will also automatically happen:

1. The build pipeline will build a new version of our application that contains the change we just made.
2. The release pipeline will take that latest version and deploy it to a Docker container where it can be further tested.

Give it a bit of time and you should be able to check the results of the build/release pipelines.

By completing this chapter, you've now set up a full CI/CD development process! Great work!

There's more...

While setting up branch policies is definitely something you'll want to do in your own environments, sometimes, you may find that there is a need to bypass those policies. These times should not happen often, but when they do, there is a way to handle it. You can allow specific users (or a group of users) to bypass branch policies by configuring their branch access control settings.

To do that, you can set one or both of the following policies, depending on your requirements:

- Bypass policies when completing pull requests.
- Bypass policies when pushing code changes to the repository.

If the need to bypass branch policies arises, then my recommendation is to temporarily set these settings, and do it only for the users that need to perform the required task(s). Once the users perform the task(s) they need to do, turn off the preceding settings so that the branch policies are adhered to once again.

You can read more about this situation and how to handle it at `https://docs.microsoft.com/en-us/azure/devops/repos/git/branch-policies?view=azure-devops#bypass-branch-policies`.

See also

Check out Microsoft Docs for more information on configuring branch policies, at `https://docs.microsoft.com/en-us/azure/devops/repos/git/branch-policies?view=azure-devops`.

There's also some good information on other things you'll need to know when it comes to managing your branches. You can read all about that at `https://docs.microsoft.com/en-us/azure/devops/repos/git/manage-your-branches?view=azure-devops`.

Time to Share Your Application! 9

You've built your application and now you want to send it out into the wild to be used. There are just a few things you need to know in order to do that. Some of the things we'll explore in this chapter include digitally signing your application and making sure that your source code is protected from prying eyes. We'll also look at how you can deploy your application to both cloud and on-premises systems.

In this chapter, we will cover the following recipes:

- Developing for multiple platforms
- Protecting your Intellectual Property
- Signing your application
- Installation logic
- Upgrade logic
- Installing applications with PowerShell
- Upgrading applications with PowerShell
- Deploying a tenant customization

Technical requirements

A few of the recipes in this chapter require a Business Central sandbox environment. Each recipe describes what type of environment you'll need, as some of them require different types.

To complete all of the recipes, you'll also need the following installed and functioning:

- The PowerShell ISE (search your Start menu, you already have it!)
- **Docker** (grab it here: `https://www.docker.com/products/docker-desktop`)
- NavContainerHelper (grab it here: `https://www.powershellgallery.com/packages/navcontainerhelper`)

Code samples and scripts are available on GitHub. Some of the recipes in this chapter build on recipes from previous chapters. You can download the complete recipe code from `https://github.com/PacktPublishing/Microsoft-Dynamics-365-Business-Central-Cookbook`.

Developing for multiple platforms

When you initially build your application, you'll build it against whatever the current version of Business Central is at the time. As time goes by, of course, there will be updates to the Business Central platform, and those updates won't always be backward-compatible. As new features are released in the Business Central product, and new features are introduced in the AL Language extension for Visual Studio Code, you may find it necessary to build your application against specific versions.

This recipe will show you how to configure your Business Central application so that you can specify which versions of Business Central it supports.

Getting ready

For this recipe, you need to download and extract `ch9/ch9-start.zip` from the GitHub link at the start of this chapter.

How to do it...

1. In Visual Studio Code, open the `televisionShow` folder that you extracted from `ch9-start.zip`.

2. In **Explorer**, select `app.json`.

3. Find the `"runtime"` property and hover your mouse over it to see information about it, which should look like this:

> The version of the runtime that the project is targeting. The project can be published to the server with an earlier or the same runtime version.
>
> The available options are:
>
> - 3.0: Business Central Spring '19 Release
>
> - 2.2: Business Central Fall '18 Release CU 2
>
> - 1.0: Business Central Spring '18 Release
>
> `"runtime": "2.3",`

The `"runtime"` property specifies the minimum platform version on which your application can be installed. The number in front of the decimal represents the major platform version, and the number afterward represents the minor platform version, or in other words, the cumulative update number. For example, the project you are working in is currently set as `"runtime": "2.3"`, which means that the minimum platform version allowed is Business Central Fall 2018, Cumulative Update 3.

4. Change the `"runtime"` property value to this:

```
"runtime": "3.0"
```

The preceding code block means that the application cannot be installed unless the platform is at least the Business Central Spring 2019 version or higher.

How it works...

You can target specific platform versions for your application by using the "runtime" property in the app.json file. This property allows you to define the minimum allowed platform version that your application can be installed on. The "runtime" value is set using a standard major/minor structure, like this:

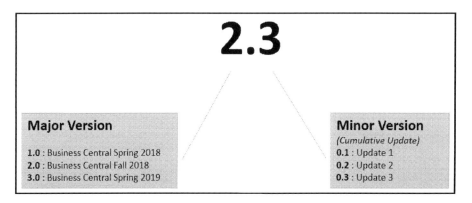

Setting the "runtime" property also controls features that you are allowed to use in the AL Language extension, as *not all features are supported on all platform versions.*

 If you change the platform version, then you will receive warnings in Visual Studio Code if you have used any features that are not compatible with the platform version you selected.

When you publish a Business Central application, the verification is done to make sure that the "runtime" version specified in the application is compatible with the actual version of the platform. If it is not, then you will get an error similar to the following one:

```
The runtime version of the extension package is currently set to '3.0'. The
runtime version must be set to '2.3' or earlier in the app.json file in
order to install the extension package on this platform.
```

See also

You can read more about developing multiple platform versions on Microsoft Docs at `https://docs.microsoft.com/en-us/dynamics365/business-central/dev-itpro/ developer/devenv-developing-for-multiple-platform-versions.`

Protecting your Intellectual Property

Any developer with Visual Studio Code, and access to a Business Central system with your application installed on it, can debug your application. This is great from a support standpoint, but it means that they'll see all of your source code, which isn't so awesome. As a developer or a partner, you may have put great effort into creating the application, so putting the source code out for anyone to see is probably going to be a less-than-ideal situation.

This recipe will show you how to configure your application so that your source code can be protected.

Getting ready

If you haven't already, make sure that you download and extract `ch9/ch9- start.zip` from the GitHub link at the start of this chapter.

How to do it...

1. In Visual Studio Code, open the `televisionShow` folder that you extracted from `ch9-start.zip`.
2. In **Explorer**, select `app.json`.
3. Find the `"showMyCode"` property and set it to `false`, like this:

   ```
   "showMyCode": false
   ```

That's all! Now when you deploy the application, anyone that debugs the system will not be able to see your source code.

The exception to this is if you install the application using Visual Studio Code. No matter what the "ShowMyCode" property is set to, when you install applications this way, you will always be able to see the source code. For this reason, be careful who you give the app files to!

How it works...

In order to protect your source code and hide it from the debugging process, you can set the "ShowMyCode" property in the app.json file. If this property is set to false, then none of the applications will be able to be debugged, and therefore, nobody will be able to see your source code. Breakpoints will not be able to be set in any of your applications, and no variable values will be able to be inspected. This makes it possible to deploy applications and you don't have to worry about anyone else seeing your code and potentially using it in another solution.

 If you do not specify the "ShowMyCode" property in the app.json file, then it is assumed to be false.

There's more...

With the "ShowMyCode" property, you can control whether or not all of the source code in your application is hidden or not, but you can also control this at the function and variable levels. If you are only concerned with hiding the code in specific functions or hiding specific variables in your code, then you can use the NonDebuggable attribute for a function, like this:

```
[NonDebuggable]
local procedure MyHiddenFunction()
var
    myVariable: Integer;
begin

end;
```

The following code is for a variable:

```
local procedure MyFunction()
var
    [NonDebuggable]
    myHiddenVariable: Integer;
```

```
begin

end;
```

Using the `NonDebuggable` attribute stops a developer from being able to do any of the following:

- Debugging the function
- Setting a breakpoint in the hidden code
- Inspecting the values of the hidden variables

You can read more about the `NonDebuggable` attribute at `https://docs.microsoft.com/ en-us/dynamics365/business-central/dev-itpro/developer/methods/devenv-nondebuggable-attribute`.

See also

Check out some more information on protecting your IP on Microsoft Docs at `https:// docs.microsoft.com/en-us/dynamics365/business-central/dev-itpro/developer/ devenv-security-settings-and-ip-protection`.

Signing your application

When you are delivering solutions to customers, it's nice to be able to provide peace of mind that the code that is being loaded into their systems is legitimate and has been created by the right source. By the way, if you plan to publish your application on **AppSource**, then signing the app is mandatory.

This recipe will show you how to digitally sign your Business Central application.

Getting ready

For this recipe, you will need the following installed and configured:

- `NavContainerHelper`
- Docker container (image: `mcr.microsoft.com/businesscentral/sandbox`; use whichever localization you want)

You can refer to the *Option 3 – Sandbox in a local container* section in `Chapter 1`, *Let's Get the Basics Out of the Way*, in the *Setting up your development sandbox* recipe, for information on how to set all of this up. You can use a local container or an Azure-hosted one.

The other thing that you'll need before you can perform this recipe is a **code signing certificate**. If you work with a partner, then you may already have access to one, but if not, then you can create a self-signed certificate using PowerShell to complete the recipe. You can download `ch9/3-signing-your-application/scripts/CreateSelfSignedCertificate.ps1` from the GitHub URL at the start of this chapter to create the certificate. Make sure that you launch PowerShell as an administrator.

How to do it...

1. In Visual Studio Code, open the `televisionShow` folder that you extracted from `ch9-start.zip` and have been working on in the previous recipes of this chapter.
2. Press *Ctrl + Shift + B* to build the Television Show application. Take note of the folder location of the application file.
3. Open the PowerShell ISE and create a new script.
4. Enter the following code:

```
$containerName = '<yourContainer>'
$applicationFileFolder = '<yourAppFileFolder>'
$certificatePassword = '<yourCertifictePassword>'
$certificateFile = '<yourCertificateFile>'

Get-ChildItem -Path $applicationFileFolder -Filter '*.app' |
ForEach-Object {
    $containerAppFile =
    "C:\ProgramData\NavContainerHelper\Extensions
    \$containerName\my\$($_.Name)"
    Copy-Item -Path $ .FullName -Destination $containerAppFile -
    Force
    Sign-NavContainerApp -appFile $containerAppFile `
        -containerName $containerName `
        -pfxFile $certificateFile `
        -pfxPassword $(ConvertTo-SecureString -String
        $certificatePassword -AsPlainText -Force)
}
```

In the previous code, make sure you populate the correct values for the following variables:

- `containerName`: The name of the container that you created as your AL sandbox
- `applicationFileFolder`: The folder in which your application file exists (for example, `C:\temp`)
- `certificatePassword`: The password for the certificate you are using
- `certificateFile`: The full path to the `pfx` code signing certificate (for example, `C:\temp\certificate.pfx`)

 This code will copy the original application file to a folder that is shared with the container, and will then sign the application file using the certificate provided. The certificate will automatically be loaded into the container for you, and the signing tool will also be installed in the container automatically.

5. Save the script as `SignAppFile.ps1`.
6. Run the PowerShell script. You should see a message like this when the application has been successfully signed:

```
Copy C:\temp\certificate.pfx to container release (c:\run\certificate.pfx)
Signing C:\ProgramData\NavContainerHelper\Extensions\release\my\Default publisher_ALProject1_1.0.0.0.app
Done Adding Additional Store
Successfully signed: C:\ProgramData\NavContainerHelper\Extensions\release\my\Default publisher_ALProject1_1.0.0.0.app
```

How it works...

By signing your Business Central applications, you are providing peace of mind to your customers that the code has indeed been created by you, and that it has not been altered in any way.

Before you can digitally sign your applications, you must obtain a code signing certificate. During the development process, you can use a self-signed certificate for testing purposes, but for production-ready applications, you need to purchase a commercial certificate, which can easily be found online.

Once you have the certificate, the easiest way to sign your Business Central application is by using Docker and NavContainerHelper. The **Sign-NavContainerApp** cmdlet will automatically perform the following tasks for you within a Business Central container:

- Install the code signing certificate
- Install Microsoft Sign Tool
- Digitally sign the application file

There's more...

Although using `NavContainerHelper` makes it very easy to sign your Business Central applications, you do not have to use it. As an alternative, you could install Microsoft SignTool yourself, load your code signing certificate, and then use SignTool to sign the file. None of this actually requires a container.

You can read more about using Microsoft SignTool at `https://docs.microsoft.com/en-us/dotnet/framework/tools/signtool-exe`.

Microsoft Sign Tool can be installed as part of Visual Studio Code, or it can be installed as part of the Windows SDK, which you can install from `https://go.microsoft.com/fwlink/p/?LinkID=2023014`.

See also

You can read more about digitally signing your Business Central applications on Microsoft Docs at `https://docs.microsoft.com/en-us/dynamics365/business-central/dev-itpro/developer/devenv-sign-extension`.

Installation logic

When an application is installed, there are times when you need to perform some sort of logic at installation time, such as validating whether the application should be installed on the system based on data, or maybe you want to set up some default or sample data for the customer so that once your application is installed, they can jump right in and start playing around with it.

This recipe will show you how to create logic that is executed at the time the application is installed.

Getting ready

If you haven't already, make sure that you download and extract `ch9/ch9-start.zip` from the GitHub link at the start of this chapter.

You'll need an AL sandbox for this recipe. You can use any sandbox type that you wish. Refer back to `Chapter 1`, *Let's Get the Basics Out of the Way*, in the *Setting up your development sandbox* recipe, for information on how to set all of this up.

How to do it...

1. In Visual Studio Code, open the `televisionShow` folder that you extracted from `ch9-start.zip` and that we've been working on in the previous recipes of this chapter.
2. Right-click on the `codeunit` folder and create a new file named `App Install.al`.
3. Create a new `codeunit` object:

   ```
   codeunit 50111 "App Install"
   {

   }
   ```

4. Add the `Subtype = Install` attribute to the `codeunit` object:

   ```
   codeunit 50111 "App Install"
   {
       Subtype = Install;

   }
   ```

   This will cause the `codeunit` object to be executed when the application is installed for the first time.

5. Add the following trigger and logic:

   ```
   trigger OnInstallAppPerCompany()
   begin
       InstallTelevisionSetup();
       EnableApplicationArea();
       InstallSampleTelevisionShows();
   end;
   ```

Now, when the application is installed, it will perform the following:

- Create the `Television Show Setup` record, which is needed before any television show data can be created.
- Automatically enable the Television Show application area that we previously added (Chapter 2, *Customizing What's Already There*, in the *Adding application areas* recipe).
- Install the sample `Television Show` entries that we previously only allowed the user to do manually (Chapter 3, *Let's Go Beyond*, in the *Assisted setup wizards* recipe).

Remember, as developers, we need to be concerned about the user experience at all times. If the application can do some setups automatically for the user, then it will make for a much nicer experience.

6. Add the following code to insert the `TelevisionSetup` record:

```
local procedure InstallTelevisionSetup()
var
    TelevisionSetup: Record "Television Show Setup";
begin
    if not TelevisionSetup.IsEmpty then
        exit;
    TelevisionSetup.Init();
    TelevisionSetup.Insert(true);
end;
```

7. Now, add the following function to enable the application area:

```
local procedure EnableApplicationArea()
var
    EnableTvApplicationArea: Codeunit "Enable TV Application Area";
begin
    if not EnableTvApplicationArea.IsTelevisionShowsEnabled() then
        EnableTvApplicationArea.EnableTelevisionShows();
end;
```

8. Add the following function to install the sample `Television Show` records:

```
local procedure InstallSampleTelevisionShows()
var
    LoadTvShows: Codeunit "Load Television Shows";
begin
    LoadTvShows.LoadTelevisionShows(true, true, true);
end;
```

9. Now, press *F5* to build and install your application. Log in to your sandbox and notice the following:
   - The Television Show List is populated with the sample data.
   - On the **Application Area** page, the **Television Shows** area is enabled.

How it works...

If you need some logic to be executed at the time your application is installed, then you can do this by creating an install codeunit. This special codeunit is executed whenever the application is installed on a system for the first time.

You create an install codeunit by following these steps:

1. Create a new empty codeunit object.
2. Assign the `SubType = Install` attribute to the codeunit.

Within the install codeunit, you have a few options for when you can execute code, and you do that by placing your code in one or more of the available triggers. These are the triggers that are executed when the application is installed:

- **OnInstallAppPerCompany:** This trigger is fired once per company. Any company-specific processing should be placed here.
- **OnInstallAppPerDatabase:** This trigger is fired only once during the installation process. Any company-agnostic processing should go here.

See also

You can read more about writing installation logic on Microsoft Docs at `https://docs.microsoft.com/en-us/dynamics365/business-central/dev-itpro/developer/devenv-extension-install-code`.

Upgrade logic

Once your application is being used by customers, you'll want to make sure that you are keeping it up to date, adding new features, and addressing issues. To deploy new features to your customers, you'll have to publish new versions of your application. Sometimes, you'll going to need to perform an upgrade to the data when moving from one version to another.

This recipe will show you how to add logic to your application that will be executed when the application gets upgraded.

Getting ready

By now, you must have downloaded and extracted `ch9/ch9-start.zip` from the GitHub link at the start of this chapter, but if not, then you need to do that before you can complete this recipe.

The scenario we'll deal with is that we are going to create version 1.1.0.0 of the Television Show application. In the new version, we are replacing the **Status** option field on the `Television Show` record with a new **Boolean** field named `Running`. When the application is upgraded to the new version, the new field needs to be populated based on the original field for all the existing records.

How to do it...

1. In Visual Studio Code, open the `televisionShow` folder that you extracted from `ch9-start.zip` and have been working with in the previous recipes of this chapter.
2. In **Explorer**, select `src/table/Television Show.al`.
3. Add the `ObsoleteState` and `ObsoleteReason` properties to the **Status** field, as follows:

```
field(4; Status; Option)
{
    OptionCaption = 'Active,Finished';
    OptionMembers = Active,Finished;
    DataClassification = CustomerContent;
    ObsoleteState = Pending;
    ObsoleteReason = 'Replaced by new field: Running';
}
```

The `ObsoleteState` and `ObsoleteReason` properties give the developer an indication when a field, table, or key is or will become obsolete, so that they can make the necessary adjustments in their solutions. You can find more information about

this at `https://docs.microsoft.com/en-us/dynamics365/business-cent ral/dev-itpro/developer/properties/devenv-obsoletestate-property`

4. Add a new field to the `Television Show` table object:

```
field(9; Running; Boolean)
{
    DataClassification = CustomerContent;
}
```

5. Right-click on the `src/codeunit` folder and create a new file named `App Upgrade.al`. Then, create a new `codeunit` object:

```
codeunit 50112 "App Upgrade"
{

}
```

6. Add the `Subtype = Upgrade` attribute to the `codeunit` object:

```
codeunit 50112 "App Upgrade"
{
    Subtype = Upgrade;

}
```

This will cause the `codeunit` object to be executed when the application is upgraded from a previous version.

7. Add the following trigger and logic to the `codeunit` object:

```
trigger OnUpgradePerCompany()
var
    CurrentAppInfo: ModuleInfo;
begin
    if NavApp.GetCurrentModuleInfo(CurrentAppInfo) then begin
        Case CurrentAppInfo.DataVersion() of
            Version.Create('1.0.0.0'):
                PopulateTelevisionShowRunningField();
        end;
    end;
end;
```

When the application is installed, if version 1.0.0.0 was previously installed, then the upgrade logic will execute in order to populate the new field.

Don't forget that you won't necessarily be able to guarantee which version your customers are upgrading from, so you will need to maintain multiple upgrade paths within your application.

8. Add the following logic to update the new **Running** field. We'll set the new field to `true`, but only if the **Status** field is set to **Active**:

```
local procedure PopulateTelevisionShowRunningField()
var
    TelevisionShow: Record "Television Show";
begin
    if TelevisionShow.FindSet() then
        repeat
            if TelevisionShow.Status =
            TelevisionShow.Status::Active then begin
                TelevisionShow.Running := true;
                TelevisionShow.Modify();
            end;
        until TelevisionShow.Next() = 0;
end;
```

9. In **Explorer**, select `app.json`.

10. Increase the version of the application by setting the `"version"` property, like this:

```
"version": "1.1.0.0"
```

Now, when the application is built, it will have the new version number.

 Any time that you release a new build of your application, always make sure to increase the version number. With a bit of effort, you can add this logic into your continuous build pipeline so the version gets updated with every new build.

Keep working through this chapter and you'll see the upgrade code in action!

How it works...

If you need some logic to be executed when your application is upgraded, then you need to create an upgrade codeunit. An upgrade codeunit is executed whenever an application is installed on a system that has had a previous version of the application installed.

You create an upgrade codeunit by following these steps:

1. Create a new empty codeunit object.

2. Assign the `SubType = Upgrade` attribute to the codeunit.

In the upgrade codeunit, you have access to a number of different triggers where you can place your code. The following triggers are available:

- `OnCheckPreconditionsPerCompany` is used to determine whether any upgrade requirements are met for each company.
- `OnCheckPreconditionsPerDatabase` is executed once during the upgrade process to determine whether any upgrade requirements are met. Only company-agnostic logic should go here.
- `OnUpgradePerCompany` performs the upgrade logic in each company.
- `OnUpgradePerDatabase` performs the company-agnostic upgrade logic.
- `OnValidateUpgradePerCompany` is used to make sure that the upgrade was successful in each company.
- `OnValidateUpgradePerDatabase` is executed once to make sure that the upgrade was successful. Only company-agnostic logic should go here.

When writing your upgrade logic, you can get information regarding the old version that was installed by using the **ModuleInfo** data type. With this, you can use the data version to determine the starting point for the upgrade, since, at the time the upgrade logic is executed, the version of the data represents the original version that's being upgraded.

More information can be found about the **ModuleInfo** data type at `https://docs.microsoft.com/en-us/dynamics365/business-central/dev-itpro/developer/methods-auto/moduleinfo/moduleinfo-data-type`.

See also

You can read more about writing upgrade code on Microsoft Docs at `https://docs.microsoft.com/en-us/dynamics365/business-central/dev-itpro/developer/devenv-upgrading-extensions`.

Installing applications with PowerShell

When installing Business Central applications to an on-premises environment, you're going to have to do that using PowerShell.

This recipe will show you how to publish and install a Business Central application using PowerShell.

Getting ready

You'll need a development sandbox for this one, but it's going to need to be a local installation since we want to simulate an on-premises environment. Make sure you remove any existing applications that you've installed in the sandbox environment. You may find it easier to start with a fresh database. You can use any 13.x or 14.x version of Business Central in whatever localization you would like.

You need to download `ch9/6-installing-applications-with-powershell/Default publisher_ALProject1_1.0.0.0.app` from the GitHub link at the start of this chapter.

How to do it...

1. Open the PowerShell ISE in administrator mode and create a new script file.
2. Add the following code:

```
$appFile = '<pathToAppFile>'
$appName = 'ALProject1'
$appVersion = '1.0.0.0'
$serverInstanceName = '<yourServerInstanceName>'
$rtcPath = "C:\Program Files (x86)\Microsoft Dynamics 365 Business
Central\*\RoleTailored Client"

Import-Module $(Join-Path $rtcPath
'Microsoft.Dynamics.Nav.Apps.Management.psd1') -DisableNameChecking
-Force

Publish-NAVApp -ServerInstance $serverInstanceName -Path $appFile -
PackageType Extension -SkipVerification
Sync-NavApp -ServerInstance $serverInstanceName -Name $appName -
Version $appVersion -Tenant Default
Install-NAVApp -ServerInstance $serverInstanceName -Name $appName
-Tenant Default
```

Make sure that you set the correct values for these variables:

- `appFile`: The full file path to `Default publisher_ALProject1_1.0.0.0.app`, which you previously downloaded
- `serverInstanceName`: The Business Central service tier name (for example, BC140) that is connected to your sandbox

The `skipVerification` parameter is required when you are publishing unsigned applications. If you have digitally signed your application, then you do not need to use this parameter.

3. Save the script as `InstallApp.ps1` and run it.

The script will perform the three steps necessary to install a Business Central application: publish, sync, and install.

When the `install` command is executed, any install logic that is in the application will be executed.

4. Log in to your sandbox and verify that the application is installed.

How it works...

In order to install a Business Central application to an on-premises environment, you'll use PowerShell. The following three commands need to be executed in order to get the application installed:

- **Publish-NavApp** makes the application available to be installed within the specific Business Central server instance.
- **Sync-NavApp** synchronizes the database schema changes required in a tenant's database.
- **Install-NavApp** installs a published application in a tenant's database.

In order to perform the previous commands, you're going to need to have the appropriate rights to the Business Central system in order to publish and install applications.

See also

You can find more information about the PowerShell commands used in this recipe on Microsoft Docs:

- `Publish-NavApp`: `https://docs.microsoft.com/en-us/powershell/module/microsoft.dynamics.nav.apps.management/publish-navapp?view=businesscentral-ps`

- `Sync-NavApp`: `https://docs.microsoft.com/en-us/powershell/module/Microsoft.Dynamics.Nav.Apps.Management/Sync-NAVApp?view=businesscentral-ps`

- `Install-NavApp`: `https://docs.microsoft.com/en-us/powershell/module/microsoft.dynamics.nav.apps.management/install-navapp?view=businesscentral-ps`

You can also find out more about installing applications here: `https://docs.microsoft.com/en-us/dynamics365/business-central/dev-itpro/developer/devenv-how-publish-and-install-an-extension-v2`.

Upgrading applications with PowerShell

Similar to installing Business Central applications in an on-premises environment, when it comes to delivering upgrades to your application, you'll need to use PowerShell to deploy them.

This recipe will show you how to upgrade a Business Central application using PowerShell.

Getting ready

You'll need a development sandbox for this one, but it's going to need to be a local installation since we want to simulate an on-premises environment. Make sure you remove any existing applications that you've installed in the sandbox environment. You may find it easier to start with a fresh database. You can use any 13.x or 14.x version of Business Central in whatever localization you would like.

You'll also need to download `ch9/7-upgrading-applications-with-powershell/Default publisher_ALProject1_1.1.0.0.app` from the GitHub link at the start of this chapter.

And finally... you need to complete the *Installing applications with PowerShell* recipe in this chapter so that you have version 1.0.0.0 of the Television Show application installed in your AL sandbox.

How to do it...

1. Open the PowerShell ISE in administrator mode and create a new script file.
2. Add the following code:

```
$appFile = '<pathToAppFile>'
$appName = 'ALProject1'
$appVersion = '1.1.0.0'
$serverInstanceName = '<yourServerInstanceName>'
$rtcPath = "C:\Program Files (x86)\Microsoft Dynamics 365 Business
Central\*\RoleTailored Client"

Import-Module $(Join-Path $rtcPath
'Microsoft.Dynamics.Nav.Apps.Management.psd1') -DisableNameChecking
-Force

Publish-NAVApp -ServerInstance $serverInstanceName -Path $appFile -
PackageType Extension -SkipVerification
Sync-NavApp -ServerInstance $serverInstanceName -Name $appName -
Version $appVersion -Tenant Default
Start-NAVAppDataUpgrade -ServerInstance $serverInstanceName -Name
$appName -Version $appVersion
```

   Make sure that you set the correct values for these variables:

   - `appFile`: The full file path to `Default` `publisher_ALProject1_1.1.0.0.app`, which you previously downloaded
   - `serverInstanceName`: The Business Central service tier name (for example, `BC140`) that is connected to your sandbox

3. Save the script as `UpgradeApp.ps1` and run it.

The script will perform the three steps necessary to install a Business Central application: publish, sync, and upgrade.

When the `upgrade` command is executed, any upgrade logic that is coded into the application will be executed.

4. Log in to your sandbox and verify that the ALProject1 application is installed and has been upgraded to version 1.1.0.0.

How it works...

Similar to installations, PowerShell is also used when performing an upgrade on a Business Central application in an on-premises environment. The involved are similar to the installation process, with the exception of the final command:

- **Publish-NavApp** makes it possible for the application to be installed within the specific Business Central server instance.
- **Sync-NavApp** synchronizes the database schema changes required for the app to a tenant database. Make sure to use the version parameter to specify that you are syncing the new version of the application.
- **Start-NAVAppDataUpgrade** upgrades an existing application in a tenant's database. Use the version parameter to specify which version you are upgrading to.

    In order to perform the preceding commands, you're going to need to have the appropriate rights to the Business Central system in order to publish and install applications.

When you are building new versions of your application, you *must* make sure that the "id" property value in app.json does not change between the application versions.

The "id" value is used by the system to determine that you are upgrading an existing application. If you change that value, then you will break that link and the system will think you are simply installing a brand new application.

See also

You can find more information about the PowerShell commands used in this recipe on Microsoft Docs:

- **Publish-NavApp**: https://docs.microsoft.com/en-us/powershell/module/microsoft.dynamics.nav.apps.management/publish-navapp?view=businesscentral-ps
- **Sync-NavApp**: https://docs.microsoft.com/en-us/powershell/module/Microsoft.Dynamics.Nav.Apps.Management/Sync-NAVApp?view=businesscentral-ps
- **Start-NAVAppDataUpgrade**: https://docs.microsoft.com/en-us/powershell/module/Microsoft.Dynamics.Nav.Apps.Management/Start-NAVAppDataUpgrade?view=businesscentral-ps

Also, you can also find out more about installing and upgrading applications at:

- **Installing applications**: https://docs.microsoft.com/en-us/dynamics365/business-central/dev-itpro/developer/devenv-how-publish-and-install-an-extension-v2
- **Upgrading applications**: https://docs.microsoft.com/en-us/dynamics365/business-central/dev-itpro/developer/devenv-upgrading-extensions.

Deploying a tenant customization

In the previous recipes, we looked at deploying your applications to an on-premises environment, but what about the online Business Central system? Since this environment exists in an Azure environment that is managed by Microsoft, accessing it using PowerShell commands is not going to be possible.

This recipe will show you how to deploy an application to an online Business Central environment.

Getting ready

You're going to need a Business Central sandbox, and it has to be an online Business Central one for this recipe. If you need help, then you can always refer to the *Setting up your development sandbox* recipe in Chapter 1, *Let's Get the Basics Out of the Way*, for information on how to set all of this up. If you've already been installing apps in your sandbox, then you can remove them all or simply delete that sandbox and create a new one.

You also need to download ch9/8-installing-tenant-customization/Default publisher_ALProject1_1.1.0.0.app from the GitHub link at the start of this chapter.

How to do it...

1. In your web browser, log in to your Business Central online sandbox.
2. Use the 💡 icon and search for *extension*, and then click the link to open the *Extension Management* page.
3. Select **Manage | Upload Extension**.
4. Click the ... icon to the right of **Select .app file**.
5. Click **Choose** and select the Default publisher_ALProject1_1.1.0.0.app file that you downloaded from GitHub.
6. Set the following options:
   - **Deploy to**: **Current version**
   - **Accept**: **Yes**
7. Click **Deploy**.

> Your application file will now be uploaded and queued to be installed in the system.

8. Click **OK** on the dialog.
9. Click **Manage | Deployment Status**. Here, you can monitor the deployment status of your application:

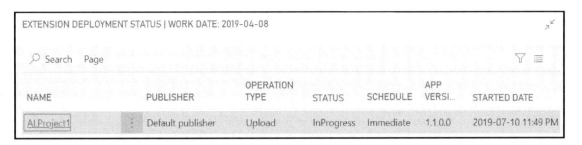

Pressing *F5* will refresh the status page.

The installation is successful once **Status** changes to **Completed**.

How it works...

Deploying an application to a specific tenant is easily done through the Business Central web client, using the *Extension Management* page.

When you deploy the application to the tenant, you have some options as to when the application will get installed:

- **Current version:** The application will be queued to be deployed right away.
- **Next minor version:** The application will be queued to be installed the next time the Business Central system has a minor update applied to it (for example, monthly cumulative updates).
- **Next major version:** The application will be queued to be installed the next time the Business Central system has a major update applied to it (for example, moving from platform v13 to platform v14).

Using the previous deployment options allows you to control how you release your applications, in the event you have to release updates to them that need to coincide with Business Central updates.

In the event that there are multiple languages available within the application, you can also choose which language you wish to deploy.

See also

You can read more about deploying custom applications to Business Central online tenants at `https://docs.microsoft.com/en-us/dynamics365/business-central/dev-itpro/developer/devenv-deploy-tenant-customization`.

Other Books You May Enjoy

If you enjoyed this book, you may be interested in these other books by Packt:

Implementing Microsoft Dynamics NAV and Business Central - Fourth Edition
Alex Chow, Roberto Stefanetti

ISBN: 978-1-78913-393-6

- Explore new features introduced in Microsoft Dynamics NAV 2018
- Migrate to Microsoft Dynamics NAV 2018 from previous versions
- Learn abstract techniques for data analysis, reporting, and debugging
- Install, configure, and use additional tools for business intelligence, document management, and reporting
- Discover Dynamics 365 Business Central and several other Microsoft services
- Utilize different tools to develop applications for Business Central

Programming Microsoft Dynamics 365 Business Central - Sixth Edition
Mark Brummel, David Studebaker, Et al

ISBN: 978-1-78913-779-8

- Programming using the AL language in the Visual Studio Code development environment
- Explore functional design and development using AL
- How to build interactive pages and learn how to extract data for users
- How to use best practices to design and develop modifications for new functionality integrated with the standard Business Central software
- Become familiar with deploying the broad range of components available in a Business Central system
- Create robust, viable systems to address specific business requirements

Leave a review - let other readers know what you think

Please share your thoughts on this book with others by leaving a review on the site that you bought it from. If you purchased the book from Amazon, please leave us an honest review on this book's Amazon page. This is vital so that other potential readers can see and use your unbiased opinion to make purchasing decisions, we can understand what our customers think about our products, and our authors can see your feedback on the title that they have worked with Packt to create. It will only take a few minutes of your time, but is valuable to other potential customers, our authors, and Packt. Thank you!

Index

.
.NET interoperability
  about 126, 127, 128, 129, 130, 131
  reference link 132

A

AAD authentication
  reference link 226
  using 226
admin center
  reference link 137
agent pool 291
AL Language extension
  installation link 9, 14
AL project
  connecting, to Azure DevOps 284, 285, 286,
    287, 288, 289
  creating 21, 22, 23
AL
  CAL, converting to 170, 171, 172, 174, 175
API endpoints
  types 240
API pages
  reference link 241
API query object
  reference link 241
API, TV Maze
  reference link 217
application areas
  adding 79, 80, 81
  reference link 82
Argument Table design pattern
  about 209, 210, 211, 212
  reference link 214
  working 213
assisted Setup wizards 102, 103, 104, 105, 106,

    107, 108, 109, 110, 111, 112, 113
Automated Testing Toolkit (ATT)
  about 147
  references 150
  using 147, 148, 149
automated testing
  reference link 167
automated tests
  creating 153, 154, 155, 156
Azure Active Directory (AAD)
  about 224
  reference link 226
Azure DevOps account
  URL 277
Azure DevOps project, users
  reference link 280
Azure DevOps project
  creating 277, 278, 279, 280
Azure DevOps
  AL project, connecting 284, 285, 286, 288, 289
  using 289
Azure Functions
  consuming 266, 267, 268, 269, 270, 271, 272
  reference link 273
  URL 266
Azure Pipeline Agent
  installing 290, 291, 292, 293, 294, 295
  Microsoft-hosted agents 294
  reference link 295
  self-hosted agents 295
  types 294
Azure Repos
  reference link 284, 289
Azure Resource Manager (ARM) 10
Azure subscription
  reference link 11
Azure web portal

URL 12
Azure-hosted sandbox 10, 11, 12, 13, 14

B

base application business logic
  modifying 59, 60, 61, 62
base application interface
  modifying 56, 57, 58
base application reports
  reference link 71
  replacing 68, 69, 70, 71
base application tables
  fields, adding 54, 55
basic authentication
  enabling 224, 225, 226
basic entities
  creating 24, 25, 26, 27, 28, 29
branch policies
  enabling 316, 317, 318, 320, 321, 322, 323, 324
  reference link 325
build pipeline, job
  reference link 305
build pipeline, stage
  reference link 304
build pipeline, step
  reference link 305
build pipeline, trigger
  reference link 305
  types 305
build pipeline
  creating 296, 297, 298, 299, 300, 301, 302, 303, 304, 305
  implementing 304
  reference link 305
  structure 304
Business Central Admin Center 137
Business Central API
  custom endpoint, publishing in 237, 238, 239, 240
  data, retrieving 229, 230, 231, 233
  exploring, with Postman 227, 228
  reference link 234
  used, for creating data 234, 235, 236
Business Central application

installation link 346
installing, with PowerShell 343, 345
signing 333, 334, 335, 336
upgrading, with PowerShell 346, 347
Business Central applications, signing on Microsoft Docs
  reference link 336
Business Central Flow Connector
  reference link 255
Business Central platform, developing on Microsoft Docs
  reference link 331
Business Central platform
  developing 328, 329, 330
business events 192
business logic
  creating 29, 30, 31, 33, 34

C

CAL objects
  data, upgrading from 181, 182, 183, 185, 186, 187
CAL
  converting, to AL 170, 171, 172, 174, 175
  post-conversion cleanup 177, 178, 180, 181
code repository
  creating 281, 282, 283
  creating, with Git 282
  creating, with Team Foundation Version Control (TFVC) 283
code signing certificate 334
code
  events, publishing in 190, 191
codeunit object 60
Common Data Model (CDM)
  about 265
  reference link 265
Common Data Service (CDS)
  about 265
  reference link 265
Continuous Delivery (CD)
  about 314
  reference link 316
Continuous Integration (CI) 304
control add-in object

reference link 89
control add-in style guide
   reference link 89
control add-ins 84, 85, 86, 87, 88, 89
controls
   types 264
custom applications, deploying to Business Central
      online tenants
   reference link 352
custom endpoint
   publishing, in Business Central API 237, 238,
      239, 240
Custom Report Layouts feature
   about 50
   reference link 50

D

data classification methods, Business Central
   reference link 36
data
   classifying 34, 35
   creating, with Business Central API 234, 235,
      236
   retrieving, from Business Central API 229, 230,
      231, 233
   upgrading, from CAL objects 181, 182, 183,
      185, 186, 187
debugger
   launching 140, 141, 142
delta links
   reference link 233
   using 233
dependencies 90, 91, 92, 93, 94
development sandbox
   Azure-hosted sandbox 10, 12, 13, 14
   hosting, in Business Central 9, 10
   in local container 15
   local sandbox, using installation media 18
   reference link 20
   sandbox, in local container 17
   setting up 8, 9, 20
DevOps 275
Discovery design pattern
   about 196, 197, 198, 199, 200
   reference link 202

working 201
discovery pattern 101
Docker image 16

E

End User License Agreement (EULA)
   download link 11
enums
   about 192, 193, 194
   reference link 196
   working 195, 196
Event Recorder
   about 65
   reference link 68
   using 65, 66, 67
events
   business events 192
   integration events 192
   publishing, in code 190, 191, 192
   reference link 192
Execution Policy
   reference link 17
Extension Management 92
external web services
   consuming 216, 217, 218, 219, 220

F

fields
   adding, to base application tables 54, 55
filter tokens
   adding 76, 77, 78
   reference link 78

G

Git 282
Git, versus TFVC
   reference link 283
Given-When-Then format 156

H

Handled design pattern
   about 202, 203
   working 204
Hello World application 21

help links
  adding 50, 51
  reference link 52

I

In-client Designer
  reference link 65
  using 62, 63, 64, 65
Install-NavApp
  about 345
  reference link 346
installation logic
  about 336, 337, 338, 339
  reference link 339
integration events 192
Intellectual Property
  protecting 331, 332, 333
  reference link 333
isolated storage
  about 114, 115, 116, 117, 118
  reference link 118

M

manual setups
  adding 100, 101, 102
Microsoft Docs article, on debugging
  reference link 143
Microsoft Dynamics 365 Business Central sandbox
  URL 9
Microsoft Dynamics Lifecycle Service
  reference link 99
Microsoft Flow, learning materials
  URL 255
Microsoft Flow, pricing page
  URL 254
Microsoft Flow
  using 247, 248, 250, 252, 253, 254
Microsoft Power BI
  using 241, 244, 246
Microsoft PowerApps
  using 255, 256, 257, 259, 261, 262, 263, 264
Microsoft SignTool
  reference link 336
Microsoft SQL Server 19
Microsoft SQL Server 2016 Express 20

ModuleInfo data type
  reference link 343
multi-root workspaces
  reference link 153
Multilingual App Toolkit Editor
  about 99
  reference link 99

N

NavContainerHelper
  about 15
  reference link 176
  using 171
NonDebuggable attribute
  reference link 333
notifications
  about 118, 119, 120, 121, 122
  reference link 123

P

page extension object
  about 58
  reference link 58
pages
  reference link 29
PATCH request
  reference link 237
  sending, to update records 237
permissions
  reference link 41
Personal Access Token (PAT)
  about 290
  reference link 290
Postman application
  installation link 227
Postman, using with basic authentication
  reference link 229
Postman, with AAD
  reference link 229
Postman
  used, for exploring Business Central API 227, 228
Power BI, learning materials
  reference link 247
Power BI

features 247
URL 247
Power Platform
  Microsoft Flow 247, 248, 250, 252, 253, 254
  Microsoft Power BI 241, 244, 246
  Microsoft PowerApps 255, 256, 257, 259, 261,
    262, 263, 264
PowerApps
  URL 266
PowerShell commands, used on Microsoft Docs
  reference links 349
PowerShell ISE
  about 171
  using 230, 234
PowerShell
  about 15
  used, for installing Business Central application
    343, 345
  used, for upgrading Business Central application
    346, 347, 348
profiles
  adding 71, 72, 74, 75
projects, configuring in Azure DevOps
  reference link 281
Publish-NavApp
  about 345
  reference link 346
pull request 318

R

release pipeline, job
  reference link 315
release pipeline, stage
  reference link 315
release pipeline, step
  reference link 315
release pipeline, triggers
  continuous deployment 315
  reference link 315
  scheduled 315
release pipeline
  creating 305, 306, 307, 308, 309, 310, 311,
    312, 313, 314
  reference link 315
Remote Desktop Protocol (RDP) 11

reports
  creating 41, 43, 44, 45, 46, 47, 48, 49
  dataset 49
  layout 49
  reference link 50
role centers
  adding 71, 72, 74, 75
  reference link 76

S

sandbox type
  Microsoft Cloud Sandbox 21
  server 21
self-hosted pipeline agents
  interactive mode 295
  service mode 295
Software as a Service (SaaS) 127
SQL queries 146
SQL, debugging with AL debugger
  reference link 146
SQL
  debugging 143, 144, 145, 146
standard REST API filtering syntax
  using 233
subscribers, to events
  reference link 62
symbols 93
Sync-NavApp
  about 345
  reference link 346

T

table extension object
  about 55
  reference link 56
tables
  reference link 29
task scheduler
  reference link 126
  using 123, 124, 125, 126
Team Foundation Version Control (TFVC)
  about 283
  local workspace 283
  server workspace 283
telemetry events, with SendTraceTag function

category 136
DataClassification 136
message 136
tag 136
verbosity 136
telemetry events
  about 132
  implementing 132, 133, 134, 135, 136, 137
  reference link 137
tenant customization
  deploying 349, 350, 351
  deploying, options 351
test application
  creating 150, 151, 152, 153
test library
  creating 164, 165, 166
test pages
  about 160
  reference link 160
Test-Driven Development (TDD)
  reference link 167
tests, Microsoft Docs
  reference link 157
TFVC, migrating to Git
  reference link 284
translations
  about 95, 96, 97, 98, 99
  reference link 100
triggers
  about 305
  reference link 34

U

UI handlers
  reference link 164

using 160, 161, 162, 163
UI
  testing 157, 158, 159, 160
upgrade logic
  about 339, 340, 341, 342, 343
  reference link 343
user permissions 37, 39, 40
user types, access levels
  reference link 280
users
  types 280

V

Variant Façade design pattern
  about 205, 206, 207, 209
  reference link 209
  working 209
Visual Studio
  using 289
vmadmin value 11

W

web service
  publishing 221, 222, 223
  reference link 224
web services, publishing in Business Central
  reference link 247
Windows 10
  URL 296
Windows Server
  URL 296

X

XML Localization Interchange File Format (XLIFF)
  95

51771202R00213

Made in the USA
San Bernardino, CA
03 September 2019